BETWEEN WORLDS

BETWEEN WORLDS

GERMAN MISSIONARIES AND THE TRANSITION
FROM MISSION TO BANTU EDUCATION
IN SOUTH AFRICA

Linda Chisholm

WITS UNIVERSITY PRESS

Published in South Africa by:

Wits University Press
1 Jan Smuts Avenue
Johannesburg, 2001
www.witspress.co.za

Copyright © Linda Chisholm 2017
Published edition © Wits University Press 2017
Photographs © Copyright holders 2017
Maps redrawn by Wendy Job

First published 2017

978-1-77614-174-6 Print
978-1-77614-175-3 PDF
978-1-77614-178-4 EPUB

Project manager: Hazel Cuthbertson
Copy editor: Lynda Gilfillan
Proofreader: Elsabé Birkenmeyer
Indexer: Tessa Botha
Cover designer: Peter Bosman Guineafolio Design
Typesetter: MPS

CONTENTS

ACKNOWLEDGEMENTS

Without the financial support of the National Research Foundation's Incentive Programme for Rated Researchers, the research for this book would not have been possible.

In South Africa a range of friends and colleagues provided insights, advice – and good company. I would like to single out Robert Balfour, Adrienne Bird, Catherine Burns, Keith Breckenridge, Mary and Robin Crewe, Ivor Chipkin, Natasha Erlank, David Fig, Brahm Fleisch, Crispin Hemson, Mudney Halim, Mondli Hlatshwayo, Isabel Hofmeyr, Preben Kaarsholm, Sue Krige, Arianna Lissoni, Gerry Maré, Lebo Moletsane, Noor Nieftagodien, Georg Scriba, Nafisa Essop Sheik, Stephen Sparks, Jane Starfield, Raymond Suttner, Salim Vally, Tony Vis, and Heinrich Voges. A special word of thanks is due to Ulrike Kistner, who so generously shared her wealth of knowledge and experience. During the initial stages, conversations in Germany with Helmut Bley, Klaus-Peter Horn and Eckhardt Fuchs were helpful, while the friendship of the following people made a qualitative difference to my research visits to Germany: Helmut Bley, Hans and Christine Bickes, Tim and Ellen Grünkemeier, Inga-Dorothee Rost and Jacob Jones, Henning and Johanna Marquardt and Susan and Guido von Schöning.

Various archivists and librarians were unstinting in their assistance, and here I wish to thank Rainer Allmann, archivist at the Evangelisch-Lutherisches Missionswerk archives in Hermannsburg, Germany, Alison Chisholm, Gabi Mohale and Sophie Motsewabone at Wits University, Roedina Desai and Riette Zaaiman at the University of Johannesburg, and Annelise Zaverdinos at the Lutheran Theological Institute in Pietermaritzburg. Inge von Fintel at the Hermannsburg, South Africa, archive kindly permitted me to copy the maps, which Wendy Job of the University of Johannesburg re-drew for the book. I am greatly indebted to Heinrich Voges, as well as Horst Meyberg, Georg Scriba and John Aitchison for photographs they placed at my disposal, though regrettably not all could be used; thanks also to Tony Vis and Kim Ludbrook for assistance in improving their quality.

Earlier versions of Chapters 2 and 10 were first published in the *South African Historical Journal*. My thanks to the Taylor and Francis Group for permission to include the following as reworked chapters in this book: 'Bantustan Education History: The "Progressivism" of Bophuthatswana's Primary Education Upgrade Programme, 1979–1988', *South African Historical Journal* 65 (3) (2013): 403–420, and 'Fate Comes to the Mission Schools: Fire at Bethel, 1953', *South African Historical Journal* 69 (1) (2017): 121–137.

Thoughtful comments offered by two anonymous reviewers greatly improved the draft, and the scrupulous attention to detail and expression by the copy-editor, Lynda Gilfillan, are appreciated. I also wish to thank the Wits University Press team for their assistance and support. Finally, my thanks to Ralf Krüger who first drew my attention to the Hermannsburgers, and whose good humour and support accompanied me every step of the way.

LIST OF MAPS AND FIGURES

FIGURES

MAPS

LIST OF ABBREVIATIONS

Acc.	Accession number (References)
ANC	African National Congress
ASA	Ausland: Südliches Afrika
BMS	Berlin Mission Society
BO	Bantoe onderwys
CAD	Central Archives Depot
CLM	Cooperating Lutheran Missions
DET	Department of Education and Training
ELM H SA	Evangelical Lutheran Mission Hermannsburg South Africa
ELCSA-SER	Evangelical Lutheran Church of South Africa – South Eastern Region
Fedsem	Federal Seminary
GOV	Government Correspondence (References)
HINO	Hoof Inspekteur Naturelle Onderwys (Chief Inspector Native Education)
HMB	Hermannsburg
IFP	Inkatha Freedom Party
IMC	International Missionary Council
INK	Inkanyezi (References)
LTC	Lutheran Theological College
LTI	Lutheran Theological Institute
LTS	Lutheran Theological Seminary
MI	Missiological Institute (References)
NATU	Natal African Teachers' Union
NEUM	Non-European Unity Movement
NTS	Naturelle Sake (Native Affairs)
OBE	Outcomes-based education
PAC	Pan Africanist Congress of Azania
PEUP	Primary Education Upgrade Programme
PMC	Property Management Company
SA Acc. 76	South African Acquisition made in 1976
SRC	Students' representative council
SASO	South African Students' Organisation
STUDS	Students (References)
UED	Union Education Department
Unibo	University of Bophuthatswana
Unisa	University of South Africa
ZAR	Zuid-Afrikaansche Republiek

INTRODUCTION

The question of transition is central to how we understand educational change in moments of rupture. South Africa's great moments of rupture, change and transition in the twentieth century occurred in 1910, in 1948 and in 1994. Each transition was accompanied by dramatic processes of social and educational change. The first, Union in 1910, created a unified system of state control and provision for white education. Mission education was increasingly directed and financed by the provinces on vastly inferior terms to those for an expanding white system. The second, the shift to apartheid in 1948, brought mission education under full state control. This change officially ended more than a century of provision by a number of different mission societies which had become a growing power in the land. By 1994, the third moment, when apartheid was officially dismantled and a democratic state brought into being, new crises borne of inequality were tearing the society apart. A democratic state set about resolving these tensions. The process of this transition has been fraught, its results an apparent failure, the continuities with the past still painfully present.

This book focuses not on the 'why', but the 'how' of educational change over time. It does so by addressing this historically, at another moment of great rupture and change, and specifically, through the experience of one mission institution involved in change. The period of change is that of the transition from segregation to apartheid, from mission to Bantu Education. The transition from mission to Bantu Education was a traumatic process with long-term consequences. It is commonly understood as constituting a deep break between liberal segregationism and apartheid. Yet what it meant for specific missions and schools in practice is poorly understood.

This book approaches the question of the transition from the perspective of how the transnational, colonial project of mission education was, perhaps paradoxically, both part of, and transformed, during the apartheid period. The project crossed geographical, national and racial boundaries. Notably, the case-study is not the larger, well-to-do and prominent mission societies and schools whose opposition to apartheid was vocal, but rather the smaller, less-visible German mission schools of the Hermannsburg Mission Society in Natal and the Transvaal. The Mission was active in providing education in KwaZulu-Natal and the Transvaal from the time of its arrival in South Africa in 1854. It was a society marked at the outset by its isolationist attitude towards its sister Lutheran societies, its closed conservatism, and its reluctance to take a stance on political matters of the day.

Although one of the more compliant rather than oppositional mission societies, the Hermannsburg Mission was as anxious about the loss of control and change signalled by Bantu Education as the other societies. Accordingly, this book focuses on the experience of a community that both agreed and complied with the change but also had something to lose by it. The book considers what Hermannsburgers did to shore up change. But it also shows how contextual changes and growing cooperation in resisting apartheid increasingly changed the Mission Society as well as its schools.

Missionaries in education

The role of the missions and mission education has been hotly debated since at least 1952 when Dora Taylor (who wrote under the pseudonym 'Nosipho Majeke') argued in *The Role of the Missionaries in Conquest* that missionaries were central to processes of colonial conquest and capitalist incorporation. This perspective reflected not only the critical Marxist approach of the Non-European Unity Movement (NEUM) mobilising against apartheid, it was also of a piece with a much wider antagonism of the time towards missionaries that intensified during the next two decades.

The explosion of social history in the 1970s and 1980s focused on the role of missions and mission education in the creation of African nationalism as part of a broader focus on African agency, initiative and response to Christianity.[1] African responses to the mission message have since then been central to discussions of the ambiguous relationship between missionary and convert. John and Jean Comaroff's analysis of the 'conversation of conversion' between missionaries and the Tswana people in the nineteenth century shows that Africans were generally uninterested in the mission message and deliberately misread mission metaphors.[2] The attempted 'colonisation of consciousness' was precisely that: a half-successful attempt that embodied a continuous battle over the terms of engagement, especially in relation to temporal, spatial and bodily relations.[3] Patrick Harries's study of the nature of literacy practices among missionaries and African mineworkers was similarly concerned with showing that Africans were not passive recipients but active users of literacy. Reading 'the Word' meant one thing to the missionaries and quite another to the recipients. For missionaries it represented a personal interaction with God, and teaching reading was 'a cheap and effective means of spreading the Gospel'.[4] For mineworkers, reading was a collective act of sociality and a source of power that could be harnessed to ends quite different from those intended by the missionaries. Moving from the sphere of informal to formal learning and schooling, Isabel Hofmeyr's study of the transnational circulation and use of Bunyan's *Pilgrim's Progress* similarly demonstrates that while missionaries at Lovedale intended its use for didactic ends, students used it as a 'political resource'.[5] Without its active adoption by African students and teachers on their own terms, in whatever way the message was received, Christianity, as Stephen Volz has shown in his study of African teachers and evangelists, would not have spread as widely as it did.[6] In the process, as Peter Limb has subsequently also argued, the line between resister and collaborator was often blurred, involving complex relationships that saw both contestation and negotiation.[7]

Both the political economy and social historical approaches sketched above are concerned with the impact of missionaries and the reception and interpretation of their message by Africans. Ongoing themes in the literature on missions and mission education therefore include the processes of 'conversion' and the disjuncture between missionary intentions and the results of their actions. Richard Elphick's recent work centres on the contradiction between the vision of equality held out by missionaries and the reality of racial segregation experienced by converts. In the same vein, Ingie Hovland refers to the colonial 'double-vision' that held out two identities for Africans, at cross-purposes with each another: the promise of becoming an equal member within a universal brotherhood, and the promise denied.[8] More recently there has been a shift back to examining the mission itself – on the one hand as part of the growing field of the study of religion[9] and on the other as part of a post-colonial emphasis on the impact of the encounter on the mission itself. The literature suggests that neither convert nor missionary was unchanged by the encounter; if hybrid forms of Christianity emerged among Africans, so too were missionaries themselves altered in the process.[10] And as Hovland writes of the Norwegian missionaries in Natal: 'There was a world of difference between the Umpumulo mission station and its Zulu surroundings. But there is also no doubt that there was a world of difference between the station at Umpumulo and the houses and churches and way of life that the Norwegian missionaries remembered from Norway'.[11] Approaches such as these raise questions for the standard interpretations of the impact of Bantu Education and suggest we ask: how did the missionary education project and schools change under the impact of apartheid and in response to their interaction with African students during a period when they were no longer in control, but relinquishing control?

There has been a long-standing recognition of the gendered character of both mission and Bantu Education. Earlier work concentrated on the role of black and white women in mission education and the gender-differentiated purposes of educational provision for boys and girls.[12] Particularly fertile for this study has been more recent work on the Norwegian Lutheran Mission Society in South Africa that has focused on mission masculinity, exploring how different kinds of hegemonic 'manly' mission masculinities were constructed in relation to subordinated 'unmanly', female, settler and Zulu masculinities.[13] 'Proper mission masculinities' distinguished between direct and indirect mission work, the former focusing on the inner world and the latter on external worlds. This suggests that even the narrowly conceived industrial and agricultural education promoted by the British and American missions for Africans conflicted with a Lutheran notion of appropriate mission endeavour. Within Lutheran theology, mission work should focus on the inner, 'spiritual' rather than external, 'temporal' spheres. It restricted the Church and mission from becoming involved in secular projects and thus 'did not wholeheartedly encourage' and embrace the promotion of an independent African peasantry in the same way as the other missions did.[14] Lutheran mission work and strategies were deeply patriarchal and gendered in all respects. The nature of the gender system changed only gradually and unevenly, as will be illustrated in this book through discussion of curricula, sexual and moral disciplinary regimes, and the work assigned to men and women in the mission.

Transition from mission to Bantu Education

There is a substantial literature on both mission and Bantu Education as well as on continuities and discontinuities between them. We know that when the Bantu Education Act (No. 47 of 1953) finally did make provision for the transfer of control of mission schools, there was nothing new about the idea: it had been much discussed and debated, in colonial conferences and journals, throughout the 1930s and into the 1940s when the Eiselen Commission was in process, and also after it reported in 1951. Werner Willi Max Eiselen, the author of its report, which became the basis of the Bantu Education Act, expressed one of the dominant educational wisdoms of his time[15] in an 'anti-humanist and deeply racialized tradition of cultural study'.[16] Although there was opposition to Bantu Education as segregationist, there was also much agreement that things had to change. Indeed, the crisis in the mission schools, manifested in food and discipline riots in the years immediately after the Second World War, underlined this fact.[17]

This consensus about the need for change explains, in part, why leading missionary schools 'capitulated' when confronted with the option of either retaining control of their schools at reduced subsidy or relinquishing them to the state.[18] In the closing pages of his monumental overview of Protestant missions in South Africa and their racial politics, mission historian Elphick shows how, one by one, the great mission schools decided to close their doors, doing so without much protest. These schools included Lovedale in the Eastern Cape, St Peter's in Johannesburg, Grace Dieu in Pietersburg (now Polokwane), and Adams College near Durban. There was no opposition from the German Berlin Mission Society (BMS) branch of the Lutherans. The only significant opposition from among the missions themselves came from the Roman Catholic Church, which chose to go private. And so, within this grand narrative of history of Bantu Education, its implementation went relatively smoothly, despite a schools boycott organised by the ANC in 1955. The Bantu Education system achieved the massification of schooling for Africans, by expanding provision in the 1950s and 1960s, thereby 'stabilising' provision, particularly in the urban areas, albeit on the basis of paltry state resources and community financing by Africans themselves.[19]

While Jonathan Hyslop has illuminated the broad contours and features of how a policy and system responding to a crisis in social reproduction was called into being and resisted, Meghan Healy-Clancy has cast light on its particularly gendered character through the case study of Inanda Seminary for Girls in Natal.[20] Not many studies exist of the actual internal processes which accompanied the process of state take-over, closure or going private, and how schools actually changed. Healy-Clancy is an exception, although here, as in much of the literature on the process, the focus is on the prominent and more well-to-do mission schools. It is the counterpoint to this study: as an American Board mission school, Inanda chose closure rather than adaptation to the new regime. Attention here is fixed on the – rather different – Lutheran Hermannsburg Mission Society. The latter provides insight into the complexities of the politics of accommodation to Bantu Education among more compliant missions. In his recent book on apartheid, Saul Dubow[21] points out that one of the major historiographical advances of the post-apartheid decades has been an exponential growth in histories of resistance. While such histories are important, it is equally important to keep histories of the state, of governance and compliance, in view. These histories also continue to shape the present.

With some exceptions, the cumulative effect of the literature is to see an obliteration and corresponding romanticisation of the past mission education rather than its continuity into the Bantu Education present. This may be because, with few exceptions, the majority of studies have focused on the fate of the well-known, elite, oppositional, English-speaking mission schools that produced the leaders of the African nationalist movement. And the dominant understanding is a major break with little continuity from the past. Central to post-colonial approaches has been the recognition first that colonial and post-colonial are not neatly separated, but interpenetrated, in the sense that the past is part of the present much as the present constructs the past. It has involved a move away from binary oppositions of coloniser/colonised, first/third world, and black/white, through recognising the 'unstable', 'fractured' and 'hybrid' nature of such identities.[22] What these approaches suggest is that there are no neat divisions between past and present, mission and Bantu Education, resistance and compliance – rather, they interpenetrate one another, and the picture is a far more mixed and hybrid one than our current political discourse allows us to see. This perspective is reinforced by recent approaches to transnationalism and colonialism, which constitute subsidiary themes in this book. The title *Between Worlds* tries to capture these interconnections.

Transnationalism, colonialism and education

Although there is a significant literature on transnationalism and education in the British Empire, this is much less the case for Germany. As in studies on missions, the emphasis has shifted from concern with 'cultural imperialism' or the influence of mission ideas on the colonised conceived as passive victims, to the reverse process – how ideas and practices in the colony influence the imperial homeland[23] and how colonial ideas traversed colonial boundaries and were adopted and modified in each context.[24]

Transnational studies try to break down dividing lines between national units. They emphasise networks spanning national boundaries, the 'centrality of linkages' and the 'transoceanic flows of people, goods and ideas'.[25] South Africa's educational history has over time been significantly informed by such networks of people and ideas crossing national boundaries. One significant recent study that does examine networks created by former mission schools is Timothy Gibbs's *Mandela's Kinsmen: Nationalist Elites and Apartheid's First Bantustan*.[26] Gibbs is interested to show how one small set of mission schools continued to create a national elite in the Eastern Cape during the apartheid years. The focus on networks of people traversing different political positions, who had attended the same schools, is an important one in South Africa. This study intends to extend this and other approaches by looking at institutional and individual processes of change and adaptation in contexts shaped by transnational and inter-Lutheran currents.[27]

From a gender perspective, the theory of men and women occupying separate spheres has also been questioned, showing particularly in the Norwegian Lutheran case in South Africa that these were neither clear-cut nor neatly divided. For Kristin Fjelde Tjelle, this was linked to Lutheran ideas about three distinct hierarchies or orders within Christian society: the household, the state, and the church.[28] Missionary men exercised authority both in the spiritual realm and as heads of households. Male missionaries often performed women's work in the home, which was also considered their sphere of authority, and missionary wives participated fully albeit unequally in the work of their husbands.[29] Missionary wives 'did not conduct any independent mission work, however; their service was always related to the position of their husbands'. The work of missionary women was also restricted to teaching and nursing. And yet women's involvement in 'devotions, religious education, reading, writing and arithmetic lessons' had the effect of disrupting 'the traditionally strict distinctions between the direct and indirect mission work'.[30]

This book is thus deeply informed by the post-colonial approach spanning mission, transition and transnational studies that seeks an understanding of the interpenetration and entanglements of worlds and identities and the ways in which the colonial legacy has involved 'cultural mixing and hybridisation'.[31]

The Hermannsburgers' move to South Africa was, indeed, part of a larger, nineteenth-century transnational, diasporic movement of people from Europe to different parts of the globe. The Hermannsburg Mission established missions not only in South Africa but also in Botswana, Ethiopia, India, Australia, the United States and Latin America. But their relationship to the de facto colonial power was an ambiguous one – simultaneously distant and close.

In the first instance, Hermannsburgers were Germans in South Africa, a country deeply marked by British colonialism, and towards which they felt some antipathy. Germany's nineteenth-century colonial Empire was short-lived and not as extensive as that of the British or the French. Germany was a colonial power from the Berlin Conference in 1884 to the end of the First World War in 1919 when its former colonies were distributed to other colonial powers. Hermannsburgers were not subjects of the British Empire, a major theme of recent historiography, and did not see themselves as such.[32] The founder of the Hermannsburgers, Louis Harms, opposed British colonialism. Part of his vision was to arm Africans to fight colonial powers so that they could be independent.

More significantly, and in the second instance, the role of the Hermannsburgers in the local context placed them in a colonial relationship to Africans. Although Louis Harms was indeed opposed to British colonialism and sought the establishment of independent African polities and an independent Lutheran African church, his faith was vested in the power of the mission and Christianity to effect this. As much as his vision opposed colonialism, it was ensnared in it. In addition, despite the often close alliances with African polities, the Hermannsburgers' eventual close identification with Afrikaners and colonial authority, as well as their appropriation of notions of themselves as Prussian feudal lords – 'of a past that had never been their own'[33] – meant that Harms' original vision was lost, and in practice rarely fought for. Hermannsburger history, being part of European social history, must therefore, as Fritz Hasselhorn argued, be considered part of colonial history.[34]

The Hermannsburg Mission Society and education

Within the substantial corpus of work on Christian missions in South Africa, there has, until recently, been relatively little regarding the Lutheran and specifically German missions that has not been written by Hermannsburgers themselves. Missionary-historian Heinrich Voges's organisational history of the Hermannsburg Mission provides a contextual history of the mission in South Africa, focusing on key missionaries and events in its educational history,[35] while Georg Scriba and Gunnar Lislerud cast light on Hermannsburgers within the broader history of Lutheran division and cooperation in South Africa.[36] Two important scholarly exceptions, which pay some attention to education, are those by Hasselhorn and Kirsten Rüther, with the former reflecting a political economy approach and the latter a social history approach.[37] For Hasselhorn, the main focus is on relations of power established between the mission, settlers and Africans, within a colonial framework; for Rüther, it is on processes of adoption by Africans of Christianity. Each provides important insight into the educational approach of the mission up to 1939. These studies are significantly deepened by the results of a comprehensive research process begun in 2007 by the German churches to come to terms with the history of complicity of Protestant missions in the history of colonialism and apartheid in southern Africa.[38] Volumes edited by Hanns Lessing et al. consist of contributions by scholars from within and outside the church and mission network.

Hasselhorn's political economy, appearing in 1989, situates the Hermannsburger history within processes of colonial conquest. The study shows how the Hermannsburg Mission was founded in 1854 as a *Bauernmission* (peasants' mission) which became enmeshed in local struggles over land. The original intentions of Louis Harms to create independent African polities able to resist the negative impact of British imperialism, colonialism and industrialisation, were radically altered over the next century as missionaries adjusted to and became embedded in local social relations. German settlers accompanied the missionaries, and they retained close relationships with one another. From the beginning, German farmers, artisans and missionaries identified with the racial thought patterns and practices of whites in general and Afrikaners in particular. Based on the need for African labour, missionaries restricted African aspirations for schooling and struggled against growing state requirements that missions provide instruction in English.[39] In this regard, they were no different from the Dutch Reformed Church missions.[40] By the late 1930s they were supportive of Christian National Education, which later became the foundation of Bantu Education. Several missionaries suspected of having sympathies with the Nazi cause were interned during the Second World War. Hasselhorn's study raises the issue as to whether the approach developed in this period changed in the second half of the twentieth century or not.

There were differences, however, between the mission in Natal and that in the Transvaal, which had much to do with the different land-holding patterns and relations with the missionaries.[41] These differences would later have implications for the fate of the schools under Bantu Education. In Natal and Zululand, mission schools were established on mission farms where Africans were often labour tenants, or on mission glebes which were reserves allocated to different mission societies by the colonial government for the purpose of continuing their work. In the Western Transvaal, by contrast, land was initially bought by the mission on behalf of African chiefs who paid for it through levies imposed on their subjects.[42] In a detailed thesis, Graeme Simpson explores the relationships between missionaries, local African communities and the Native Affairs department. He demonstrates how political and ideological battles within African polities during the 1920s and 1930s were shaped by the social differentiation that emerged among land-holding, landless, wage-earning and migrant workers in the Tswana polities of the Hermannsburg Mission.[43]

Simpson traces the role that the Hermannsburg missionaries played, as invitees of Tswana chiefdoms, in purchasing land on their behalf. Ernst Penzhorn, whose father had arrived as the first invited missionary in 1867, was the resident Hermannsburg missionary until his death in 1940. By virtue of this land-buying role and the provision of schooling, the Hermannsburgers became, Simpson argues, a form of 'state church' of the polities in the area.[44] Almost all of the conflicts in the 1920s and 1930s, mostly within chiefdoms, and against chiefs' efforts to extract the levies and taxes to pay for land so bought, can be traced to conflicts between chiefs and Christianised migrants or wealthier peasants. In almost every district, the latter resisted and disputed 'traditionally defined' communal responsibilities and obligations, refusing to perform labour services and pay levies.[45] Mission-education Christians formed a substantial part of the leadership of these resistance movements. Resistance was almost always expressed in terms of traditional Tswana law and custom. Few connections were formed with others, and opposition remained 'local and introverted'.[46] And seldom was white authority consciously challenged. Rather, both chiefs and rebels appealed to officials of the Native Affairs and Justice departments to settle disputes.

Penzhorn always took the side of the chiefs, regardless of whether the accusations against them were the – presumably anti-Christian – practices of financial mismanagement and drunkenness.[47] In resulting court cases, the concept of 'traditional law' and whether chiefs had absolute power or were beholden to the *lekgotla*, which exercised a more democratic form of power, became deeply contested. As Simpson shows, missionaries, the Native Affairs department and appointed chiefs all promoted a rigid, formalistic and legalistic view of the absolute authority of the chief that suited the Native Affairs department, whereas the so-called 'rebels',[48] or dissenters, often drawing on Sol Plaatje and like-minded critics of this approach in support of their court cases, argued for more democratic forms of power rooted in the *lekgotla*. This all provides valuable background to the conflicts that persisted into the period when Bantu Education was introduced. It suggests that many of the conflicts and processes that congealed around the transition also had roots in these earlier conflicts.

Simpson's analysis of the role of the missionaries in education is mainly concerned with the conflict that developed between Penzhorn and Rev. Kenneth Spooner, a clash also taken up by Belinda Bozzoli (with Mmantho Nkotsoe) in *Women of Phokeng*.[49] According to Bernard Mbenga and Andrew Manson, the two missionaries remained 'implacable foes until their respective deaths in 1937 and 1940'.[50] This was a conflict on the one hand between Penzhorn's more conservative emphasis on the use of mother tongue and religious instruction and the more radical approach taken by Spooner, who promoted English and industrial education with a dose of Africanism as well as Joint Council involvement.[51] Both Simpson and Bozzoli (with Nkotsoe) show that, despite the challenge that Spooner posed to the Hermannsburgers, and despite the widespread popularity that Mbenga shows Spooner enjoyed, the Hermannsburgers remained the mission endorsed by the chiefs. Moreover, Simpson and Bozzoli (with Nkotsoe) both make extensive use of Naboth Mokgatle's *Autobiography of an Unknown South African* to cast light on mission-African relations at this time.[52] Both show that Christianisation did not involve abandonment of Tswana customs such as polygamy, bride-price and initiation schools, or of 'diviners', the medicine-men frowned upon by missionaries, but that it was rather adopted in a 'contradictory' manner, combining elements of both.[53]

Writing more than a decade later, Kirsten Rüther's main concern is to recognise that mission ideologies and ideas were not imposed but adopted. Her main contribution is a comparison of the Hermannsburg and Berlin Mission Society approaches. In the process, she casts light on the educational practices and processes of the society and the communities with whom they worked. Focusing on the period from the 1870s to the early 1900s, Rüther shows that the Hermannsburg schools were oriented 'along the concept of pre-industrial peasant schooling' but became 'spaces for colonial encounters . . . in which people who were geographically and historically separated came into contact with each other and established ongoing relations, although in the long term these proved to be based on radical inequality and intractable conflict'.[54] Schools were principally aimed at ensuring baptism. As such, religious instruction in the Lutheran catechism was considered much more important than reading, writing and arithmetic, which as a rule did not go beyond basic addition and subtraction. Schooling, as Simpson also emphasised, ended with the confirmation ceremony.

Schooling was regularly interrupted by labour demands of the homestead. Like Simpson, Rüther shows that by the beginning of the twentieth century, parents were making strategic use of schools, carefully selecting schools for their children. Choices were increasingly made on the basis of language, resulting in competition among Lutheran schools, which provided for instruction in the mother tongue, and nearby schools where English was the medium of instruction. Eventually, in order not to lose more congregants, the mission relented and began teaching also in English. By the 1920s the schools were forced to use English in exchange for government recognition and subsidy. All provinces during the 1930s and 1940s prescribed English as the medium of instruction. Hermannsburgers used English as the medium of instruction but had a firm belief in education through the mother tongue, so Tswana was taught in the Western Transvaal and Zulu in schools in Natal and Zululand. At first they used the London Missionary Society readers for their Tswana schools, but later developed their own.

Although the mission trained African men and women as teachers to supply the expanding network of schools, such training was rudimentary and the status of these teachers was low: they were trained to be 'helpers', or *baruti*, as opposed to teachers or *moruti*, which was the appellation reserved for missionaries. Teacher trainees were between the ages of 14 and 16 and their syllabus consisted of Bible and Catechism classes, Church and Mission History, South African and Palestinian Geography, Arithmetic, and Reading and Writing in Tswana and Dutch.[55] In 1924 the Bethel Institute was established near Lichtenburg to train evangelists as well as teachers. It did not go beyond Standard 6, and like most other grant-aided mission schools, it used the provincial syllabus. Rüther's book ends in the early nineteenth century. It nonetheless provides a valuable insight, along with that of Hasselhorn's, into the gendered colonial character of education provided before and immediately after Union.

The focus of contributions within the second Lessing volume is somewhat different, since the aim is to explicitly confront the history of German missions in South Africa.[56] Contributions are concerned with the Nazi heritage and expression in educational ideologies. They discuss the mixed relationship of the Hermannsburgers to Nazi Germany in the 1930s, the significance of the notion of *Volkstum* or ethnic identity to notions of education in the 1940s and 1950s, and the role of the wider Lutheran and Christian church movement in breaking the link to apartheid in the 1970s. The concept of diaspora is important to the contributions in Volume 1 on the origins, development and identity of German language communities in southern Africa and the consequences in terms of settler, mission and African identities. Here Hasselhorn's contribution looks at the gradual, inexorable process up to the 1930s by which the congregations in Hermannsburg became socially, spatially and educationally segregated on the basis of notions of the superiority of whites.[57] Martin Eberhardt shows how German-speakers in South Africa during the 1930s and certainly from the Hermannsburg Mission largely shared the racist and anti-Semitic attitudes of their Afrikaner neighbours'.[58]

There is some debate about the specific character and role of the German missions in South Africa. Kevin Ward argues that, by contrast with the Anglicanism which institutionally was 'almost exclusively an English affair,' the missionary work of Lutheran missions, including the Norwegians, Swedes, Finns and Germans, contributed greatly to creating a 'Lutheran cosmopolitanism'.[59] He describes the milieu of the Hermannsburgers as being rather more detached from British rule and closer to the Afrikaans-speaking world than either the Anglicans or, indeed, the Wesleyans. Ward later argues that 'it is too simple to contrast a positive "liberal" approach to African Christianity (exemplified by English-speaking missionary activity) to the negative "apartheid" ideology of the Afrikaner churches, in which German mission is seen as collusive' as this 'fails to recognise the complicity of British capitalist imperialism in South Africa's development and the inadequacy of "Anglo-Saxon" liberal Christianity to address the enormous social and political, as well as cultural and religious, contradictions inherent in the shaping of South Africa'.[60] This is similar to the view expressed by Norman Etherington in 1978 that the 'subtle chemistry of racial prejudice' and the colour-line had become a 'universal characteristic of Christianity' by the 1880s.[61] Nonetheless, there were specificities of the German mission approach, particularly from the 1930s to 1960s: it was based on essentialist and anti-universalist romantic notions celebrating cultural and national particularity.[62]

Volume 2 of Lessing et al. documents the complicity of the German churches and congregations in apartheid. In an unvarnished reconstruction of the attitudes of the 1930s, Gunther Schendel shows how Hermannsburgers at first welcomed Nazi Germany as a source of pride and statement of German recovery from the losses of the First World War, but declined to accept the proposed co-option of churches by the Nazi state, and so gradually distanced themselves. At an individual level, however, he suggests that there were some strong sympathisers. Both Schendel and Peter Kallaway draw attention to the idea of *Volkstum* in the development of educational ideas, and support for the segregationist policies of J.B.M. Hertzog, with Kallaway focusing specifically on the Berlin Mission Society while Schendel also includes the Hermannsburgers.[63] Schendel's work on how the conservative milieu and 'social practice' of the Hermannsburgers shaped their approach is insightful.[64] These ideas about ethnicity as nationhood, and the necessity of educating Africans in their own language and for identification not with Europe but African ethnic identity, underlay the approach in education that later developed into Bantu Education. Rudolf Hinz shows how the German churches became integrated into and consolidated relations with apartheid during the 1950s, but that the massacre that took place at Sharpeville in 1960 was a turning point. By the early 1970s, despite the separation of black and white Lutherans into different organisational structures,[65] younger anti-apartheid missionaries and the presence of African representatives at international Lutheran and church gatherings were decisive in shifting the church response to condemnation of apartheid.[66] Joining the anti-apartheid struggle 'relatively late',[67] Hermannsburgers like Wolfram Kistner and Manas Buthelezi nonetheless played a key role once they had done so.

Conclusion

The break with mission education, the book argues, was deeply conflictual and contradictory including many continuities but also changes over time. First, it situates the mission in its broader Lutheran context and discusses differences among them over their educational politics. Second, it examines how power relations shifted between the mission, the state, and communities, and how the mission's influence was gradually and differentially eroded in Natal and the Transvaal. Third, it explores the politics of continuities and changes in curricula, medium of instruction and textbooks in schools and teacher training. And fourth, it traces the paradoxical effect of apartheid in uniting and radicalising a previously quiescent and isolationist educational community. This was in part a consequence of strengthened transnational networks and post-war generations asking new questions which enabled the educational endeavour to interrogate the intentions of apartheid. It resulted in the creation of an institution in 1963 that contradicted much that apartheid stood for, the Umpumulo Theological College. The offspring of Hermannsburg missionaries, working in the secular, 'temporal' world of Lutheranism, played a key role in driving the Primary Education Upgrade Programme promoted in Bophuthatswana from the late 1970s. Though it was, similarly, a progressivist educational project in intent, in its association and alliance with ethnic nationalism it was doomed to failure. But Hermannsburg-connected people played no comparable role in the educational project of Inkatha, *Ubuntu-botho*. Here the book looks at transnational networks of influence outside schools but nevertheless impacting on schools. Umpumulo and the Primary Education Upgrade Programme were both distinguished by their transnational connections – in the one it fostered opposition to apartheid, while in the other it bolstered the apartheid ethnic project. Both were deeply gendered projects, the former dominated by men, the latter by women. Tracing African responses throughout, the book ends with three very different routes taken through the mission by Micah Kgasi, Paulina Dlamini and Naboth Mokgatle.

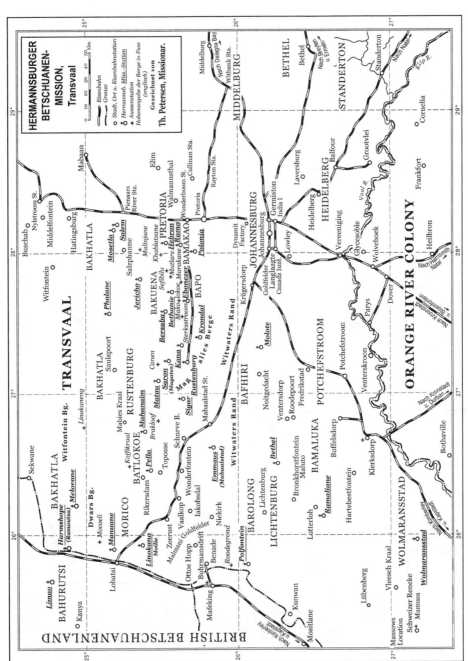

Map 1: Hermannsburg Mission, Transvaal (redrawn by Wendy Job). The map is an exact replica of the original, and includes its spelling particularities and errors.

Natal, Hermannsburger Missionsgebiet.

Map 2: Hermannsburg Mission, Zululand and Natal (redrawn by Wendy Job). The map is an exact replica of the original, and includes its spelling particularities and errors.

CHAPTER 1

TRANSNATIONAL COOPERATION, HERMANNSBURGERS AND BANTU EDUCATION

In order to understand how the Hermannsburgers positioned themselves in relation to Bantu Education it is necessary to provide a picture of who they were, their relationships with other Lutherans and the approach they took to politics, since this defined their approach to education.

Who were the Hermannsburgers?

The Hermannsburg Mission was one of the smaller, Lutheran, German societies founded by Louis Harms in Hermannsburg, a small village in a picturesque but rural and agricultural area in northern Germany known as the Lüneberger Heide.[1] Its missionaries arrived in British colonial Natal in 1854. The Hermannsburg Mission has been described as a *Bauernmission* – a mission of peasants, or *plattelanders*. Although they shared a highly gendered, patriarchal social organisation with the Berlin Mission, they differed in their social origins and theology. They were from humble rural agricultural and artisanal backgrounds, and not from the aristocratic, military or civil service, the upper strata of Prussian society.[2] Unlike the Prussian Berlin Mission Society, whose Lutheranism was an amalgam of Lutheranism with the Calvinism of the state church, the Hermannsburgers chose a more 'original' form of Lutheranism.[3]

Support for mission work for both Hermannsburgers and the Berlin Mission came from country districts, where the influence of the pietist movement that had spread across Protestant Europe in the 17th and 18th centuries was strong. Its 'simple piety' corresponded to Methodism or non-conformism in Britain and was characterised by an 'avers[ion] to orthodoxy and dogmatism in the Church'.[4]

Once ordained and sent out to South Africa, missionaries were sent to a mission station for a year to learn the local language, either Zulu or Tswana, and then given a posting either in the Marico or Magaliesburg district in the Western Transvaal or the Zulu mission in Natal. Missionaries were normally accompanied and assisted by their wives, usually women within and drawn from the Hermannsburg community.[5] The majority of missionaries were not highly educated, and had attended their local village schools. None were trained teachers. Yet they established a network of mission stations with satellite outstations in Natal, Zululand and the Western Transvaal, on land granted either by chiefs, the Natal colonial government, or the President of the Zuid-Afrikaansche Republiek (ZAR). They were accompanied by German colonists, who would assist in ensuring that the Hermannsburgers were a self-sufficient Christian community serving as an example to the 'heathen'.[6] In Zululand and Natal, Hermannsburg and Moorleigh – the latter being the Natal seat of the Hermannsburg Mission Press – became the base for German missionaries and settlers. In the Western Transvaal, Kroondal near Rustenburg served this purpose. The Mission Press also established itself at Rustenburg. Hermannsburg women seldom enter the missionary record. Missionary wives played a secondary and supportive role to the missionaries, whose working lives and networks were exclusively male. Not distinguishing between missionary wives and wives of German settlers linked to the Hermannsburg mission, Christina Landman argues that family was at the centre of Hermannsburg women's lives and that they 'gave priority to marriage and domestic duties'.[7] Tjelle, writing specifically about Lutheran missionary wives, has by contrast argued that they played a more active, albeit unrecognised and unseen role alongside the male missionaries.[8]

Conversion was initially extremely slow – evidence of the widespread resistance to missionaries. However, as in other missions, girls and women were the first to convert, dominating school enrolments from the start.[9] Segregationist practices and assumptions meant that, from the late nineteenth and early twentieth century onwards, Hermannsburgers were as much struck by black separatism as were other missions.[10] The role of the Hermannsburgers was ambiguous, however, as they also played an intermediary role between Africans and ruling white societies. Fluency in local languages also marked them off from other whites, facilitating a degree of closeness that was often rudely disturbed by the latter's assumptions of difference and inequality.[11] Particularly well-known is the story of Penzhorn and the Bafokeng: as Africans were not allowed to buy land in the ZAR, the mission bought land on behalf of the Bafokeng throughout the late nineteenth and early twentieth centuries when the Land Acts were being put in place – a development that would have huge consequences in later years.[12]

Studies of the early encounters between German missionaries such as the Hermannsburg Mission Society and the Tswana showed that the patterns of response included both resistance and cooperation.[13] For example, African chiefs made it clear to the missionaries that they 'should support royal authority and . . . serve as intermediaries between them and the white colonists',[14] and they entered into alliances with missionaries whereby missionaries bought and held land in trust for Africans. But mass conversions did not occur as hoped for, and five separatist movements emerged between 1870 and 1910.[15] Alliances with Boers were just as important to the Hermannsburgers as those with chiefs, on whose goodwill they depended for access to local communities. The alliances with Boers derived at first from the Hermannsburg Mission aim of building African polities independent of British imperialism and then as a consequence of their own integration into property and land-holding white communities. The Hermannsburgers sided with the Boers against the British during the South African War (1899–1902) and the First World War.

The Hermannsburgers established a network of mission schools separate from the well-known German schools for their own children.[16] In Natal and Zululand, mission stations carried Zulu names such as Ehlanzeni, Enyezane, Etembeni, Emlalazi, Emhlangane, Emvutjini, Emhlangubo, Ekombela, Entombe and Endhlovini. In contrast to this, nearby towns established for German communities replicated the names of villages in the Lüneburger Heide, from which the people came, names such as Hermannsburg, Lüneburg, Müden, Harburg, Bergen and Lilienthal. In the Western Transvaal, names of mission stations included ones of Afrikaans, Tswana and religious origin: Polfontein, Emmaus, Manuane, Pella, Mahanaim, Jericho, Mosetla, Polonia, Saron, Kana, Melorane, and so on.[17] While Hermannsburg in Germany was responsible for salaries of missionaries and pastors, the salaries of teachers and evangelists, as well as the construction of school buildings and maintenance were covered by local parishes.[18] Given the mostly strained financial circumstances of the missions, churches often doubled as schools, especially on the outstations. By 1949 there were altogether 36 missionaries covering 59 mission stations assisted by 921 Africans working in various capacities. The Marico district boasted 6,338 children in its schools, the Zulu mission 4,597 and the Magaliesburg district 4,430.[19] In the absence of exact figures, evidence provided by Dehnke seems to suggest that girls and women were preponderant from the beginning.[20]

Transnational cooperation

Cooperation between Lutherans from Germany, Sweden, Norway and America began in the context of the emergence of African separatist movements and the feminisation of religion. Strengthening their Lutheran identity in this way was a strategy, according to Tjelle, that Norwegian Christian men adopted against these external threats.[21] While development was slow during the first half of the twentieth century, the Second World War and the advent of apartheid provided a further boost to cooperation among Lutherans in South Africa.

1880-1912

In 1951 the Lutheran Publishing House in Durban published a history of the cooperation among Lutheran missions in Natal from 1912 to 1951.[22] It was a significant moment, marking the full entry of the Hermannsburg Mission Society's members into the international community of Lutherans.[23] When cooperation initiatives first began between Norwegian, Swedish, Berlin and Hanoverian Missions in 1889, the Hermannsburg Mission Society kept itself aloof. It was only in 1939 that divisions over its participation in local and international bodies were resolved in favour of joining. In 1949 the first deputy chairman of the Lutheran World Federation Commission on World Missions was a Hermannsburger, A. Elfers, as was the secretary. This marked a turning point that would eventually result in decisive shifts in the nature of its educational activities. Up until this time, however, its participation was desultory and focused on joint publishing and teacher-training ventures. The teacher-training activities tell us something about the nature of teacher training before the transition to Bantu Education, and also indicate how it was affected by the advent of Bantu Education.

Lutheran missions associated with the cooperative initiative had first started work in Natal and Zululand in the nineteenth century. From the beginning, joint work was divided among them. The Norwegian Mission Society's Bishop Schreuder arrived in 1844. A colourful character, he came, left, and then returned to Natal, establishing close links with Chief Mpande, through whose good offices he established a station at Empangeni. Differences with his Home Board in Norway led to his forming his own society. This breakaway society did not join the Cooperating Lutheran Missions (CLMs). In 1928 the Norwegian Mission Society was taken over by the American Lutheran Mission, which consisted of Norwegians who had emigrated to America. Schreuder established a mission station at Umpumulo in 1850. The subject of a fascinating study of the nature of relationships forged between missionaries, mother body, local mission societies and Africans in this new space,[24] Umpumulo also became a teacher-training establishment of some repute for the Lutheran Societies in Natal. Its complex transition during the 1960s and 1970s from mission teacher training to theological institute for the training of pastors is related in Chapters 6 and 7.

The Berlin Mission Society, founded in 1824, first started mission work in the Eastern Cape in 1834. It began work in Zululand in 1846 and in 1847 established a station at Emmaus, close to present-day Bergville. In 1860 it started work in the ZAR. Emmaus became the base for the training of evangelists for all the Natal Lutheran societies. Evangelists were distinct from pastors in that they were not ordained, and were in effect the local assistants of missionaries. The Church of Sweden Mission arrived in 1876 and established its main station at Dundee. Its mission station at Oscarsberg near present-day Rorke's Drift became the base for training Lutheran pastors. The Hanoverian Free Church Mission was founded in 1892 and emerged as the result of a split within the Hermannsburg Mission Society, a split that continues to the present day.

Although there were personal and informal contacts among the Lutheran missions in Natal from the beginning, the reasons for formal cooperation were both local and international. Internationally, mission conferences were all the rage. In 1881 a Natal Missionary Conference was held. Eight years later, stimulated by this activity, a specifically Lutheran Conference was held at Umpumulo.[25] African disengagement from missions from the 1880s, through the establishment of separatist churches known as Ethiopianism, spurred Lutherans to find ways of stemming the bleeding. The solution was to train teachers, evangelists and pastors. A related factor was the growth of the Reformed Missions' educational work as represented in the highly successful Lovedale Institute. Also, because institutions such as Lovedale provided education to a higher level than that provided by the Lutherans, they attracted more Africans than their Lutheran counterparts. African Lutherans who wanted further education were welcomed in institutions such as Adams College. This represented a threat for the Lutherans.[26] Definitive, perhaps, was the indication by the Natal Education

Department that it would not fund multiple institutions, and that only one grant would be made to Lutherans.[27]

Pressures both internal and external thus contributed to initiatives to provide education beyond the 'small seminaries for the training of evangelists and . . . small primary schools of the common inferior type'.[28] At the start of the twentieth century these schools were still focused primarily on teaching the tenets of Lutheranism through the Bible and the Lutheran small catechism. The production of literature to support this teaching, such as the production of a common hymn book compiled in 1897, had been one of the main early cooperative undertakings. In that year, a joint Lutheran newspaper, *Isithunywa*, was also begun.

Between 1900 and 1910 discussions and consultations proceeded apace, but all that eventuated was the establishment of the seminary for training evangelists at Oscarsberg in 1908. After Union in 1910, the broader impulse towards unification among whites in the country probably pushed the Lutheran societies into a meeting at Dundee in 1910 where the Swedish, Norwegian and Berlin mission societies agreed to turn Umpumulo into a joint Lutheran Normal or teacher-training school, Emmaus into a seminary for training evangelists, with pastors being trained at Oscarsberg. The Scheme of Cooperation upon which they agreed in 1911 included rules and regulations regarding the number of staff, their accommodation and salaries, buildings and equipment for classes (up to Standard 6) and a curriculum.[29] The curriculum provided for was a fairly liberal one. Secular instruction was to consist of Zulu (reading, dictation and composition), English (reading, translation, letter writing and elementary grammar), Arithmetic (based on the syllabus of government-aided schools), Geography (outline of the continents and countries of the world, especially South Africa and Palestine), History (outline of the history of Natal), Hygiene, Writing (the 'semi-upright style'), and Singing. Religious instruction would consist in Bible knowledge, the New Testament and Church history.

The three missions that stood apart at this time were the Hermannsburgers, Hanoverians and Bishop Schreuder's Church of Norway mission. Although the former two faced similar pressures and threats as the Norwegians, it has been argued that doctrinal differences – more pronounced at home than in South Africa – militated against joining together. For the Hermannsburgers, the Berlin Mission Society's close links with the form of Prussian Calvinism represented in the Hanoverian Church, to which they were opposed, was apparently persuasive. In addition, the Hermannsburgers were resistant to state control and being obliged to follow state syllabi, including the teaching of English.[30]

Once their respective Home Boards had approved the proposals for cooperation, the three cooperating partners began meeting regularly in Durban as the CLMs. Ironically, this was in 1912, the same year as the founding of the African National Congress (ANC).

1912–1939

For almost two decades after the founding of the CLM, the work limped along, significantly disrupted by the effects of the First World War. If German missions had suffered severe losses as a result of having supported the Boers in the South African War, the main consequence of the First World War was the loss of revenue from the mother country. The reduction of income meant that Oscarsberg and Emmaus were closed during the war. The extreme financial straits in which the Berlin Mission Society found itself as a result of the post-war slump in Germany contributed to cooperative activities in South Africa being constrained for several years. The main work at this time included the production of a Zulu grammar, reading charts, an ABC spelling book, and Zulu readers for use at Umpumulo.[31] The syllabus followed at Umpumulo followed the Natal Education Department syllabus for the Native Teacher Training Certificate introduced in 1910. It was narrower than the CLM curriculum, excluding for example History and Geography – limited as these were – and including only the teaching of Zulu and English, as well as Writing, Arithmetic and Drawing, up to and including Standard 4.[32] But this changed again in 1918 when, despite objections from the Berlin Mission Society about the expense involved, Chief Inspector of Native Education in Natal, C.T. Loram, revamped syllabi in an attempt to make them more 'relevant' to students' lives.[33] This meant removing subjects such as Algebra, Geometry and Translation and including subjects considered to have a practical value for students, such as Physiology, Hygiene, Nature Study, and agricultural and manual work.[34] Whereas the main objection from many missionary societies and intellectuals was the anti-intellectual orientation of the syllabus, the Hermannsburgers' main complaint was state control and instruction in English.

In 1929, things began picking up again. By this time the Hermannsburgers' differences with the Berliners had become more muted, and they had started sending pupils to Umpumulo despite the medium of instruction being English. The matter of Hermannsburg's full participation was discussed at the General Lutheran Conferences in 1932, 1934 and 1936, but it stalled until 1938 when the Hermannsburg leadership changed. The Hermannsburgers joined the CLM in 1939, but the Hanoverian Free Church remained outside, ostensibly on financial grounds.[35] What role a more confident Germany, led by National Socialists pushing a nationalist agenda, played in this is unclear. But transnational cooperation within South Africa, including among Swedes, Norwegians, Americans and various Germans, had become a reality. During the Second World War, cooperative activities by members of the German Lutheran mission societies were once again constrained by finances as all contributions from Germany declined dramatically. In the 1920s, inflation and economic crisis had been the principal reasons for such financial constraints; during the 1930s, Hitler imposed currency restrictions and cut off allowances, particularly to churches such as the Hermannsburgers and Berlin Mission Society, which were not prepared to accept the 'volkisch neo-paganist' and 'Aryanised version of Christianity' under state control promoted by Hitler, even as they might have been sympathetic to an apparently revitalising Germany and its views on race.[36] During this period, when cost-cutting was the order of the day, teacher training at Umpumulo – to which was added a secondary school programme – as well as evangelist preparation at Oscarsberg, and Bible translation and revision work continued as the main activities.

By this stage, however, South Africa was also much changed. Not only were segregationist land, labour and social policies in place, but the influence of the numerous mission societies in African education had grown significantly. Their representatives and voices were always present and heard at the plethora of colonial, regional and national conferences held across the British Empire on African education. They were also represented on advisory bodies such as the Natal Native Education Advisory Body, where they came into contact and exchanged views not only with missionaries from all denominations, but also with university intellectuals and government officials. Their relationships with the provincial departmental officials and inspectors were strong. There were certainly differences among the different mission configurations. While, for example, English-speaking missions associated themselves with the liberal Joint Councils for Europeans and Natives, the Hermannsburgers were less enthusiastic about participation in such liberal bodies. They were, nonetheless, aware of them.

The main rift that emerged in the 1930s in the educational field was, however, over state control of mission education. Within this overarching issue there were many other smaller considerations, all responding to broader political divisions. The question of state control, and the form this should take, not only divided all missionaries from the Union government's powerful four provincial chief inspectors of Native Education, it also caused divisions among mission societies themselves. With some exceptions, chief inspectors of Native Education were themselves the offspring of missionaries. But they sought to end the division and to bring mission schools within the ambit of the state. The main expression of this approach was the 1935–36 Welsh Report.[37] Natal's Broome Commission on Education (1936–37), chaired by the Chief Inspector of Native Education, D. McMalcolm, agreed with the position taken by the Welsh Report that the Union government should take over from provincial councils the control and administration of Native Education.

The differences over the form that state control should take aligned with the pro and anti-segregationist positions of proponents and antagonists. Many of the inspectors who were in favour of state control asserted the needs of the temporal and secular world against the spiritual, and thus also a different form of masculinity – one that challenged missionary notions. Thus, as Sue Krige has shown, chief inspectors McMalcolm from Natal, Welsh from the Cape, and Kuschke from the Orange Free State aligned themselves with liberals such as Victor Murray, W.M. MacMillan and Edgar Brookes who promoted an integrationist view of education. This approach wished to place African education on an equal footing with that of whites. They therefore argued for African education to be brought under the control of provinces and rejected the 'retribalisation' they argued would occur if African education was removed from Union provincial control and placed under a separate Native Affairs department, as proposed by segregationists and educationists such as W.W.M. Eiselen, chief inspector of native education in the Transvaal, as well as E.G. Malherbe, P.A.W. Cook and others. For the latter, the argument was that a Native Affairs department would deal with African economic, political and social issues as a whole.[38] Missions were deeply affected by these proposals, and they discussed and debated them extensively, alarmed at the prospect of loss of power and control, whatever form the change might take. Nonetheless, when the proposals were discussed in the Natal Native Education Advisory Board meeting in 1938, at which Lutherans were present, the Board accepted the principle proposed by the Welsh Report.[39]

1939-1955

The Cooperating Lutheran Missions were in a stronger position to develop and advance joint positions once the Hermannsburgers had joined. And this they did. The disquiet they felt was vividly expressed in a paper read out at the General Lutheran Conference (probably of missions in Natal) on 26 October 1939 on state efforts to take over control of teachers in schools. Titled 'Our

Reaction to the Attempts of the Education Department to take control of Native Teachers out of the Hands of Grantees' the paper addressed regulations sent to missions spelling out the conditions under which the superintendent general/director had the right to 'terminate services of a teacher, reduce his salary or remove his name from the Good Service list, or to transfer him to another post of equal or lower grade on account of proven neglect of duty of incompetence'.[40] The concerns were less with the threat to integration than to their religious purposes. Put another way, the objection was not framed in terms of the segregationist import of the recommendations, but to state control as a threat to the religious control exercised by schools.

For the author of the paper the intentions amounted to 'shifting the centre of control from the missions to the state'.[41] It meant the 'turning of government-aided mission schools into mission-aided government schools on the lines laid down by the Interdepartmental Committee on Native Education (1935–36)'. The paper was a strong rebuttal of the position. The question for the author was whether missionaries 'can accept this new policy in regard to our educational work without compromising the spiritual purpose for which the missionary enterprise exists'.[42] The answer given was that 'the enormous expansion of the functions of the State during the last 50 years and the increasing secularisation of modern life' had to be acknowledged, and also that 'some increase in state intervention in Nat. Ed. is simply inevitable'.[43] Ultimately, however, the 'objection to the scheme is based on the conviction that the uncompromising Christian character of the mission schools must be safeguarded'.[44]

The approach adopted in this paper amounts to one of neutrality as regards the much bigger question of the implications of the form that state control might take. A much stronger and more negative position was taken towards the Eiselen Report once it was made public. In 1952 the Cooperating Lutheran Missions in Natal issued a memorandum stating their views.[45] It was signed by W.O. Rindahl, B. Schiele, and O. Sarndal. Rindahl was from the American Lutheran Mission and had been principal at Umpumulo before taking up the post of principal at the Eshowe Zulu Lutheran High School. No Hermannsburgers were officially party to the signing or compiling of the memorandum.

The 1952 memorandum provides a carefully worded but sustained critique of the principles and recommendations of the Eiselen Commission Report, unequivocally aligning itself with the integrationists, and opposing removal of control to a separate department. It begins with a critique of the idea that Bantu Education should be made an integral part of a plan of socio-economic development. The problem with such 'planning', it suggests, is exemplified by communism and its elevation of 'society' over the individual and democracy. The memorandum notes: 'We therefore endorse the statement of Senator Brookes in his speech in the Senate on the Report: "The object of education is not to mould people to a pattern; the object of education is to set the great creative forces in every man free"'.[46] On the Eiselen Report's 'correlation of Bantu education with Bantu culture', the authors maintain that African culture cannot be the foundation of education because it was in the process of breaking down and could not be reconstituted. The future would not lie in bolstering this culture but rather in strengthening Christianity. In this regard, the critique of mission education and the proposal to do away entirely with mission control was considered illogical and impractical. The memorandum continued: 'If however Union control is to be introduced, then we definitely favour Bantu education being placed under the control of a Union Education Department. We fear that Bantu education might get lost in the maze of multitudinous interests that would be involved in the proposed Division of Bantu Affairs. Education would not receive the attention it merits'. The authors did however endorse proposals for a strong research organisation, and steps for the production of Bantu literature.[47]

The memorandum went on to question 'whether placing all Primary Education under the proposed Local Authorities would be in the best interests of Bantu education at present'.[48] Those against this were opposed to the power of traditional authorities, largely non-Christian and uneducated, being increased with regard to education:

> The local chief will hold the key position in the Bantu membership of such Local Authorities. It is well known that many chiefs in the Reserves still have little interest in education and Christianity. And those who may want education have, in most cases, no real qualification for discussing and deciding on school matters. Chiefs, too, are depending on the views of their councillors. Here again it seems that non-Christians have the greatest influence, with the Christian men of the community either not getting a chance to have a say in the tribal council, or else not daring to oppose the anti-educational or anti-Christian views of their chief and the majority of his council. The chances, therefore, of education, and particularly, Christian education, receiving the support and attention it deserves from such authorities, may be in question.

This did not mean that the opponents disagreed with the proposal that 'the local Bantu people should be given a more direct interest in their schools'.

Indeed, they believed that this 'could be achieve(d) by extending the responsibility and authority of the present advisory School Committee elected by the
parents possibly renaming it School Board), this Board to consist of European
and Bantu members, with definite provisions for Mission and Church presentation. Consideration might also be given to an extended use of suitable Bantu
as managers of schools'. In general, it was felt that, 'local control should be
orientated to the local Christian community, rather than to the tribal authority'.

On financial matters, the memorandum questioned 'the justice of requiring
the local Bantu people to provide a portion of the funds for their own education', since this was not a requirement in the case of other races:

> Why require it from the poorest section of the country? We have no
> objection to voluntary contributions towards the erection of school build-
> ings, or towards "extras" in a school, but everything in the nature of a
> separate school tax for regular school expenses we feel is unfair under
> present circumstances as the Bantu already contribute to the total income
> of the country through taxes, and through their contribution to the gen-
> eral economy of the country.[49]

While the feasibility of the proposed restructuring of schools into lower primary, higher primary, and secondary schools was questioned, it was also accepted
in part. Of greatest concern was teacher-training colleges, which should remain
in mission hands: 'This implies full use of well qualified Mission personnel
on the staff, sufficient time allowed on the time table for religious subjects
(including training in teaching), as well as time and freedom outside regular
school hours for extra-curricular religious activities which are so important in
the development of . . . Christian "personality and devotion"'.[50]

Regarding medium of instruction, the principle of mother-tongue instruction was endorsed, particularly in lower standards.[51] So too was its continued use in high school and training colleges for Religious Instruction. But
in relation to other subjects severe problems were perceived, such as lack
of textbooks or higher cost of books in the vernacular, lack of staff trained
in the vernacular, and lack of terminology. Because of the general need to
use one of the official languages (i.e. English or Afrikaans) as a medium
of instruction in high schools and training colleges, they considered that 'it
might be necessary by way of preparation to introduce the language gradually as a medium in the classes of the Higher Primary, in order to avoid too
sudden a change-over'.

The authors of the memorandum agreed with the recommendations on official languages 'with the exception that we believe that reading and writing of the first official language could begin with profit after one year of only oral work'.[52] They also believed that the teaching of the second official language should be postponed until Standard 3, at least. As the aim in the lower primary was to provide a well-balanced basic course for the large numbers who leave schools at the end of Standard 2, they did not see much use 'in burdening this course with a year of second language study which really cannot help the pupils much, but which may take considerable time from other subjects'.

Religious instruction was a matter of great importance.[53] Accordingly, they recommended the continuance in aided schools of the practice then in use in Natal, namely, that missions be allowed to teach their own catechism or church doctrine in addition to the government scripture syllabus. Any such syllabus should be drawn up in consultation with mission authorities and avoid the teaching of any doctrine not generally accepted by all denominations.

It is possible that the memorandum did not exactly reflect the views and positions of all the members of the CLM. Its views were more liberal than those normally associated with the Lutheran missions, and its approach to the mother tongue more nuanced and critical of government policy than much of the literature and evidence suggests it was, particularly among the Hermannsburgers. That the document went out under the name of the CLM is significant. Whether it was a consensus document is unclear, but if it was, it constitutes a remarkable piece of evidence that within their ranks there existed more critical voices, as well as significant ambiguities, in the approach to race, culture and education. If it was not a consensus document, this would suggest that there were differences among Lutherans themselves over the principles underpinning the proposed new system of education. Differences existed among the Hermannsburgers themselves and between them and the CLM. This will be demonstrated in the discussion below concerning the mission's overall approach to the relationship between politics and education and the divergences among black and white Hermannsburgers regarding the image and role of European and African elements in education in South Africa.

Hermannsburgers, politics and education

As suggested above, the Hermannsburgers' approach to politics was shaped by the Lutheran notion of the separation of the 'Two Kingdoms' of God and the state, of matters spiritual and temporal.[54] This was a doctrine that committed them to non-interference in worldly or political affairs.[55] It predisposed them to a 'less activist attitude towards the state' than that taken by British and American missionaries who were, as a result, 'more inclined to come into open conflict with white settler societies or with Christian African rulers'.[56] In effect, however, this stance of neutrality drew them closer to identification with and support for segregationist policies and practices. After the Second World War, a schism developed among and between missions and German communities over politics. As white power was consolidated, German communities and congregations identified ever more closely with the policies and practices of the apartheid government, whereas German missions were torn apart by challenges articulated by younger missionaries, and increased questioning of the Two Kingdoms doctrine in the face of repression, removals and resistance by Africans.

The mission's approach was marked by obedience to the state, a belief in white supremacy, and the passivity implicit in the Two Kingdoms notion with respect to the political and temporal world. Nonetheless, even though many older missionaries justified apartheid, none of them, according to Voges, defended it on theological grounds.[57] But neither did they give active support to the Church Council of South Africa's opposition to apartheid legislation.[58] Moreover, they were sympathetic to the Bantu Education Act as it emphasised and took over aspects of Lutheran policy such as mother-tongue education. And instead of resisting the resettlement of African people occupying their land, they worked to ensure that it involved the resettlement of whole communities and families so as to avoid separation. Yet despite this cooperative attitude, the state acted without regard to the Hermannsburgers: when, for example, the residents of Lemgo were resettled, this was done without consultation with Fritz Scriba, whose negotiations with the state over such matters had been extensive and meticulous.[59] In practice, Hermannsburgers did not resist segregationist and apartheid policies until the 1970s and 1980s, and then only through people such as Wolfram Kistner who worked within the South African Council of Churches, often in tension with the mainstream approach of Hermannsburgers.

Accordingly, their approach to education also changed over time. The 'imagined communities' of Europe and Africa were, in the Hermannsburger view, not hostile entities insofar as they were perceived as sharing similar histories and possibilities. Louis Harms himself was deeply influenced by the process of Christianisation of Germanic societies in his own region, and projected onto African societies a desire for a similar process. He saw both early German and African societies as beset by evils that could be redeemed and civilised by Christianity.[60] However, this Christianity had its roots not in a modern, industrialising, conflictual and secular Europe but rather in rural and organicist communities. Deeply embedded in this romantic nationalist imaginary was a binary notion of Europe as the corrupting influence, and simultaneously holding out redemption through Christianity. And if African heathendom was constructed as the evil to be brought under Christian control, then the African was also constructed as the Noble Savage who needed to be returned to his true and pure nature. This essentialised notion of an original essence, or 'true nature', was captured in the notion of *Volkstum* or ethnic identity as defined by culture and language. It was a notion that tolerated no form of mixing, which was derogatorily referred to as 'bastardisation'.[61] During the 1930s and 1940s, as many have argued, Hermannsburgers were preoccupied with using education to develop *Volkstum*, a form of cultural authenticity based on an imagined unity of ethnicity, culture and language.[62] In effect, however, this amounted to a belief in the role of education being to bolster racial difference, as each 'race' was seen as having a culture and language unique to it. Inequality and racism was deeply implicated in this perspective of racial difference.

Europe and Africa as imagined by Hermannsburgers

The particular Hermannsburger approach to this ensemble of ideas relating to culture, language and ethnicity was developed in their response to a questionnaire that the Eiselen Commission sent to all mission schools. The approach exemplifies the paternalistic notion of a corrupting European and Western civilisation from which Africans need to be protected, and an original (traditional) cultural source to which they should be returned. The contradiction between, on the one hand, the negative perception of African paganism, and, on the other, the positive valuation of African culture or *Volkstum*, enables a construction of Europe as at once 'foreign body', 'destroyer', and redeemer. This is light years away from the collective response sent via the Cooperative Lutheran Missions that problematises African culture, seeing it as undergoing dramatic change and providing an inadequate basis for the reorganisation of education.[63]

The memorandum sent by the Hermannsburg Mission in 1949 argued that, while the principles underpinning 'native' education should be the same as those of education in general, the education provided should 'not be based on a dream of an ideal humanity' and should 'distance itself from . . . a blind admiration of foreign achievement and thus creating a feeling of inferiority'. Secondary schools, training colleges, and especially universities were considered 'to estrange their students from native life'. Education should be in the hands of Africans themselves, and they should carry the main responsibility for it.

While as a race Africans shared characteristics in common with other races and could not be considered inferior, 'they have however their own dynamics, their own tradition and their own future'. Education should be based on these differences. All careers should be open to Africans, but mother-tongue education was of vital importance: it should comprise the first four years of education, followed by the introduction of one official language in the fourth year of schooling, and a second official language in secondary school. Such ideas were entirely consistent with the new approach to education shortly to be implemented by the state.

Images of Europe and Africa: Heinz Dehnke and Micah Kgasi

Although the Hermannsburgers were not an 'intellectual' mission society, two of their members, Heinz Dehnke and Micah Kgasi, published short works on education in 1949 and 1939 respectively – one in German, the other in Tswana.[64] It is highly likely that the two missionaries would have known each another, as the Hermannsburgers were a close-knit community. Dehnke's father was based at Hebron, near Pretoria, where Kgasi himself had started his teaching career and with which he would no doubt have retained some links. Although there was an age difference between Dehnke and Kgasi, and a ten-year gap between the books they had written, there are discernible links between their respective approaches to education, one from the mission perspective, and the other from a 'convert' point of view. Their writing suggests a debate among black and white male Hermannsburgers over universal and culturally-specific solutions to educational crises current at the time in which differing constructions of Europe and Africa played a key role.

Heinz Dehnke was born in 1910, the son of a Hermannsburg missionary, and grew up on the mission station of Hebron.[65] He undertook his missionary training in Hermannsburg in Germany and then proceeded to study Bantu Studies and Native Education at the University of Pretoria from 1932 to 1933. During this time, he writes, 'I was swept off my feet and spent long evenings in discussing' the work of German anthropologist Bruno Gutmann.[66] Gutmann's numerous anthropological publications on the Chagga people in Tanzania were based on organic notions of family, community, ethnicity and nation. These clearly appealed to Dehnke, who was a language teacher at the Hermannsburg Bethel Training Institute from 1933 to 1938, the year he was married. During the war years he worked as an auxiliary preacher in Lady Selborne, Atteridgeville, Kwaggaspoort and Eastwood in Pretoria before becoming principal at Hebron until 1945, and later principal at Bethel from

1955 to 1962.[67] He was the representative of the Hermannsburg Mission on the Transvaal Advisory Board of Education, and it is possible that the memorandum placing indigenous control and mother-tongue education at the forefront of its education policy, cited earlier, was the product of his work. Whatever the case, Dehnke believed in race theory, that some races were superior to others, and in racial segregation. He kept company with the main proponents of Christian National Education, who would increasingly shape education policy.[68] The focus of his life's work, according to his biographer, was 'indigenisation'.[69] In education, Dehnke's main concern was that Africans and particularly 'communities' and 'parents' should run schools. A close friendship developed between Dehnke and Lucas Mangope, who was awarded his primary teacher-training certificate at Bethel during Dehnke's tenure. From early on, Mangope played a key role in what eventually became apartheid's Bantustan edifice of Bophuthatswana.

In 'The Mission and the School: with special consideration of the Transvaal mission', Dehnke provides a perspective on the history of schools set up by the Hermannsburg Mission in the Transvaal as read through reports dealing with schooling in the mission newspaper, *Hermannsburger Missionsblatt*. In this history, Dehnke emphasises links with the ZAR, the contradictory purposes of schooling as seen by the missionaries and local people, the great diversity and uniqueness of each school in the early years, the dominance of girls in enrolments, the rudimentary character of the syllabus and textbooks, as well as the increased use of teaching auxiliaries (mainly women) and the growth of uniformity as the state took greater control after the South African War. Long before the social historians of the 1970s and later, Dehnke recognised that while missionaries saw teaching reading as the route to reading the Bible, Africans saw it as a means of becoming equal to whites. As a history of formal schooling, Dehnke's study pays attention to the growth as well as the deficiencies of schools thus far established, one of which is worth highlighting: his notion of the school initially being 'like a foreign body in the life of the tribe' and his corresponding criticism of syllabi for being insufficiently indigenised. Even as he makes somewhat disparaging and embarrassed remarks on the nakedness and 'unclothed' bodies of the school children, wishing for properly clothed bodies, he also decries the missionaries' failure to incorporate African song, seen as heathen, into a syllabus of which a large part was taken up by singing.[70] But the greatest difficulty, as far as he was concerned, was the introduction of English or Dutch numerals 'as a makeshift solution . . . a miserable crutch' to compensate for the difficulty caused by the inconsistency of Tswana numerals: they were very long, sometimes adjectives and sometimes nouns, and multiplication tables were 'masterpieces of oratory'.[71] The answer, he felt, lay within the existing linguistic heritage and not in the adoption of foreign elements which would corrupt the 'pure' and original forms.

Dehnke also promoted the idea of parents taking active responsibility for the education of their children.[72] Indeed, he is reputed to have disagreed with the proposed administration of Bantu Education by a central Department of Native Affairs rather than the provinces. Likewise, he was appalled at the powers given to chiefs as well as the removal of teacher training from the purview of missions. He believed that the minister's power was absolutised, that central control was bureaucratised, and that the way in which chiefly control was implemented would amount to a 'dictatorship of the chiefs' in education.[73] It is not difficult here to be aware of echoes of the Lutheran Cooperating Mission's 1952 memorandum which identified and drew parallels between centralised control and the approach taken in communist countries. As time went on, Dehnke became increasingly ill at ease with some of the effects of apartheid on his parish, but nevertheless retained a belief in the destructive power of Europeanisation on Africans, and in the fundamental idea underlying separate development, namely the purity of ethnic entities.

Micah Kgasi's book *Thutô ke Eng?* (*What is Education?*), was published by Lovedale Press in 1949 [1939]. He started work as a teacher at the Hermannsburg school of Hebron, just north of Pretoria in the Western Transvaal, before being called to become an evangelist for the mission in Kgabalatsane (place of hunger) in 1894, where he remained until his death. The preface to *Thutô ke Eng?* gratefully acknowledges African Studies intellectuals of the time, including Professor G.P. Lestrade of the University of Cape Town and Professor Z.K. Matthews of Fort Hare. The publication by Lovedale further suggests Kgasi's integration into liberal intellectual and political circles. Subordinated as a black man to the missionary, he yet found wider networks to exercise influence.

Thutô ke Eng? provides a very different interpretation of the history of education among Hermannsburgers from that of Dehnke. The contrast reveals that, despite Dehnke's aspirations regarding educational indigenisation, his approach was in fact deeply Eurocentric. Kgasi's account begins with the history of education among the Tswana before the arrival of missionaries, and focuses on dressmaking, metalwork, agriculture, medicine and woodwork. Far from seeing the body of the African as 'unclothed' and 'naked', Kgasi sees a person clothed with various kinds of blankets, dresses and beadwork. In this way, he self-consciously affirms traditional informal forms as 'education'; similarly, he goes on to describe the learning of various skills and crafts that occurred through working for whites. His story is an affirmation of African agency, also pre-dating social historians of the 1970s. He emphasises the role of one David Modibane – whose story is also briefly told by Dehnke – in spreading Christianity before the arrival of the Hermannsburgers. Modibane had been captured by Mzilikazi,[74] whose army was wreaking havoc in the area. Modibane managed to escape, and was trained by Wesleyans in the Eastern Cape before returning to establish his own church among the Bakwena at Phokeng. Though Kgasi's account is filled with images of heathen darkness and Christian light, Africans are portrayed not only as part of the darkness, but also as bringing light to heathendom. *Thutô ke Eng?* is also replete with Christian imagery of God's plan revealing itself in the suffering and humiliation of people at the hands of whites as well as Mzilikazi. This fate was necessary, he argues, to ready the fields for ploughing and also for the sowing of the seed, which was done by the missionaries.

The ambiguity of Kgasi's view of Western civilisation and of missionaries becomes evident, however, in the chapter on education. Throughout it, Western civilisation is presented as good and necessary progress that requires hardships to be endured for its benefits to be enjoyed. But Kgasi criticises the limitations of the Bible-based mission education prior to the 'resolution' of the state – 'at the request of Chief Mamogale' – to 'give black people access to education'.[75] He distinguishes between mission education and the progressive, secular, Western education that he identifies with the teaching of English. Despite it being pro-secular and anti-Biblical, he nonetheless places his confidence in the latter form. He describes how 'we' (the African Lutherans) 'really struggled with this progressive education', recounting a government training programme provided entirely in English and hence incomprehensible to its recipients until an interpreter was found. Kgasi also describes the humiliation and degradation he was subjected to at Kilnerton when English-speakers identified 'the German ones' as 'the weak ones'. Progressive education, he writes, 'started feebly', but 'it has grown, teachers are strong and have certificates. The visiting white can no longer identify our teachers by their weakness. The interpretor [*sic*] is not needed any more. . . . We thank the Government which took us out of the depth of ignorance to lead us to the light'.[76] He goes on to show how Africans have, through the hardship of working for whites, learnt to make items that they could sell, thus accumulating wealth and starting to live like white people. What matters here is not so much the hardship or humiliation, but the fact that these things 'were learnt through observation by Africans as they

were working'.[77] Despite Kgasi's affirmation of African agency and initiative
in grasping opportunity, in adopting the posture of grateful supplicant he rep-
resents the mirror image of the paternalist: 'we still need guidance . . . to cling
to the breast and suck from it . . . so that we can be robust [and] strong in
all learning'.[78]

If the good resides in civilisation and learning, then Kgasi's enemies of education are identified as certain communities that oppose education, as well as
some chiefs and clergymen. He calls on them all to unite in the service of
education. He concludes with a paragraph on the unjust manner in which the
church treats its ministers, and particularly its retiring ministers, who leave with
nothing. They are, he says, treated 'without regard for their duties but according
to skin colour'.[79] Kgasi did not see the racism and racial discrimination of the
church as part and parcel of the Western civilisation he so admired. The educational and administrative issues that concerned Dehnke did not concern him,
and nor did the strengthening of ethnic or community control over education.
Although he did not express himself on the matter, Kgasi's overall approach
suggests that it is likely that he would not have supported Bantu Education.

The tensions and constructions of 'Europe' and 'Africa' within both Dehnke
and Kgasi's work signal public identifications that each wished to make from their
respective positionings as 'European missionary' and 'African convert'. Dehnke
tried to overcome his manifest Europeanness through an imagined identification
with an 'Africa' that emphasised its uniqueness, while Kgasi tried to overcome
his positioning as 'African' and 'heathen' through an imagined identification
with, and desire for, inclusion in Europeanness. Even as the politics of the one
entailed segregation, and integration in the other, each was in effect the mirror
image of the other, with each constituting itself in terms of the other.

Conclusion

Although closed and isolationist in their everyday practices, declining to join
the Cooperating Lutheran Missions in South Africa until 1939, and cultivat-
ing a sense of German community through close interaction, including marriage with one another, Hermannsburgers were nonetheless part and parcel
of broader transnational and national debates about politics and education.
Lutherans in South Africa consisted not only of different branches of North
Europeans such as Swedes, Germans and Norwegians, but also of Americans.
The Hermannsburgers themselves comprised both black and white Lutherans.

Concerning the tenets underlying Bantu Education, there were differences, as this chapter has shown, both within the Lutheran body, between

regions such as Natal and the Transvaal, as well as among black and white male Hermannsburgers differently positioned in the social, political and religious hierarchy. Dehnke's argument tended towards making the 'foreign body' of schooling more meaningful to African communities by making it locally relevant. Kgasi's argument, by contrast, was concerned with overcoming political and social inequality through an education that was secular and open to the world. The 'foreign body', in his approach, needed to be mastered. The next chapter will explore further differences among Lutherans and Hermannsburgers over the running of schools after an incident that exploded before them at Bethel in 1953.

CHAPTER 2

BURNING BETHEL IN 1953: CHANGING EDUCATIONAL PRACTICES AND CONTROL

At 11:15 on the night of 14 May 1953, the district commandant of the South African Police force based at Lichtenburg in the Transvaal received a report that trouble was brewing among the African students at Bethel Training Institute, situated between Ventersdorp and Coligny. Nine constables, five white and four African, were immediately dispatched to the scene, arriving about an hour later. En route, they noticed that buildings were 'on fire and burning seriously'. Upon arrival they discovered that approximately 200 students were in uproar, and called for police reinforcements. By 2:30 a.m. a further 18 white and 12 African police officers had arrived to help quell the uprising. By that stage the school had already been reduced to glowing embers. The police moved to the dining hall where the students had gathered, held a roll call, and searched the students as well as the dormitories. They found pamphlets stating their grievances: inadequate diet, bad accommodation, and the unjust expulsion of a student. In all, 184 students were arrested, of whom 69 were female and 115 male, with ages ranging from 16 to 39. The students were charged with arson, alternatively public violence or malicious injury to property. They appeared in court on 16 May, when all but two pleaded not guilty to the charges. The case was remanded to 29 May.[1] The entire school and pump house had been destroyed, as well as the homes of the headmaster and two teachers.

The events of that night, as well as the underlying reasons and the consequences, are important for a number of reasons. First, there is the timing: this event happened one month before the reading of the Bantu Education Bill in Parliament and in the context of the Defiance Campaign that had been launched across the country in 1952 in protest against the new apartheid laws. Fire had played a role in the campaign too in the burning of passbooks by Nelson Mandela and other activists.[2] Second, the event provides insight into the relationship between the mission and the state at that point, and the conditions under which the transition from mission to apartheid education and control occurred within institutions more compliant than others to the state and yet still wishing to retain a degree of control. Third, the immediate causes, course and eventual outcome of this uprising provide insight into the different approaches as well as practices by this mission with regard to authority, rights, and democracy at the time. Fourth, these differing approaches corresponded to, and indeed represented, conflict between different manifestations of missionary masculinity – the spiritual and the temporal. In asserting control over the 'unruliness' of both male and female African students, dominant mission masculinities were affirmed as the normative ideal in the mission.[3]

Neither at Bethel in particular nor at mission schools in general were these kinds of disturbances unusual. They were typical of student riots wracking mission institutions across the country at the time.[4] This chapter focuses on the regimes of belief and practice that existed in one of the principal Hermannsburg institutions. The 1953 fire not only threw these into sharp relief but also revealed how turbulent local conditions and internal dynamics within educational institutions facilitated the take over by a state already intimately involved in these schools. It marked a turning point in more ways than one. It crushed the conflicts underlying the educational regime at Bethel, bringing to an end the conflicting signals about student participation. It asserted the power of students in a context fraught with powerlessness, indecision and uncertainty. But it also helped to precipitate the birth of a new order – integration into the system of Bantu Education. For a brief period, the fire dramatically threw into the air the existing educational regime, though it soon settled back into familiar patterns, albeit within a significantly altered broader context, with immense implications for the school and education in the country as a whole. The incident provides a concentrated and condensed image both of what had been and of what was to come. It also draws attention to the historical role of fire and burning in student resistance in South Africa, an issue of continuing contemporary significance.

This chapter will provide a brief history of the Bethel Institute, and show how the tensions that gave rise to the arson were generated many years before. It will look at the immediate and longer-term consequences through an examination of the actions of the mission, the education department and the courts, as well as the eventual fate of the students, the institution and its leadership. It argues that tensions around different approaches to discipline, student control and rights were manifested in a conflict between the mission superintendent on the one hand, and the principal and some of the teachers on the other. The former represented a 'softer', more spiritual mission masculinity, and the latter a 'harder', more masculinist, secular and temporal one. The investigations conducted and the numerous reports on the incident from various angles all provide the basis for a range of insights into what transpired. The voice of the missionaries and the state are dominant in these sources, and consequently their perspectives are too. The voices and perspectives of the teachers and students involved are mediated through these records. Only in their statements to the commission of inquiry are the teachers' voices directly heard. But these, like all the other sources, have to be read against the grain, not as 'truth', but as truths produced within a context, and for a specific purpose.[5] Students' voices are completely silent in the sources. But their voice, as expressed through their actions, was loud.

Bethel Training Institute 1920-1953

Bethel was a seminary consisting by 1953 of a secondary school, teacher-training college and hostels, and should be distinguished from Bethal, the town in present-day Mpumalanga.[6] Bethel's origins go back some years, however. According to Breutz, the Hermannsburgers started a mission station on the nearby farm of Rooijantjesfontein (near present-day Gerdau) in 1871. Three years later, in 1874, a missionary moved with the Barolong Boo Rapulana chiefdom to Polfontein, neighbouring the farm Holgat, to establish a mission station there. Chief Matlaba invited the Hermannsburg Mission to open a school for its children, and thus it was that in 1877 the mission station of Bethel was founded on Holgat. Shortly thereafter some 1,000 people moved there, with the number eventually increasing to 3,000. These people joined the local Batloung group, which had long been associated with the Hermannsburgers.[7] Between 1938 and 1940 a number of trust farms were bought in the area, one of them being Polfontein.[8] The people living there were mostly squatters, renting land for the purposes of ploughing and grazing.[9]

Missionaries of the Hermannsburg Mission Society started planning the establishment of a seminary on the mission farm Holgat in 1920.[10] In the context of financial distress occasioned by post-World War I conditions in Germany, the mission participated in the short-lived alluvial diamond diggings in the area by buying claims on Holgat and the adjoining farm in May 1924.[11] The seminary opened as a teacher-training institution that year with four students, to whose number three more were added in the coming weeks. In 1929 a seminary for evangelists was built. From its inception, the students were the children of people from neighbouring white farms as well as trust farms occupied by Africans. Students ranged in age from 16 to 39. In accordance with departmental requirements for registration, instruction was provided in English, with the exception of religious instruction, which was in Tswana. The institution was built with some difficulty, given the lack of resources, but in 1924 a boarding house for the scholars was also opened. The school included primary schooling as well as Standards 5 and 6 (Grade 7 and Grade 8), which were the necessary teacher qualifications. In 1938 the mission also began training pastors in a separate building.

The first school strike occurred a mere nine years after its founding. Principal Ernst Karberg described it as something of a palace revolution.[12] The incident was triggered by a teacher's action of removing answers to class exercises which were provided at the back of the London Missionary Society's Tswana grammar book. He did so on the grounds that the students were continually cheating, copying from the book instead of providing their own answers. The students felt they had been denied their rights to books that were their personal property and demanded to be paid or their money back for the seven torn-out pages. The teachers and students finally agreed, after a discussion, that the offending pages would be put back into the book once the students had left the school. For the missionaries, this compromise saved face. But the morning after the agreement, the students appeared, holding up placards that read: 'Industrial Commercial Workers' Union'. The Industrial Commercial Workers' Union was at the time a militant union active particularly in the rural areas of the Transvaal. It is possible that students were exposed to its influence in local communities and families. Their action indicates a readiness to link broader social issues with those at the school.

In 1933 there was a mini-revolt when, one morning, students were served only bread and no porridge for breakfast owing to a broken chimney flue. Although they were given two helpings of porridge at lunch-time to compensate, this incident, so small in the eyes of the missionaries and so large in the eyes of the students, developed into a 'great protest action' resulting in 22 students being sent home.[13] In 1938 seminarists went on strike over the making of bricks, an activity in which they refused to participate. Discussions with those in charge failed. The spokespersons of the strike were dismissed and the seminarists were instructed to submit to the rules or leave. The male seminarists chose to leave. In this context, Dehnke left the school for Hebron, claiming to disagree with the leadership in its manifestly authoritarian handling of the matter.[14]

The seminary received departmental recognition in 1935, mainly because it appointed as head of the educational side of the institution a person who, though from the mission, had the necessary professional qualifications. Tensions immediately emerged between the mission and the department. On the occasion of the 1937 visit to the school by Werner Eiselen, chief inspector of Native Education at the time, he insisted that the principal take over leadership of the institution as a whole. The governing body of the school refused, however, preferring that the superintendent accountable to the mission should adopt this role. This signalled the beginning of an extended conflict between the state-appointed principal, who was responsible for the school, and the mission-appointed superintendent, who was responsible for the institution as a whole, including the hostel.[15]

In 1945 Hermann Greve took over as superintendent and hostel house father in charge of 144 pupils.[16] He was not pleased at the prospect, as talk of a 'bolshevist spirit' among the school pupils had disturbed him.[17] This defiance had asserted itself over a dispute with the school over the compulsion to do manual labour. Shortly before Greve's transfer,[18] the institution had sent a circular to parents, informing them that students had been given work such as chopping wood, carrying water for the kitchen, fetching post, building the institution's roads, and so on, in exchange for low boarding and lodging fees. Students had, however, complained that the work was onerous, refused to fulfil these duties, and demanded that the institution appoint labourers, and so the school gave parents an option. Either their children continued as before, with no additional fees beyond an extra £1 for board and lodging to compensate for rising food costs, or they did not, but at a cost of an additional £3 per student per year to cover the cost of hiring labourers. Unsurprisingly, parents voted for the former.

For the missionaries themselves, asking students to do this kind of work was a perfectly normal expectation – it was after all work that they themselves did at home in their rural hinterland of the Lüneberger Heide in Germany as peasant farmers and artisans; moreover, it accorded with the role of Africans as workers in South Africa. But for the students it was a different matter altogether. With the support of two teachers, they petitioned the institution on 12 June 1945, demanding the removal of the principal as well as answers to specific questions. They were given answers to their questions, but the demand for the removal of the principal was ignored.[19] The school instituted a discipline committee to deal with the incident and any such future incidents. But by 1947, Superintendent Greve was reporting that the 'bolshevist' spirit was no longer manifesting itself at the institution,[20] that the discipline committee had 'shown little sign of life', and that there would be no harm if it died off completely. He busied himself with building a dormitory for the girls' hostel, concerned about the shortage of space, mounting debt, the high turn-over of teachers, and student rejection of church teaching: 'The Bible,' he wrote, 'doesn't contain the "Education" that they want'.[21] A massive building programme had begun. During the course of 1946, the mission completed two homes for teachers and started building four classrooms, an office for the principal, a staffroom and a library. The hall that had been burnt down was rebuilt in 1947. With departmental help, the missionaries were planning also to create more dormitory space for boys and a space for the teaching of domestic science.

A system of student governance existed similar to those at other mission institutions such as Kilnerton.[22] A students' council met at frequent intervals and discussed student problems in the institution. Certain members of staff attended the meetings of this council ex officio. Any changes to rules and regulations were generally first discussed with the students' council and thereafter announced by the superintendent or his deputy in a full assembly of students. If a student faced disciplinary action, a full enquiry was held into complaints against that student; the accused was present and given the opportunity to state his or her case and even to cross-question the accusers.

In 1948 the National Party was voted into power on its apartheid ticket. The state acted increasingly repressively towards African opposition movements even as it moved to implement its policy with immediate effect. The recommendations of the Eiselen Commission, appointed in 1947, were well known. Even though students might not have known that, two months later, the Bantu Education Bill would be read in Parliament, state control of mission institutions had long been mooted and it was clear that the state was moving in this direction. Opposition movements continued to mobilise opposition, holding mass meetings and demonstrations, and launching the Defiance Campaign on 26 June 1952. During the early 1950s tensions were also at fever pitch between the Lutheran Mission and communities in Phokeng.[23] Most significantly, the community on the adjoining farm Holgat was marked for resettlement in 1953.[24]

Even though tight linkages cannot be drawn between these national and regional developments and what happened in the school, it is possible that they set the conditions for upheaval at the institution. I found no actual evidence of networks or organisation between outsiders and those in the school, either at this time or in the earlier periods. Nor was there any documentary reference at the time to the forced removals at Holgat. Nevertheless, incidents throughout the history of the school suggest that, despite the institutional isolation, students were responsive to and inspired by wider currents of discontent and organisation. These general conditions do not however explain the specific conditions within the institution that led to the fire and to which I now turn. These require closer scrutiny.

Rising tensions, conflagration and immediate reactions: April-May 1953

Tensions began rising at Bethel in early 1953. In January, three young male students were suspended after returning to the institution having spent the night on the train drunk. One had moreover spent the evening in a compartment harassing a young girl and making 'declarations of love' to her.[25] These incidents represented unruly and 'inappropriate' forms of masculinity, a challenge and threat to its more disciplined and controlled expressions by the missionaries.[26] Possibly more than usually sensitive to challenges to their authority, the institutional leadership began discussing tightening up disciplinary measures. This provoked conflict between those who believed students ought to be informed of these discussions and those who did not, with the principal and superintendent on opposite sides of a divide where the surrounding community, parents and teachers also took sides.

The first inkling Superintendent Greve had that something was brewing at Bethel was at a Sunday service on 12 April 1953. Small acts of disobedience suggested something was afoot. A monitor responsible for church services refused to put out benches as he normally did; furthermore, students were coughing and talking throughout the service. As the students left the service, they sang and threw stones onto the roof. Greve's attempt to extract an explanation from the seniors and those responsible for the service came to naught. The next morning he discussed the matter with the student committee, who informed him that their dissatisfaction stemmed from the introduction of new regulations without being told about them. Greve called a meeting of the school's welfare committee which accused the students of having no real complaints. He then asked the principal, Georg Meyer, to call a meeting with the teachers, though this request was simply ignored.[27] Greve's superiors, to whom he wrote for advice, gave cold comfort. Their response was that teachers should take greater responsibility for discipline as students' motivations in these matters were both 'political and material'.[28] Greve was advised that a meeting of the council of friends of the institution, consisting of representatives from Ramakokstad (near Brits), Luka (near Rustenburg), Bethanie (near Brits) and Hebron (near Pretoria) would be held soon to discuss the matter. But this was all too late.

There was a long weekend from 14 to 17 May, and about half the staff were away on leave. Student noisiness was observed in the church parade on the morning of the 14th.[29] That evening there was a small incident in the dining room, though the prefects managed to calm the situation. A tense and restive atmosphere prevailed, however, with one report saying that just after lights out all the students were ordered under threat, by a small group of students, to the sports fields. The horror at what happened next, as far as the staff were concerned, was described by the superintendent. Also evident in this account is the existence of differences and fissures among students:

> Shortly after 11 pm on the evening of the Ascension we went to bed. After about five minutes, noise and shouting and howling broke out and simultaneously stones started thundering onto the roofs of the Tswana teachers. The school bell started ringing and in a short while the whole yard seemed to be alive. Before I could get dressed, the Seniors arrived to inform me about a revolt. Another scholar also sought protection in our house. Noise and thundering stones on the corrugated iron roofs, the shrieks of women and whistling also awoke the sleeping. It was like a bomb attack during war. Mr Peters and teacher Kgomongwe crashed into the house and commanded me to shoot. I refused, and also refused to give them my gun, but hurried to my office to inform the police by telephone. In the yard, the confusion was like a wild attack of bees. I couldn't believe that it was our scholars who were responsible for this. I couldn't get through to the police in Coligny, so I phoned Lichtenburg . . . While I was on the telephone, the light of the fire appeared over the school yard. They started by breaking the doors and windows of the houses of teachers Sephoti and Kgomongwe. Then the perpetrators divided themselves into two groups – one went to the house of the school principal . . . and set it alight. The other group was busy at the school where they set alight the

Principal's office and staff room. One classroom after the other started burning, including the school hall beside which we had our book depot. There was no possibility, as I saw it, of calling a stop to it. Mr Volker had driven to Bodenstein to fetch the police as he was of the opinion that the telephone lines had been cut. On his return, his car was stoned, such that he feared for his life. Without switching off the engine, he jumped out of the car and arrived unharmed in our house. Finally, at about 12.30 am a police car arrived from Lichtenburg, but it had to turn around to fetch reinforcements. In one hour the scholars had done their work. A few apparently went back to the hostels, the large majority to the house of Kgomongwe, who had of course fled. And then the train moved with lamps over the sports-fields to the lands of Mr Thiele. About 2 hours later they returned and went to the dining hall for boys. Shortly thereafter the police arrived.[30]

The situation was probably worse for the students. But it is clear that the incident drew a line between the authorities and the students. It profoundly disorganised the missionaries, and in so doing gave the state the space to insert its interpretation of events and what needed to be done.

The next day, local people and the press streamed to the site to observe the damage. The event was a sensation in both local and international media.[31]

After a week of turmoil, on 22 May an extraordinary meeting of the council was held to discuss the situation. It decided to rebuild the seminary, call on the department for 'an objective investigation into the educational questions and relationships at the seminar', and to call a meeting of the council of friends to discuss the situation. Each student would need to reapply and each would be checked individually. The possibility of a fine would be discussed with the friendship council and a decision taken with the parents of the students. The council of friends – Africans associated with the church, students or tribal authorities – supported the institutional authority.

A week later, on 28 May, the mission managed to secure a meeting with G.H. Franz,[32] son of Berlin missionaries and also chief inspector of Native Education in the Transvaal.[33] An investigation was planned for the following week, on 3 June, with the hope that the results would be in the hands of the department no later than 6 June. A committee consisting of four people – two departmental and two mission representatives – would be set up and chaired by a representative who was also a member of the department, and hearings would be held at Bethel.

The investigation

Based on the committee investigation, several reports were prepared.[34] Each source provides different insights into the incident as well as the foci of interest and discourses of particular parties. The department gave a secular interpretation of the events. In its view, educational leadership and roles and responsibilities were of principal importance.

Missionary discourses

The missionaries, as illustrated in Wickert's report for the *Hermannsburger Missionsblatt*, were besieged by a confused mix of guilt, despair and determination not to be cowed by the event.[35] Wickert discounts political causes and the suggestion that it might have been an outbreak of racial hatred (*Ausbruch des Rassenhasses*). For him, it was a matter of 'good vs evil' in which good would surely triumph. Themes of 'the Devil's work' and dark forces threatening to possess African hearts are counterposed with 'God's work' and the Christian (missionary) spirit of love and forgiveness. The blackened ruins of the institution were testimony of God's hand allowing Satan to overcome the missionaries, and now God demanded repentance. Accordingly, the missionaries would rebuild the institution, and pupils and students would be readmitted after 'spiritual examination of each case', the demonstration of remorse, and a monetary contribution towards rebuilding. This was a battle for the soul of Africa that should not be left to dark forces.

Official discourses

Official departmental discourses were more mundane, seeing neither the hand of God nor Satan but of Man at work. This was evident in the terms of reference of the investigation, which included: inquiring into relationships between the superintendent, principal and staff of the institution; ascertaining whether these relationships had a bearing on the discipline in the institution and made a contribution to earlier or the most recent disturbances; and deciding whether any other aspect of the control of the institution had a direct or indirect relationship to the earlier incidents.[36]

The confidential report of the committee focused on the roles, relationships and responsibilities of principal and superintendent. The report concluded that, though the respective responsibilities were clearly laid out on paper, they did not work in practice. The principal felt hemmed in by the superintendent, and this created tension. In the exercise of discipline, the superintendent consulted with the principal, while the principal acted independently of the superintendent. The latter failed to take full advantage of his position to exercise authority to enforce his view, which meant that he acted hesitantly, and this in turn had a negative impact on discipline in the institution. Aware that differences existed between the two, students took advantage of the lax rules in place after hours, as well as the lack of proper controls. The students were left much to their own devices in the hostels, and without proper supervision the prefect system was unable to function effectively. The relationship between prefects, superintendent and principal was not satisfactory. Loyalty was shown to the principal and superintendent by the teachers, except for Mr Pooe,[37] who was considered to be 'very intimate' with the students. It was evident that he had reported the meeting to the students, as there was damage to the property of the two other teachers, Kgomongwe and Sephoti, who were in the meeting that had expelled the student Morule. The system of having two authority figures at an institution of that kind was clearly unsatisfactory.

The committee's recommendations were, accordingly: to rebuild the institution with funds from the department; students should reapply for admission and pay £30 upon readmission, £10 of which had to be paid immediately and the remainder by means of stop orders; students who refused readmission should be blacklisted, that is, not be admitted to any other institution; everything necessary should be done to resume work in the third quarter of 1953; the dual-head system had to end, and a single principal should be appointed to head the institution; the services of teacher Pooe should be terminated as soon as possible.

The memorandum on the chief inspector's interview with the governing body provides more specific information about the nature of the disciplinary measures that were at the root of the problem. Some teachers had, since 1950, felt that discipline was declining, especially during students' free time, and that it should be tightened. But this did not happen until 1953, when it was decided that teachers would be in constant supervision during students' study periods. Weekend activities on Saturday and Sunday evenings were now organised and placed under the supervision of teachers. Students were also required to go to church in an orderly manner, again under the supervision of the teachers. At the insistence of the teachers, these regulations were not discussed with the students. All that was discussed with senior students was difficulties with discipline, though the regulations themselves were not communicated to seniors. The superintendent had however discussed with prefects the rules in relation to going to church. Neither male nor female students objected to the new rules concerning supervision of study, but they were surprised and offended at not being informed beforehand. With respect to church attendance, students felt the rule to be a sign of mistrust, and so one Sunday, when a teacher was unable to march them to church, 'they broke into noisy behaviour in which they even gave the Africa salute'.[38] When the superintendent called the prefect body together after the stone-throwing incident at the service in April, they were aggrieved about not being informed in advance about the new regulations. The climax was the evening of 14 May, as described above.

Those conducting the interview with the governing body, which perhaps influenced their perceptions, described the sense of suspicion and paranoia that prevailed: it was 'completely clear that the riots were organised by a small group of students' who used 'agitation' and 'mass hysteria' to drag other students into the matter. It was not however possible to identify 'the ring-leaders'. The memorandum also considered the possibility of outside influences and con-cluded that, while the superintendent and principal were not aware of any con-tact with outsiders, one of the six teachers at the institute was 'under suspicion': he was aware of currents and undercurrents, and himself worked in an under-mining manner. Furthermore, relationships between the local community and the institute were not good – it was evident that men from the community had refused to help put out the fire.

The judgment of the Education department, in the figure of Chief Inspector G.H. Franz, was decisive. This son of a Berlin missionary now represented a secular rather than religious form of authority in education. His position ulti-mately sanctioned the religious head of the institute, the superintendent, rather than the secular authority appointed by the department: the school principal. Franz used his position to limit staff numbers until such time as enrolments increased.[39] He viewed the position of the principal in a very negative light,[40] noting that he 'did not have the confidence of the African parents and church community'. On 11 June he recommended that the governing body be asked to give reasons why the principal, Mr Meyer, should not be charged with lack of professionalism and negligence.[41] Franz argued that there was not enough evidence to charge Mr Pooe, but because he had been appointed on a tem-porary basis he could be given 24 hours' notice in terms of the conditions of his appointment. The full weight of Franz's displeasure was reserved for the principal.[42] The reasons he advanced for asking that he be charged included his failure over a period of 17 years to draw the lack of clarity of his posi-tion to the attention of the department; also, his negative attitude towards the superintendent and the running of the institution, and his concomitant failure to assist the superintendent and allowing a situation to develop in which staff took sides. His opposition to the superintendent's wish to make the new rules known to the students he saw as 'inexplicable from both the education per-spective as well as the perspective of reasonableness and justice . . . Under such conditions the cooperation of the students couldn't be expected'. The principal had, moreover, expelled a student for an offence that took place outside of school hours and was therefore technically not under his jurisdiction, and he had done so without any preliminary investigation. Franz also found it 'difficult to understand' why Meyer had not called a meeting of teachers when the superintendent requested it, interpreting his reasons for the long delay as 'idle excuses' and 'irresponsibility'. He concluded that the principal had exercised poor judgement in leaving everything outside of school hours to the superintendent; also, his attitude and uncooperative behaviour had undermined the general disciplinary tone of the institution and he had thereby made himself guilty of charges of incompetence and dereliction of duty.

Rights of students

On discipline and freedom, Superintendent Greve and Principal Meyer had taken diametrically opposed positions. It is probable that the superintendent's approach was informed by his pastoral role and accountability to the mission, while that of the principal was informed by accountability to the department. Their differences were also linked to different educational principles in turn associated with the nature of their power and authority within the institution. The superintendent's approach was consultative and anti-authoritarian, 'softer' than that of the principal. Serious disciplinary measures, such as expulsion of a student, he always discussed with the principal. Superintendent Greve consulted teachers through a teachers' committee, and students through the students' council. His approach to the implementation of the new rules advocated transparency and openness as well as recognition of the right of students to be informed. Principal Meyer, on the other hand, was unequivocal about standing for 'strict discipline and application of punishment'. He characterised the superintendent's view as one where 'the scholars won't be disciplined by the rules', seeing him as a 'representative of the view that students should be given greater responsibility and that they should control themselves. By implication students should be given greater freedom to manage their affairs themselves'. Greve was not greatly disturbed by the freedom students enjoyed outside school hours, and did not see a need to supervise their free time closely. These differing approaches were particularly significant when the ages of students are taken into account; the principal's approach, for example of marching 30-year-olds to church, can be read as a form of racial paternalism or as a masculinist assertion of power, a staging of his 'manliness' against the 'unmanliness' of a superintendent unable to exercise control – and of African youth unable to control themselves.

The teachers held conflicting views. Mr Kgomongwe identified himself with the position of the principal. He contrasted the two approaches, with the superintendent being 'too lenient', admonishing rather than punishing a student for wrongdoing, while the principal held that a student must suffer the consequences of his wrongdoing. Kgomongwe expressed the view that discipline had declined greatly, largely due to the lack of cooperation between various staff members, and that the students were aware of differences on this matter among the staff. Mr K.K. Sephoti likewise identified with the principal who, he said, 'is strict and so am I. We both like to enforce rules and students who do not obey should be punished . . ..' The Superintendent differs from us in that he is more lenient'. Pooe, whose statements are characterised by opaqueness, gave nothing away, apparently agreeing with everything that was put to him. Mr Volker, whose statement was in Afrikaans, was the only teacher who identified himself with the position of the superintendent on matters of discipline, 'as it depended on cooperation with students'. Linked to this was a disapproval of teachers becoming 'too intimate' with students as this undermined hierarchical relationships.[43]

The trial

What, in the meantime, was the fate of the students? Upon being arrested, the students were taken to the Lichtenburg gaol. But the police cells could not hold all 184 students, and so 80 were remanded to police cells at Elandsputte. There they remained until the court case commenced on 5 June, while the commission of inquiry was conducting its investigations at Bethel. Those at Elandsputte were transported to the court in a ¾-ton open truck. They had no rights to legal representation or appeal.

The students were at first undefended, but then a firm from Krugersdorp, Gladwyn, took over their defence on a pro bono basis. As the trial proceeded, the case was withdrawn against 7 students, so 177 finally stood trial.[44] Soon into the trial, the defence persuaded the trialists and representatives of the families that some 50 accused should plead guilty so as to avoid the trial dragging on for another 6 months. As a result, the matter was brought to a swift conclusion. In the end, 52 students were found guilty of public violence, 1 of malicious injury to property, and 124 were discharged. Sentencing varied according to age and gender: 28 males and 3 females between the ages of 19 and 39 years were sentenced to 6 months' hard labour each; 10 males between the ages of 16 and 19 were each sentenced to 9 cuts with a light cane, whereas 4 females between the ages of 16 and 18 years were each sentenced to £5 or

1 month's hard labour; 6 girls and 1 boy under the age of 16 were cautioned and discharged.

After the verdict, the released students went to the seminary to collect their things, and the younger boys were given a pass to go home, though they were given no date for their return.[45] The missionary council was disappointed with the verdict because there was no attribution of individual guilt.

Consequences

Students

In addition to the punishments meted out by the court, the mission chose to impose a financial punishment. There was a long discussion at the meeting of the council of friends held on 3 June about the amount that returning students should be expected to pay.[46] In the end, the council decided that each pupil would pay £30 on readmission. The council also decided that, from the following year, the annual fee would be raised to a staggering £20. Both the council of friends and the council of the Bethel Institute agreed on this.

The students also suffered in terms of education. Many students requested permission to go to other schools or colleges. No one who was involved in the strike or who was arrested by the police was given this permission, as this would have deprived the mission of compensation for damages. Nonetheless, when the school reopened in January 1954, only 90 out of 140 reapplications were successful.[47] According to reports, however, the spirit of the students had changed: they were obedient and cooperative, both inside and outside of the school. As far as the mission was concerned, the heavy weather had lifted and the air had cleared.[48]

Withdrawal of registration and transfer

The mission suffered financially: because of the strike and the fact that exams were not written, neither fees nor exam monies were paid.[49] Bethel temporarily lost its departmental registration, though on appeal it managed to regain it.[50] The suspension of students also had financial implications as the school was funded on the basis of enrolments. Funding for renovations was made up of a donation of £258 11s 7d given jointly by the then South West Africa and *Deutsche Presse Agentur* (German Press Agency), the recovery of an additional £1,060 from students, £5 5s 0d from Supervisor Mokone, £13 from teachers, and £159 10s 8d from the parish. By completion, however, there was still a deficit.

In the process of getting back onto its feet, major changes were under way in the education system. The disturbances at Bethel in 1953 provided the right conditions for the 'restructuring' desired by the Education department. The state cancelled the matriculation class.[51] Later on, Bethel became a secondary school and the matric class was restored. In the short term, however, state planning played havoc with the school.

But in some respects the new plans came at the right time for the Hermannsburg Mission in the Transvaal, beleaguered as it was by student opposition, financial losses and other constraints. It was with some joy, then, that Heinz Dehnke wrote on 9 May, after hearing it announced on the radio that government wished to take over mission schools: 'The solution to Bethel seems to be at hand . . . .. In that way fate comes to the mission schools . . . .. In any case we won't be able to continue with the schools, as we don't have the finances'.[52]

The school immediately entered into negotiations with the state when the official August 1954 Circular on the Transfer of Control of Teacher Training Schools arrived.[53] Despite the relief that part of the burden would be lifted, the mission wished to retain some degree of influence. Its generally positive response emphasised that Bethel had grown into a 'great unity of teacher-training school, secondary school and hostels', and was an entirely Tswana institution, with a close relationship between parents and school. The parents should thus have a say.[54] In many ways, Bethel already conformed to what the state wanted.

There was very little time for negotiation, but eventually a compromise was reached[55] in which the mission remained in charge of the hostels, while the buildings for teaching were rented out to the department. A person linked to the mission, with the requisite professional educational qualifications, was appointed to run the hostel as well as the buildings for the period 1955 to 1962. Relations with the new tribal authorities were also consolidated. In 1955, Lucas Mangope, who had attained his Higher Primary Teachers' Diploma at the institute in 1951, became chairman of the Bethel board and wrote to the department requesting 'more representation to the Bantu in full conformity with the Bantu Education Act'.[56] Born in 1923 at Motswedi, north of Zeerust, Mangope had worked for the Department of Native Affairs between 1947 and 1949, and was 'advancing in traditional rank, having become the leader of the Mathlatlhowa'.[57] A primary school teacher in the 1940s and a second-ary school teacher during the 1950s, he had begun to position himself for a role within the Bantustan apparatus. The school board that was established consisted of the rector, the housefather, a minister of religion, representatives of parents of alumni, of the Tswana church and mission, as well as the Tswana chief and a farmer from the Western Transvaal.

Conclusion

The transition to Bantu Education was rapid and relatively unproblematic. In the process, the state asserted its particular form of governmentality[58]: it temporarily denied registration to the school, teachers lost their jobs, both the principal and superintendent were asked to leave, and the matric class was discontinued. In this way the events at the institution facilitated, rather than hindered or blocked, a change of regime.

There were distinct continuities with the past, however, in that the influence of the mission continued for at least another three decades. It continued to be represented on the board, and the principal and some staff continued to be drawn from a mission background so that links with the German home mission remained. The Tswana character of the mission, of which it was so proud, also remained intact. But there were also changes. The chairman of the board, no longer a religious appointment, was now Lucas Mangope, an ambitious young man earmarked for a position within the Bantustan apparatus.

The matric class was reintroduced in the early 1960s. With Mangope's support, departmental approval was given for the addition of the necessary classrooms, a library and laboratory.[59] Ironically, the school would diversify significantly. By 1982, in the wake of the 1976 student uprising, the largest proportion of pupils and students still came from small towns, farms and 'tribal' areas, but now 76 out of a total of 600 also came from cities. The majority were still Tswana-speaking, though there were many whose home languages were Sotho, Zulu and Xhosa, with a few whose mother tongue was Tsonga or Swazi.[60] Half the teachers were white, with many being the wives of farmers in the area; the rest of the teachers were African. As before, the school had great difficulty attracting African teachers on a permanent basis.

The events at Bethel in 1953 were momentous, not only in terms of the history of the institution but also in revealing the conflict between relationships based on different ideals of masculinity within the mission, and between the mission and the department. The events also revealed different approaches to discipline and freedom ('feminine' versus 'masculine') and exposed the nature of relationships among staff at the institution, and between mission authorities and students. The spark that lit the fuse was lack of consultation or proper communication with the students about the introduction of new disciplinary measures, an approach that is likely to have chafed considering that the students were in effect adults. There were deep divisions within the institution, with different rules applying not only in the spheres for which the superintendent and principal were responsible, but also in the hostel and school; moreover, there were different ways of enforcing the rules. Divisions existed among staff too, and among the student body. Some representatives of the local African community dissented from the student action, while others appeared to support the students. In the midst of all this, secular authority in the form of the department affirmed Greve, the 'man of the Word', and not Meyer, the 'man of the world', despite the latter being one of their own. The gentler, more marginal masculinity of the 'man of the Word', however, together with the temporal, secular authority of the department, was arraigned against the students, who were portrayed as the sexually and socially out-of-control antithesis to the social and disciplinary regime of the school.

To summarise, this chapter has explored the differentiated character of responses within the mission to the transition to Bantu Education. While much of the work to date has focused on the grand policy and resistance narrative, with few exceptions, very little has focused on what actually went on in schools and how school actors resisted, complied, accommodated and changed. In this instance, student resistance and mission compliance with the department's objectives enabled a rapid transition to Bantu Education. Local case studies of schools can provide insight into not only the impact of policy and broader political dynamics, but also the invisible beliefs and practices that constructed internal regimes of schooling and the conditions constraining and enabling change in particular directions. In order to understand the legacies of both mission and Bantu Education, we need much closer examination of how this transition occurred within specific contexts. We also need far greater understanding of how, in both the mission and apartheid periods, local, community and traditional authorities were harnessed to different types of schools.

CHAPTER 3

CHIEFS, MISSIONARIES, COMMUNITIES AND THE DEPARTMENT OF NATIVE EDUCATION

Lucas Mangope, a local traditionalist who was later installed as a Bantustan leader, continued the practice of chiefly alliance with the mission, which had been established by earlier generations of chiefs. The close relationship the Hermannsburgers enjoyed with Mangope did not, however, characterise all relationships between the mission and the chiefs. Indeed, relationships were often tense and conflictual, and became increasingly so during the 1950s. Much of this conflict emerged in the preceding decades when local communities challenged chiefly authority on the grounds of financial mismanagement or efforts to extract levies from communities who belonged to the ethnic group but did not have any interest in the land, to pay for indebted land.

Particularly in the 1940s and 1950s, there is evidence that these conflicts spilled over into schooling. If in the earlier period conflict had centred within the ethnic group, in the later period the mission was identified as a problematic locus of authority alongside the chief. As schools became central to conflicts between communities, missionaries and chiefs, their authority was increasingly challenged and their position became more vulnerable. The chief inspectors of Native Education and the Native Affairs department were recruited by both sides in these battles and played a critical mediating role.

The Bantu Education Act (No. 47 of 1953) envisaged a removal of control from missionaries, not only to the state, but in rural areas also to local African communities linked with traditional authorities recognised by the state. While many African schools did have some form of school board or committee before the Act was passed, the Act now specified their composition: in rural areas two of their seven members were to be nominated by the secretary for Bantu Education to represent religious or other interests, while the rest were to be nominated by the tribal authority or by the chief subject to the secretary's approval.[1] The 'retribalisation' purposes of the Act have been well-documented: to situate Africans 'psycho-ideologically where the Bantustans placed them physically and politically'.[2] Some of its intellectual roots were discussed in Chapter 1. And yet the Act can also be seen as a response to the intense pressures that were building up against missionaries by some chiefs and local communities, and also to the demand by local communities and some chiefs for state control. State response was one that chose to recognise and work with those chiefs compliant with the new directions undertaken by the state. In this sense, the 'crisis' to which the Bantu Education Act responded included not only rebellions in schools,[3] but also deep conflicts between missions, chiefs and local communities over the nature of the education that missions were providing. As in the previous chapter, these conflicts can also be seen as power struggles between rival forms of masculinity. Although this chapter deals only with the Western Transvaal, it is likely that such conflicts were not isolated to the Hermannsburg Mission.[4]

Three incidents during the 1930s and 1940s between chiefs, local communities and missionaries in the Western Transvaal set the scene for the transition from mission to traditional authority control. Often difficult to disentangle, they were bitterly conflictual, occurred in close proximity, and endured for many years. Thus the conflict at Bethanie lasted from 1938 to 1946, at Ramakokstad from 1946 to 1952, and at Saron from 1952 to 1954. In this struggle between missionaries and Africans, where necessary, both sides drew on state officials as well as legal teams for intervention or legitimation. Not surprisingly, those in support of the mission were based in the more conservative, Afrikaner-dominated Pretoria while those who supported the Africans were based in Johannesburg, home of a more progressive politics and legal practice. Alliances formed and re-formed in this process, with the chiefs playing all sides. The set of alliances that became dominant with and through the Bantu Education Act were between the traditional authority and the apartheid state. It was a battle that the missionaries lost, and that they anticipated they would lose, although they also struggled over its terms even as their fate was being sealed.

Bethanie 1938-1946

Graeme Simpson has provided a detailed analysis of how the efforts of Bethanie-based Chief J.O.M. Mamogale, of the Kwena ba Mogopa, to extract payments from Hebron and Jericho communities for land he had bought, resulted in a protracted battle in the 1930s.[5] Rival *lekgotlas* at Hebron and Jericho were established to challenge the authority of Mamogale, who was bolstered by both the Native Affairs Department and the mission. Repeated defeat of their applications, including in the courts, for intervention against the chief and recognition of their rights, finally led to intense successionist battles, as well as a secessionist movement.[6]

Matters came to a head in 1939 when J.O.M. Mamogale was 'retired' as chief and replaced by acting chief Daniel More, generally acknowledged to be a divisive choice. In 1940 Penzhorn, who had been advisor to Mamogale, passed away, and Missionary Karl Bühr became responsible for Bethanie. According to Simpson, 'dissension within the chiefdom appears to have intensified . . . and the period 1939 to 1941 witnessed intense and often violent conflict, most notably at Bethanie where the chief had his headquarters'.[7] Resistance to the chief was expressed as resistance to the mission. Two groups emerged: those loyal to the chief and mission were called 'Agtertrekkers' or 'Ma-Agter', with the rebel section calling themselves 'Voortrekkers'.[8]

The Segale rebellion exploded on the Bethanie mission station in 1938. Jehosua Segale, its leader, was the son of a Lutheran evangelist, *Moruti* Segale. Jehosua had himself taught at various schools. Gathering around himself a group of supporters who had been members of the mission church, he challenged the resident missionary over what appears to have been a clash between Christian and local burial practices and community expectations. The immediate cause of the rebellion seems to have been the fact that Bühr had refused to preside over the burial of Koos Mahuma. Even though Koos Mahuma had been a churchgoer, according to Bühr he had taken communion only once, and had moreover failed to pay his church dues. For Segale, the mission's response was unconscionable; he claimed that the Hermannsburgers had 'destroyed his [i.e. Mahuma's] life'.[9]

This was not a good time for the presiding missionary, Karl Bühr, who in that year lost not only his parents, but also his wife and three sons.[10] Born in Germany in 1887, he trained as a joiner and a nurse, and later as a missionary at the Hermannsburg Seminary in 1908. Leaving for South Africa in 1919 at the age of 32, he first went to Hebron where he learnt Tswana and was then posted to Phalane until 1928 when he went to Bethanie. Bühr responded harshly to Segale, suspending the breakaway group known as 'the rebels'. One of the suspended men, according to Bühr, was a member of the Communist Party. Whether he was or not is immaterial, though the use of the term indicates that the missionary saw his opponents as dangerous subversives. The suspension from the mission resulted in hostilities between the missionary and 'the rebels'. In the process, Bühr sought the support of Daniel More, with 'the rebels' seeking the support of a lawyer based in Johannesburg. According to Simpson, 'the conflict at Bethanie proved to be of the most violent witnessed in the district' throughout the preceding decades.[11] Eventually, 'the rebels' buried Mahuma 'with honour', singing, preaching and disrupting the ceremony. They mocked Bühr for his indifference, going to his home at night where they sang a song comparing him to Pontius Pilate.

These 'rebels' or 'Voortrekkers', as they were also known as, led by Segale, moved away from Bethanie and started a school in nearby Berseba with eight enrolments. As a consequence, and adding insult to injury, one of them was fined £5 by acting chief More. The man refused to pay and took the matter to a lawyer in Johannesburg who informed the chief that his client would act against the fine. Following this, there was another incident: during a Christmas Eve service, according to Bühr, a group of young men were causing a noise outside the church; when he tried to intervene the matter came to blows, with members of the congregation having to separate the parties. The church head then took the matter to the *lekgotla* and the chief took the matter to court.

Two years later, the situation had worsened. The community was split down the middle between those supporting the church and those supporting 'the rebels'. By now Segale had established his school. It was in this context that More started building a new school at nearby Mokolokwe. This inflamed the situation, as the chief had obtained government funding for the school, and was assisted by the Hermannsburg Mission. At a *lekgotla* he threatened to impose a fine of £5 on any community member who did not help in building the school. 'The rebels' instructed their lawyer, a Mr Sive, to write to the native commissioner to prevent the building of the school. The matter eventually went to court, with both sides claiming victory, though the situation remained unresolved.

The 1944 report of Hermannsburg preacher, Joseph Mogotsi, lamented the divisions within the community. Describing himself as a 'true believer', he wrote that he was one of those who 'stick to the church, communion, pay their church money, send their kids to school', do their work 'with joy' and help to build the school at Mokolokwe. On the other side was the 'broken-away piece' that 'hates the *baruti* [plural of *moruti*, a teacher, missionary or minister of religion], hates the chief, has separated itself from the church, has built itself a tent from sacks, is away from everyone and also does not come to communion anymore'. Their children were growing up 'without adequate education'. Every day, he reported, more than 600 children gathered at the school buildings and then went home in the afternoons without having learnt anything. He also described how the breakaway group had sent men to the *lekgotla* where they had requested teachers for their schools and also approached the native commissioner for help. In response, the *lekgotla* informed them that the schools were open, and that they simply had to send the children to the schools – as the native commissioner himself responded. On each occasion, the sticking point was the supervision of the school by the missionary Bühr. The response of the *lekgotla* to the dissidents was that Bühr was a departmental appointment and they could do nothing about it – a response echoed by the native commissioner.[12]

A battle for the loyalty of the children ensued, but it was one that Segale's school, which was not registered and so could not apply for any teachers, was bound to lose. The forces arrayed against it, including the chief, the mission and the department, were simply too great. Three years later, on 30 January 1945, Bühr reported with some satisfaction that the new school was experiencing difficulties: 'Even the principal, who has no teacher training, has left and is now the postal agent here in Bethanie'. Segale now sent his own children to the mission school – one of about 20 children who had returned to the mission school that year. In the same vein, Bühr continued: 'the [Voor]trekkers are always claiming that the Missionaries are halting their progress. Now it is the other way around'.[13]

Preceding these developments was a visit to Bethanie in November 1944, shortly before the end of the school year, by Dr Eiselen, chief inspector of Native Education for the Transvaal, accompanied by District Inspector Jansen as well as two new government inspectors. The meeting was attended by Bühr, Segale and others. Bühr kept detailed minutes. Eiselen began by listening to the story of the 'rebel' school committee, and then asking what it was that they wanted. Segale expressed the wish for secular, modern schools outside chiefly control, but complained that these always ended up affirming the positions of chief and missionary. He and his followers wanted departmental schools to be established in the area not under mission control; they also wanted elected school boards comprised of parents who would work with the department, with the power to establish houses and school buildings at their own cost, in accordance with government policy. When Eiselen questioned why they wished to take responsibility for building rather than asking the chief, they replied that it was precisely because of the chief that matters had arrived at this point. Eiselen explained that, because it was departmental policy to work with the chief, they should rather work with the chief. A member of the school committee, Koos Thage, then retorted: 'You always speak about the chief, we are speaking about the school'.[14]

At this point, Eiselen turned to the question of the mission school and the difficulties of making peace with it. The response, according to Bühr's minutes, was a categorical assertion that they were against *Moruti* Bühr, and did not want mission involvement in the school. The meeting concluded with Eiselen affirming that, together with the chief, 'a big joint school, an ethnic (tribal) school' would be built, and placed under the authority of the department. Neither the mission nor 'the rebels' were pleased. The latter threatened to form a private school, but shortly thereafter their efforts seemed to fall apart as Segale vanished after being summonsed to appear in court in Ventersdorp on a charge of neglecting to care for his children and his apparently disabled wife whom he had abandoned for another woman. Bühr offered to give up the superintendency after a six-month period, provided that the congregation sent the children back to the mission school. At the same time, having had no success with the education officials, 'the rebels' went to see the native commissioner.

Then in January, on a second visit, Inspector Jansen informed Bühr that if he could attract children back from the new school, he would get more teachers. With Segale gone, more than 20 children did in fact enrol, but 'the rebels' attacked the parents whom they accused of succumbing to departmental pressure. In the meantime, the school that the chief had built at Mokolokwe was amalgamated with two mission schools.

That year, 1945, the Allied victory brought the Second World War to an end. But the war in Bethanie continued. Bühr stated in his annual report[15] that he had attempted to strike a deal with 'the rebels': they would send their children to school while he – though without promising anything – would broach the question of his removal from the post at the next missionary conference. One member of the delegation distrusted Bühr, another said he needed to discuss it with his people, while a third seemed to put on a show of not understanding what was being proposed. Following this, a few parents once more sent their children to school, and they themselves returned to the church in the course of the year, but nothing further came of Bühr's proposition that he give up the superintendency for a six-month period in exchange for a return of the children to school. The churchgoing community and the school enrolments had, in any event, shrunk. Bühr had resumed church singing each evening, from 8 to 9 p.m.; a few children and between 10 and 20 adults attended, and he again took up the telling of Bible stories. But the overwhelming difficulty was, as he described it: 'converting Africans, their scepticism, their rejection of the Church and the school'. Among the complaints the community seemed to direct at the church and the school was 'the want of reading material'. Bühr acknowledged that, apart from the Bible, catechism, hymn books and a harp, as well as school books, the mission had little to offer them. The Tswana and Sotho tracts, which came mainly from the English missions, were also apparently widely disliked.

Within this context, the mission discussed the possibility and implications of mission superintendents of the education department taking over schools.[16] In early 1945, Otto Brümmerhoff, newly appointed in 1944 as superintendent of the Magaliesburg district of Hermannsburg's Tswana Mission,[17] appears to have written and distributed a circular regarding the role of missionaries as superintendents, to which Rev. Lange responded, referring to the tension between the roles of the state and missionaries in the running of schools as a contributory factor in community upheaval and disunity. Whereas the missionary had at the outset supervised both the 'inner' and 'outer' workings of the school, this role became confined to the 'outer' or 'external' matters once the state took over payment of teachers' salaries. This meant that the missionary remained responsible for the appointment and dismissal of teachers, the receipt and distribution of cheques, the management of accounts, the purchase of books, classroom maintenance, the provision of desks and so on – but none of this related to his spiritual vocation or position. From this perspective it was desirable to enter into an agreement with government whereby these spiritual dimensions occupied a greater place, that is, teachers should be appointed according to denomination, religious instruction should be under the supervision of the spiritual leaders, approved schoolbooks should also be used in Hermannsburg schools, and there should be time during school hours for confirmation classes.

The embattled Bühr took a slightly different position, however. He acknowledged the right of the state to take responsibility for the schooling of children, including the curriculum. But he rejected the departmental subject inspectors on the basis that they promoted English at the expense of the mother tongue; he also complained of an apparent state hostility towards the church in schools, claiming it was hindering progress. Bühr clearly felt beleaguered, and suspected that the government wanted to take over the schools. He proposed that they did so on condition that religious instruction be guaranteed, that time allocated under no circumstances be reduced, and that provision be made for Bible history instruction in the catechism and religious songs and hymns, as well as confirmation classes, and also for morning prayers in the mother tongue. Government should also, he felt, be compelled to use the Hermannsburg Tswana reader series.

In 1946, eight years after the conflict first broke out, the mission decided that Pastor Bühr would be moved to Jericho.[18] But this immediately provoked a petition of protest from his congregation, whether at Bühr's instigation or not is unclear.[19] A delegation of three was sent to plead the case. It included David Malebye (church elder), Abraham Musi (member of the school committee) and Solomon Mahuma (principal of Bethanie). The petition humbly requested that Bühr remain at Bethanie. The main reasons they advanced were that the chief, Daniel More, had passed away. Simpson may thus be correct when he argues that the Bethanie conflict 'appeared to be a struggle over control of the chieftaincy initiated by a group of "progressive natives" who were frustrated with the archaic rule of the chief and his supporters'.[20] Without the chief, Bühr was less of a threat. He understood the issues, while a new leadership, lacking comprehension, would be unable to deal with them. Bühr was, moreover, in the process of negotiating the repair of the vandalised church with the Bakwena committee. Nothing came of the congregation's plea, however, and Bühr's transfer to Jericho was effected. His last posting was in Rustenburg where he was given responsibility for the mission's book depot.

In this story, the main players were the missionary and his supporters, the chief, and 'the rebels' and their supporters. The missionary was allied with the chief, while the chief was allied both with the missionary and the department. 'The rebels' wanted neither traditional nor mission control but rather an independent school free not only from the church and its practices, but also from the chief. The Native Education inspectors supported neither the dissidents nor the missionaries, but rather the authority of the chief. There is a deep irony in communities seeking support from individuals within the state who promoted the chiefly authority which these same communities opposed, and whose struggles ultimately functioned to bolster the plan for state control of education.

Ramakokstad 1946-1952

If Bühr's troubles broke out in the year in which he buried six family members, those of Peter Meyerhoff began when he first showed symptoms of heart failure. In 1946, the year before his death, during which he was hospitalised, Chief Ramakoka wrote to the assistant native commissioner in Pilanesberg,[21] requesting the replacement of Rev. P.G. Meyerhoff 'because it was felt that he was against the Progress of the school'. Gaotingwe Betheule Ramakoka, appointed chief in August 1927, was a member of one of the more prosperous chiefdoms in the Pilanesberg district. Ramakoka's Location, where the school in question was situated, was 38 miles north of Rustenburg. The chief himself was a Hermannsburg-educated man and owned several farms. The people under his rule were less well-off, with some working on white-owned farms while others were migrant labourers. The vast majority were considered to be Christian, and most were members of the Hermannsburg Lutheran Mission. The school referred to was probably the one government-aided school in the area, with classes up to Standard 6 and a staff of 5 teachers for 370 children. An additional teacher was paid for by the community. The Native Affairs department estimated that about three-quarters of children of school-going age attended school.[22]

Ramakoka's charges against Meyerhoff all related to him failing in his educational mission. He had, the chief noted, been superintendent of the school for more than fifteen years, during which time he had done nothing for the school. The school started as a three-classroom, three-teacher school, but had expanded teacher numbers to five. The missionary, Ramakoka wrote, was against anything that the group proposed and was 'under all circumstances prepared to go contrary to our plans'. He cited several instances to support his case. First was the community's effort to increase the number of teachers as the school was understaffed. This met with firm opposition, so they resorted to the native commissioner, who communicated with the Transvaal Education Department on their behalf and paid the school regular visits when they were constructing two additional classrooms. Second was that Meyerhoff appeared to resent it when more children enrolled, and then fought to ensure that they attended confirmation classes and were confirmed by the age of 16. The result was that they left school with less than four years of schooling – a further reason why no provision was made for higher classes. Third, Meyerhoff did not support his teachers: 'if any teacher tries his best in teaching he often regards him as a bad person'. This behaviour appears to have been counter-posed to democratic principles, and Ramakoka posed the question, if teachers cannot teach and lead their own people, who did the missionary expect should do so? Fourth, the missionary attempted to restrict the educational level of the children. The *lekgotla* agreed that the children should leave school either after passing Standard

6 or after eight years of schooling, and the inspector endorsed this decision 'and signed in the logbook that he grants us Std. VI as from January 1946' – but despite this, 'what did our Superintendent do?' Ramakoka asks, clearly annoyed at Meyerhoff's subsequent dismissal of the head teacher on the basis that children aged sixteen were in the school. Fifth, Meyerhoff did not pass on letters from the principal or school committee either to the department or the inspector, and he refused to allow a feeding scheme for the school. The school had reported the matter to the assistant native commissioner in Rustenburg but had as yet received no reply.

The reason for the silence was the extensive process of consultation, both internally and with the mission, which was occurring behind closed doors. The assistant native commissioner had sent a memorandum to the native commissioner on 8 April informing him that the school belonged to 'the tribe', was built on their property and was recognised by the Transvaal Education Department, and that Rev. Meyerhoff had been appointed superintendent about fifteen years before. A month later the native commissioner sent a letter to the inspector at Rustenburg, attaching the letter from the assistant commissioner, and asking him for his views.[23] The bureaucratic process was taking its course – and also taking its time.

Almost two months later, on 28 June, Inspector C.A. Jansen from Rustenburg wrote to missionary Meyerhoff's superior, Rev. Brümmerhoff, at Saron, Phokeng, asking what the church intended to do given the fact that 'the tribe' no longer wanted the services of Rev. Meyerhoff.[24] Six or more months went by, during which time Brümmerhoff consulted his own superiors. He eventually responded that his synod had not given him the authority to handle such matters. This provoked a sharp letter from Inspector G. Dearden to both Meyerhoff and Brümmerhoff, in which he informed them that the department viewed 'with grave concern the rapid deterioration of the relations existing between you as Superintendent of the school and the parent community'.[25] A request to re-establish normal relationships had not resolved the situation and the position was 'becoming more aggravated'. In the face of inaction on the part of the mission, the department called a meeting for February 1947 at Ramakokstad 'of all the parties interested in order to allow the community to state its grievances' in the presence of the mission and to give it 'the opportunity of refuting their allegations'. The inspector said that the department would then be able to decide, in the light of the facts placed before it, whether cooperation on a basis of mutual respect between the mission superintendent and the community could be restored.

Almost a year passed before a meeting was called between representatives of, respectively, the mission, the chief and 'the tribe', the school committee and the Transvaal Education Department; it eventually took place on 11 February 1947 at 11 a.m. in Ramakokstad.[26] The matter to be discussed was the control of the school and its superintendency. Around the time of this meeting Meyerhoff was hospitalised, following which he went to stay with his daughter until his death barely six months later, on 29 July 1947.[27] Meyerhoff had finally been removed.

In this case, there is evidence of deep hostility between the mission and the traditional authority, with the latter working with the community and calling on departmental authority to assist in the resolution of disputes. In this, as in the previous case, the bona fide interest of missionaries in education was questioned – in both instances they seemed primarily concerned with 'conversion' and the rituals of conversion rather than with actual education, which was a priority for local communities and, in this case, the chief as well.

Saron, Phokeng 1952-1954

Another case concerned Otto Brümmerhoff, this time in Saron. Here the conflict was once again over religious versus secular schooling. Once again, chief and missionary were on opposite sides, with each struggling for control over the school.

Saron was the site to which one of the first Hermannsburg missionaries, Christoph Penzhorn, had been invited by Kgosi Mokgatle in 1867. The two men had established a good working relationship. Over time, this relationship between the Lutherans and Bafokeng had gone through good times and bad, mainly because of the role played by the early Hermannsburg missionaries, Ernst Penzhorn, Hermann Wenhold and Wilhelm Springhorn, in acquiring land for and with the Bafokeng between 1866 and 1899. Even though the contributions made by the Bafokeng generally exceeded those of the Lutherans, the former were not permitted to own land in their own right, a restriction that had existed in the ZAR, and was reinforced and tightened with the 1913 Land Act. As a result, purchases by the Lutherans were in the name of the Lutherans, but largely paid for in cattle and cash by the Africans. The contractual arrangements entered into were fairly informal; there were no written agreements – a situation that was open to abuse.[28] Land was bought by the Bafokeng, but registered in the name of the missionaries. In 1898, and again after the South African War, mission-owned land was re-registered in the names of the secretary and the commissioner of Native Affairs.

Land acquisition continued after the Natives Land Act (No. 27 of 1913), despite restrictions, and often with the assistance of the Native Affairs department, whose role in this regard may be seen as benevolent paternalist, i.e. 'combining the qualities of a Victorian patriarch and a "traditional" chief'.[29] This relationship and the mission's role in Saron were shattered by events that took place between 1952 and 1954, a period during which the Bantu Authorities Act (No. 68 of 1951) introduced a system of 'tribal authorities' responsible for control within African reserves, with the 1953 Bantu Education Act locating the control and administration of education in rural areas within the realm of these 'tribal authorities'. This was a fraught period for the Bafokeng, characterised by much litigation – a strategy much used in the latter half of the twentieth century 'in blunting the efforts of the government to force compliance with government policy decisions'.[30] It was also used to devastating effect to break the power of, and relationship with, the mission in Saron after almost a century of cooperation.

Between 1952 and 1954 the mission was involved in a bitter, costly and lengthy legal dispute with the Bafokeng chief over the right of the mission to the use of a church that had been built on 'tribal' land. The origins of the dispute are attributed to a rain service called for during a persistent drought. Rain services were central to local beliefs, but the missionary influence had gradually weakened these. As head of the mission in South Africa, *Kondirektor* Winfried Wickert[31] wrote in his report on the matter in the mission newspaper that the parish had requested a rain service. He complied, but the rains did not come. Then the chief ordered the entire community, parish and mission included, to hold a rain service 'to the ancestors in the heathen way'. The rains then came. The next Sunday Brümmerhoff held a church service to preach against 'heathen' ways, informing the congregation that the Christian service was the only route to God and salvation. According to Wickert, the chief was upset, and from that moment became hostile towards the missionary and the church. The chief refused any attempt at face-to-face discussion and forbade his people from attending church services on pain of punishment. For Wickert, this was a conflict between 'the will of God and that of the Chief'.[32]

These events occurred in January 1949.[33] Some three years later, on 28 February 1952, Brümmerhoff and Wickert were served with a notice from Gratus, Sacks & Bernard Melman, a firm of solicitors in Johannesburg, acting for James Molotlegi, chief of the Bafokeng tribe, Rustenburg, to vacate the church at Saron-Phokeng, the property of the Bafokeng, no later than 31 March 1952, failing which action his 'ejectment would be instituted without any further notice or demand'.[34] Between these dates, 1949 and 1952, the African National Congress (ANC) had mounted its Defiance Campaign against apartheid, and the Eiselen Commission had sat, and reported its findings. Brümmerhoff had arrived at Saron in 1946.

Schools and schooling inevitably became entangled in this conflict. During 1951 serious tensions developed between Brümmerhoff and the chief. In a letter to the chief inspector of Native Education, G.H. Franz, Brümmerhoff reveals not only his own antagonism towards the chief, but also that displayed by members of the school committee.[35] He relays the request by the Luka School Committee for the transfer of the principal, Koos Mokgatle. Their objection to him is twofold: first, he 'does what he wants without bothering about the school committee'; and second, he is 'the spy of the Chief and shuts up discussions in the Committee'. Brümmerhoff reports that when he went to see the native commissioner in Rustenburg, Mr Cronje, the latter had informed him of the chief's complaint that committee meetings were being held without him or a representative of his being present. Cronje had requested the chief to write a letter about the matter to the department so that they could act upon it. Brümmerhoff, however, found the situation outrageous, as it would give the chief 'all authority in the school'. He then begged Chief Inspector Franz to intervene on the side of the school committee as the chief was 'a seasoned diplomat' who would brook no dissent or opposition, and had in fact relieved two committee members of their positions simply because they expressed their own opinions. Jonathan Hyslop's analysis of the way in which school boards and committees established under the Bantu Education Act in rural areas enabled chiefs and homeland politicians to exercise a 'ferocious' and 'authoritarian' control over teachers and parents[36] chimes with what seems to have happened here. At this stage, however, the power of the local community was still in the process of being asserted. School committees elected by parents, as well as school boards, had been established in the Transvaal before the Bantu Education Act,[37] and some of the issues that would later undermine them were now beginning to emerge.

Another point of conflict between the missionary, the chief and the school principal was the question of confirmation classes. The missionary had asked the principals of three schools to release children on Mondays and Fridays so that they could attend confirmation classes at 3 p.m. on those days. This requirement was resented as some of the children were in Standard 6 and were anxious about passing the exam if they left school early. But the chief and at least one of the principals forbade the children to attend confirmation classes. For this reason, the missionary requested the chief inspector to make him a member of the school committee as representative of the department at Saron, Bafokeng Secondary and Luka schools. He invoked the support of committee members who felt they did not know the departmental regulations and were therefore 'in the power of the Chiefs'. Likening the power chiefs wielded over people in the schools to the despotic power of Stalin in Russia, he averred that 'what the chief wants is placed before the Committee as the wish of the Department' – for the missionary, this was an 'Impossible situation!'[38]

Brümmerhoff's efforts to curtail the power of the chief in educational matters and to increase his own were halted by the legal process in which he now became embroiled. Much of the legal battle revolved around rights to the land and to the church. The missionary case was partly based on an historical argument. The Hermannsburg Mission had been invited by Chief Mokgatle to Saron in 1866. The missionary Penzhorn then settled on land belonging to Paul Kruger, president of the ZAR. The chief was one of the first converts, albeit towards the end of his life. As Africans could not own land, the Bafokeng together with the mission bought the land upon which the mission built its church. The community contributed £700 and the mission £220.[39] Saron was described as 'a prospering mission station during the reign of Chief Mokgatle and during the ministry of Penzhorn. The native town was situated beneath the hills and to the north of it was the mission station, and between them was the great church like the centre of the whole'.[40] This church was built by congregants and the mission for the purpose of performing church services. Nearly a hundred years later, Molotlegi would state his case as follows: 'The Church building was not built by the Mission but by the Tribe irrespective of demonization and it was regarded as tribal property. It is the Bafokeng cathedral'.[41]

In the meantime, though, Mokgatle was succeeded by Tumagole, who never became a convert, though many other family members chose to remain Christians. The school grew in numbers, with several teachers coming from both missionary and African communities. But there were several periods in its history when opposition to the mission took hold. Tumagole, according to the official Hermannsburg history, was opposed to the mission. When he died in 1896, he was succeeded by August Mokgatle, a Christian, 'who immediately suppressed all kinds of witchcraft and rainmaking'.[42] Support for the mission waxed and waned during the first part of the twentieth century, but it appears that mission influence continued to grow. The son of the first Penzhorn took over from his father when he died in 1895, and remained at Phokeng until his own death in 1940. Then, for a brief period, the mission was run by Friedhold Dehnke. Brümmerhoff took over in 1946.

At the start of legal proceedings in 1952 between Molotlegi and Brümmerhoff concerning rights to the land, both parties made an appeal to the secretary of Native Affairs. His response was to support the chief. According to the department, the church building was erected outside mission grounds, on 'tribal' land, with the permission and assistance of the chief and his *lekgotla*. The building was therefore the property of the Bafokeng. The secretary thus supported the view of the chief that the church was built by the community and only lent to the mission. The department saw this as a 'personal feud between the chief and the Rev. Brümmerhoff', was reluctant to intervene, and proposed a negotiated solution.[43] Indeed, on 3 November 1952, Brümmerhoff's Pretoria-based firm of solicitors, Stegmann, Oosthuizen and Jackson, wrote to Wickert's solicitors, saying that it appeared that Chief Molotlegi and the Bafokeng would be prepared to abandon their proceedings against the Hermannsburg Mission Society if Rev. Brümmerhoff were to be replaced. This was also conveyed to Wickert by Mr Zietsman of the Native Affairs department in Pretoria on 24 April 1953. Zietsman had indeed advised Wickert to settle as it seemed likely they would lose the case. Throughout, their position was bolstered by the support they claimed the chief had from his people. The mission and Brümmerhoff, however, dug in their heels.[44] Giving in, they argued, would be to place their missionaries at the mercy of 'those native chiefs', which might mean 'destruction of the mission work'. Instead, they decided 'to fight it out'.

The case was heard in the Supreme Court in June 1953 with further appeals and papers placed before it thereafter. On 29 April 1954, a defeated Wickert wrote an angry, accusatory letter to Molotlegi. He accused him of having 'destroyed the congregation' knowing full well that Brümmerhoff had done no wrong, and of being unwilling to reconcile with him. He ended by saying that the time had come for him, as director of the mission, to take Brümmerhoff away from Saron, though he prayed that God would help him (Molotlegi) to recognise the wrong he had done. A similar letter was sent to the congregation, who responded by thanking him for removing Brümmerhoff, but leaving Moruti Moa in place; diplomatically, they said he had given them 'hope', and expressed the wish that he would again give them 'a white Minister'.[45]

Having arrived at a settlement, it was proposed that preparations for trial be held over and a later date obtained.[46] Molotlegi's response to Wickert, via the lawyers, was to raise the stakes: he communicated that, while he bore no personal grudge against the mission and was merely acting on behalf of the Bafokeng, he doubted whether his people would be prepared to accept the offer made by the mission. He would have to discuss it with them. But he

intimated that the matter could probably be settled quite easily if the mission
would agree to erect a church on its own property, in the village of Phokeng,
where it owned at least 12 morgen. If this was done, there would be no further
complaints against the mission society. The matter then went to trial. The final
judgment, delivered on 3 September, went against the mission. The judge noted
in his opening remarks: 'In one of the years 1886, 1887 or 1888, a church was
built on the tribal land about one hundred and fifty yards from the mission
station. That church, enlarged, is still there. The tribal land, after some change
in registration, is still registered in the name of the Minister of Native Affairs
in trust for the tribe'. The main point on which the case turned was the servitude between the mission and the church. The plea of the plaintiff was to have
the missionary and its society ejected since the latter 'had acquired for itself
and its various agents a servitude of user and occupation over and in respect of
the church and the site on which it is first built and a servitude of right of way
between the mission station and the church. The Society counters claims for a
declaration that these servitudes exist'.[47]

The judgment was based on the 1913 Natives Land Act and the Native
Trust and Land Act (No. 18 of 1936). The 1913 Act was cited; it provided that:

> no person other than a native shall purchase, hire or in any other manner
> whatever acquire any land in a scheduled native area or enter into any
> agreement or transaction for the purchase, hire or other acquisition, direct
> or indirect, of any such land or of any right thereto or interest therein or
> servitude thereover, except with the approval of the Governor-General.[48]

Read together with the 1936 Act, this settled the case. The judgment ejected
Brümmerhoff and the Hermannsburg Mission from the church and/or site
upon which the church was erected at Phokeng, district Rustenburg, Transvaal
Province, and the defendants were ordered to pay the costs of the action.

The case of Saron is important because of the role that the conflict over
schooling may have played prior to the case being taken up legally. While
the school itself was not in question, the control of the missionary over the
church, and therefore over the school, certainly was in question. The ejection of
Brümmerhoff from the church was a victory for Molotlegi and the Bafokeng
against not only the individual himself, but also the mission and its message.
In this case, the state, in the form of the native commissioner and inspector,
as well as the courts, were clearly behind the traditional authority who was
advancing a secular agenda similar to their own. The days of the mission were

numbered. Although Greve replaced Brümmerhoff in 1957, the power of the mission was broken, achieved not by an Act of Parliament but by local struggles between missionaries and traditional authorities.

During the standoff, a new church, the African Missionary Society, led by Rev. Moepi Ramphete, was formed, 'enabling [the congregation] to hold services separate from the Lutheran Church'.[49] Greve took over a position that had been considerably weakened. He had himself been at the centre of an upheaval at the Bethel Teacher Training Institute four years before, in 1953. He was not unscarred when he arrived at Saron. Also, since he was not confrontational, but rather easy-going, his experience at Bethel was likely to ensure that he would foster a different kind of relationship with the community than his predecessor. That the Bafokeng went on to oppose the Bantustan authority that was installed and to insist on a degree of independence from it is one of the ironies of history, since the actions of its chiefs had also assisted in the demise of missionary influence and the strengthening of departmental authority in the area. The Bafokeng would later become one of the richest groups in South Africa, as they had legal claims to their land when valuable platinum deposits were discovered there.

Conclusion

In the decades of the Penzhorns' presence in the Western Transvaal Hermannsburg Mission, relations between Tswana chiefdoms and the mission were strong, so much so that one analyst has referred to the Hermannsburg Mission as being the 'state church' of the polities in the area during this period.[50] In the 1940s and 1950s this relationship began to unravel, however. In the process, to a degree perhaps unrecognised in the wider literature on the transition from mission to state control, local demands for secular schooling played a powerful role in legitimising the case for removal of missionaries and the assertion of state control over schools. During the first three decades of the twentieth century, prosperous Christianised communities had already emerged, many of which increasingly rejected the role of the chief as autocratic power, or sought an education that was secular and free from mission control. In the first case of Bethanie, a rebel movement associating the missionary with the chief established independent schools in opposition to those controlled by the mission and supported by the chief. As controlling power, the Native Affairs department, and the chief inspector in particular, played a decisive role: in line with its function to bolster chiefly authority, it supported the chief and the mission school. In the second case, at Ramakokstad, the failings of the resident missionary in regard to providing adequate and secular schooling were grounds for the request for his removal. In the third case, at Saron in Phokeng, tensions between chief and missionary regarding the control and nature of schooling resulted in a court case which ruled in favour of ejection of the missionary from the church. The missionary feared authoritarian control of the chief; the chief sought a more secular form of schooling. In this case, too, the state supported traditional authority.

These incidents of bitter conflict between chiefs, communities and missionaries suggest that conditions for a transition to control of education by the state, in alliance with chiefs, at least in this area of the Western Transvaal, were ripe. The state consistently supported traditional and chiefly authority; and the latter consistently resorted to the state for assistance in settlement of its disputes, whether within chiefdoms or with missionaries. In this particular triad, one party was growing weaker, and increasingly superfluous. It was a matter of time before ranks would close against it in the matter of the running of schools.

CHAPTER 4

NEGOTIATING THE TRANSFER TO BANTU EDUCATION IN NATAL

When mission societies received the circular on 2 August 1954[1] notifying them that they had to make a choice about the future of their schools, they were given a deadline of the end of that year to make a decision. As Richard Elphick indicates, most missions, with the exception of the Catholics, 'capitulated' in the face of the crippling expense confronting them if they chose to maintain control. The process and path taken in each mission still need careful dissection and comparison with that discussed here. In the case of the Hermannsburg Mission, the decision was taken to transfer control to the state to ensure the continuance of the schools. However, the process of transfer did not take place as quickly or in as clear-cut a manner as envisaged. Although the missions were barely able to continue their financial support of the schools, they wished to retain influence concerning the specifically moral or Christianising mission of their schools. Formal compliance with official directives did not always translate into practical compliance, however, and so the transfer process was in many cases protracted. Eventually, missions did end up retaining a degree of control in attenuated form, some right into the 1980s. But this control was accompanied by considerable contestation on the part of Africans too.

The Hermannsburg Mission's negotiations in Natal and Zululand can be seen to fit into three distinct periods – the first around the making of the decision in 1954–55, the second until the end of the decade, and the third through the 1960s. These periods correspond to changes in the nature and implementation of apartheid. The Bantu Authorities Act (No. 68 of 1951) provided the regulatory framework for the spatialised control envisaged in the 1953 Bantu Education Act, and shaped the politics of transfer until the late 1950s. As contradictions surfaced and resistance escalated, the position of the National Party hardened. The Promotion of Bantu Self-Government Act (No. 46 of 1959) thus initiated the second phase: it provided for the reconstitution of the former reserves as self-governing Bantustans and later as independent homelands on an ethnic basis. As a 'particular politics of population . . . of social and economic engineering preoccupied with trying to reconfigure spatial ratios of blacks to whites and regulate the conditions of their association',[2] the apartheid state's transfer of control from the missions to itself also involved a dynamic of attempted spatial reorganisation, as the regulation of people affected their relationship with the mission as well as the schools. From the early 1960s, the resettlement and removal of hundreds and thousands of people began as part of the plan of the apartheid state. Such processes were achieved through a combination of 'law and violence' – as central to the apartheid project as the ubiquitous notion of race, racial governance, the regulation of the domestic sphere, and the politics of ethnicity.[3] These developments had distinct implications for those missions that still retained some control over schools. In Natal, Hermannsburg communities at Lemgo, Marburg and Esibongweni were resettled in 1963, and that at Nazareth in 1965.[4]

In the first section, this chapter will consider how the Hermannsburg Mission in Natal and Zululand responded to the state as it sought to retain control over schools over the three periods. Here conditions were very different from what they were in the Western Transvaal. Relationships with chiefs did not determine their relationships with schools in all cases, and their relationship with the department and chief inspector was not as close as it was in the Western Transvaal. The second section will analyse African responses to and conflicts with missions over this period.

Making the decision: 1954

Eiselen's circular of 2 August 1954 outlined different procedures to be adopted for primary and post-primary schools respectively in: African areas; farm, mine or factory schools on land in white areas; schools situated on white-owned land in areas which were not recognised as bona fide farm, mine or factory schools.

The circular required a response by 31 December, failing which, state subsidisation would be terminated.

The first step the Hermannsburg Mission took was to discuss the matter at its missionary conference. A number of problems were raised, as the situation seemed to be far more complex than that described in the circular. Fritz Scriba, mission superintendent of Natal and Zululand, was instructed to write to Eiselen. Scriba had been born in India in 1907, the son of Hermannsburg Mission parents. He was educated in Germany and studied theology at Göttingen before being ordained as a missionary and sailing for South Africa in 1931. He spent some time in Hermannsburg, South Africa, with Johann Kistner, the principal of the German school there and father of the well-known anti-apartheid activist.[5] Scriba himself became aware of political movements among rural Africans and the increasing influence of Shembe-Ethiopian and Zionist sects, and wrote about them in his *History of the Station Ehlanzeni 1856–1954*.[6] His successors remember Scriba as a charismatic, story-telling patriarch, respected by both black and white, but nonetheless a segregationist in everyday practice.[7] By 1954 he had considerable experience in South Africa, and as his correspondence with the Department of Native Affairs reveals, he attempted by diplomacy and all manner of tactics to stall and delay the transfer process and to reveal its absurdities while yet remaining within the framework of the law.

Scriba subsequently sent a letter to Eiselen asking for clarity and drawing attention to the multiplicity of conditions and the grey areas which existed and did not seem to fit neatly into any of the categories provided.[8] These included mission land that straddled white- and African-owned land, and land between white-owned farms and African areas that drew their schoolgoing population from both the mission land and from surrounding farms. Then there were mission stations which were in fact farms where many Africans resided either as squatters or workers. Schools on such farms drew children from both the mission farm as well as from surrounding areas. Scriba made it clear that it was difficult to determine boundaries, pointing also to schools which included children from the mission, surrounding farms and from neighbouring African reserves, and schools on small sites provided by farmers for the purpose of teaching the children of farm workers. He raised several other questions too. Were they expected now to give up any plans for building improvements and extensions on money already pledged or should they abandon such plans? In the event of the department renting buildings from missionaries, would the department take responsibility for maintenance of the rented buildings?

And who would be required to erect new buildings that might be needed at a later stage?

Eiselen responded to what he probably perceived as delaying tactics by directing the mission to the regional director. But he was also at a loss. By 13 December, very close to the deadline, Scriba had not yet received a reply. So he again wrote to Eiselen indicating that there was still considerable confusion about whose control the various schools would fall under, and whether the mission could in some instances remain as trustee, i.e. where the African community to whom the school was transferred were members of its congregation. Scriba also expressed the fear that many in the African community 'might not be interested in education or might be inconsistent [sic] in supporting it'.[9] However, in order to ensure that the schools of the mission did not lose their subsidy, he indicated that the Lutheran Missions in Zululand and Natal had agreed on three things. First, although they disagreed with several of the provisions and implications of the Bantu Education Act, they had no option but to accept the proposed alternative of relinquishing control of their state-aided primary schools to African community organisations. This was because they were unable to continue financially without the 75% state subsidy, and to close the schools would deprive many African children of educational facilities. Second, they did not want to sell their buildings, but they were prepared to rent them to the state on condition that they were not used in a manner that was contrary to Christian principles, that the department would be responsible for paying the rent, and that the mission would have full control of the buildings outside school hours. And thirdly, the letter indicated the intention of the missions to avail themselves of the opportunities offered to 'give vital Christian instruction to the pupils from our Churches'. The letter ended with a prayer and a plea that the 'good intentions of the Government might result in success to the best of the Bantu people and not be hindered by forces of darkness in this our multiracial land'. This was sufficiently ambiguous to indicate both a sense of foreboding and a degree of optimism.

Even before the deadline came round, on 17 December 1954, Minister of Native Affairs, H.F. Verwoerd, distributed regulations and application forms for the registration, recognition and subsidisation of all mission schools.[10] These regulations were aimed at Bantu school boards, or farmers, who would now take over the schools on their land. It informed them that they would now become the managers of the schools and employers of the teachers, whose contracts they would have to sign. If they did not wish to manage the school themselves, they were permitted to have a missionary do it on their behalf.

But there was much that the department had not taken into account. By early 1955, it was already taking strain. It was forced to issue new definitions of, for example, a state-aided farm school, and to request that all queries and completed forms be handed in to circuit inspectors, taking into account the fact that the national department was having to ask missionaries themselves to distribute the application forms.[11] It also admitted in April that, owing to pressure of other activities, it had not been possible to negotiate individual leases and contracts with owners of state-aided schools scheduled to become Bantu community schools on 1 April 1955. All it could provide was time-frames and responsibilities regarding rentals, use, maintenance, and so on.[12] By this time, it was also clear that all building and alteration should come to a halt because of uncertainty as to the status of the schools.

The mission continued from early in 1955 to seek clarity and to manage the confusion and insecurity that had broken out in its ranks. The mission had a broad variety of schools in different situations: on mission farms and on property in 'white areas', on the property of farmers, on mission glebes and farms, and on sites and stands in reserves, which had been allocated to missions by Africans. The question was: how were these all to be fitted into the racial map of the apartheid engineers? Many missionaries had been called to meetings and asked to fill in forms about transfer, regardless of whether there was clarity or not. Mission *Kondirektor* Wickert appealed to the regional director of Bantu Education in Natal on 2 January 1955[13] to send all questions and forms to the superintendent of the Hermannsburg Mission in Natal and Zululand, Rev. W. Kaiser, rather than to individuals. 'Our missionaries,' he wrote, 'do not wish to be rushed and have decided themselves that all decisions should be made by the Board and not by the individual missionaries'.

Wickert stated, moreover, that the mission felt fully justified in its request as the schools were the property of the mission, after all. The mission had come to certain decisions so as to resolve some of the tensions created by the state's need for racial delimitation of schools: it would register schools on mission property as farm schools, and appoint missionaries as managers; it would hand over schools on farms to the farmers, even though the department was probably aware that these schools would close 'as not all farmers will agree to build and maintain schools'; and it would hand over schools on glebes and farms, built for mission purposes, to the department to bring them under African community control. But given that the schools had been built and maintained by the mission and its congregation, the mission requested strong representation by the congregation in the school board, at least in the early years, and also continued use by the mission and congregation of the school building and the right to continue to teach reading in the baptism and confirmation classes. What was important to the mission, above all else, was education or schooling for the purposes of conversion to Christianity. While Wickert's letter indicates compliance, it is also an attempt to negotiate, through these measures, some degree of continued influence.

Less than a year after Eiselen's 1954 circular and his requests for information about the location and control of schools, the department had succeeded in reclassifying all the schools which, up to then, they were aware of.[14] By 21 April 1955, almost a thousand schools had been classified as follows: 498 Bantu community schools (i.e. more than half of all schools in Natal and Zululand); 152 aided mission schools; 65 provisionally aided with reduced subsidy for an indefinite period; 154 farm schools; 7 mine and factory schools. In all, 66 were permitted to carry on as before, though for a limited period. There were 6 closures.

However, implementing the procedures for conversion or transfer of control was a different matter altogether. The department quickly picked up on this and ensured that foot-dragging or resistance of any kind was quickly dealt with. In September 1956 the Regional Director of Bantu Education, S.R. Dent, instructed the mission community to inform owners of all farm, mine and factory schools that they were *personally* required to declare support for the Bantu Education Act and also pledge to observe it in their management of the school. This applied in particular to the provision for religious instruction according to the syllabus. But owners were also to be made aware that if a manager (i.e. missionary) in any way acted contrary to the Act, or departmental regulations and instructions, another manager should be nominated.[15] Missions were warned that educational institutions for Africans which were not situated in African areas or urban residential areas set aside for Africans would not be registered.[16]

Negotiated dispossession by contract: 1955–1968
Bantu community schools

Many mission schools situated in designated African areas were converted into Bantu community schools. Local African communities generally welcomed the move.[17] However, it had implications for the school buildings, and it was unclear to whom they now belonged. Initially, the state agreed to pay the missions rent for the buildings through the school board, which would receive a grant to pay the rent. The negotiations around this were lengthy, and in Natal and Zululand the mission developed a common contract for its 20 schools, based on one that the Methodists had developed. For the mission, it was important that the leadership rather than individual missionaries should deal with government.[18] A united response and approach was emphasised throughout the negotiations. The document eventually agreed upon leased all mission 'land, buildings and furniture . . . for use as a Native School or a Bantu school' to the government, which had the first option to purchase. Several conditions were, however, built into the lease: government had the responsibility for rental as well as the maintenance of buildings and furniture, and it was not allowed to make any structural alterations without permission from the church. Government was also responsible for paying electricity, water and sanitation. It was not permitted to cut down trees or shrubs without the permission of the church. The latter was responsible for insurance and could claim from government for damages. In the case of irreparable damage, the lease would be terminated.[19]

A crucial point arose in 1960, however. The department sent notice to the mission that it had reviewed its rental policy – from now on communities would have to pay for their own buildings. This was argued for on the somewhat dubious grounds of 'encouraging the bantu to develop more self-reliance and to assume increased responsibility in the educational field'.[20] As from 1 January 1962, all school boards were expected to assume full responsibility for school buildings hired or purchased from the owners. An ambiguous phrase indicated that 'within these limitations and . . . where necessary, assurance within the limits of available departmental funds [would] be given'. For the mission this was a heavy blow. Responding with his customary tact, Scriba asked whether the school boards would be able to pay what was owed every month, and what the consequences might be if they had no funds at their disposal. Also, it was unclear where the money would come from, as parents could not be expected to pay.[21]

In its response, the departmental representative, a Mr Potgieter, reiterated the self-reliance rationale and argued that school boards could obtain the necessary funds 'from school fees either payable by all children who attend the school; or from bazaars, concerts, etc. In other words from the community itself which in many cases includes members from different congregations'.[22] Funds collected in this way were now used to hire buildings from churches and other parties; the department had previously hired these as an interim measure only. Furthermore, if a school board was able 'to proof [sic] to the satisfaction of the Department that it has a limited or very small income or credit balance too small to cover expenses in this connection, the Department will consider its request more than like favourably [sic]'.[23]

In the short term this provision created great difficulty for the mission, and in the long term even greater difficulties for the African communities. The mission again decided to act as a collective, i.e. as Hermannsburg Mission in tandem with other Lutherans who were in the same situation – each mission in each station was advised to enter into the same contract.[24] Tensions broke out between different Lutheran bodies when some met independently with government and, anticipating failure, decided to sell the buildings rather than enter into new contract agreements with communities. There were differences also among Hermannsburgers who wanted to continue the relationship with local communities in this way, and those who did not. Among the objectors was Heini Fedderke from the Georgenau station: 'I personally think it is clear for everybody that we as a mission can't become a tool and servant, can't and may not become a tool and handmaiden of government. I have severe objections against rental contracts in general that I will explain'.

For him, the issues as set out for the Hermannsburg Mission in his lengthy discussion paper,[25] were both material and moral. The work of the mission would be deeply compromised, he felt, by the relationship that government was demanding that it enter into with communities. Acknowledging that the Bantu community and farm schools over which the mission had control 'were in many ways built and maintained in part by the parents of the children,' Fedderke nevertheless asked:

> Is it really right to burden many of our community members living in locations with asking a rent? Wouldn't the tie to the community become even looser than it is now? Why should one pay 3X – in the community, for the building of the school and now even for the rent? Won't the work be deeply disturbed or prevented? Will concerts and bazaars in favour of rents not burden our communities so that they don't have any power any more for the Synodal effort?

In the end, the Hermannsburg Mission capitulated and sent a circular to school boards that appeared very similar to that sent to the mission by government.[26] This signalled the arrival of the Hermannsburg Mission as school building landlord. The circular set out the situation and then laid down strict conditions for the hiring of the buildings: the buildings were to be used for school purposes only from Monday to Friday; no concerts were to be held in buildings reserved for divine service; the mission would enjoy free access to the buildings over weekends for religious instruction purposes. Provision was also made for appeals to be lodged. Almost immediately, several responses were received from school boards indicating that they were not able to pay.[27] The mission advised that the department be approached with a request for relief, saying that they were unable to pay the rent and that the Hermannsburg Synodal Council would not be paying the rent. At a community meeting of the Kranskop School Board, the community took a more radical position: the mission should cancel the lease as the parents had helped build the school 'by shovelling the sand, breaking stones from the rocks into small pieces, carrying water for the construction'.[28]

What had indeed been achieved within a mere five-year period after 1955, however, was the transfer of responsibility for the funding of schools from a combination of mission and government, to one of government and local African communities themselves. In the vast majority of cases, though, these communities simply lacked the means.

Farm schools

The subordination of children attending mission schools neighbouring white farms to the interests of those farmers occurred through legal means also. Mission schools on land comprising less than 400 acres had to be leased to the neighbouring farmer for one shilling a year. The missionary was entitled to become the school manager. Permission for children to attend the school had to be obtained from the neighbouring farmer: irrespective of how many neighbouring farms the children came from, permission had to be obtained for each one of them. Throughout this period, the department badgered the mission so as to ensure compliance on every point.[29] The great majority of farm schools belonging to the Hermannsburg Mission consisted of those that the mission had built on its outstations.[30] All these properties were smaller than 400 acres, so there was no farm labour as none was needed. Consequently, the farm schools could only be retained as such if they were leased to neighbouring farmers who were then registered as the owners of these schools. In most cases they were small buildings that served as both church and school.

The mission responded in the same way as it had with Bantu community schools – it consulted with the department, engaged with it, decided to act as one rather than individually, sought to have the same contract even with different farmers, and looked at what other Lutherans were doing. It attempted to get around the official requirement by registering land as a farm under the name either of the mission or of a German farmer in the area. As with the Bantu community schools, the mission adapted leases that had been developed by Methodist and Swedish missionaries. But the Hermannsburgers had serious concerns about the situation, as it was clear to them that under these conditions each person became an employee of the farmer, including the evangelist, who, from a legal perspective, could be seen as his worker, having to repair his fences and the like. More importantly, as Scriba had noted in correspondence with the regional director of Bantu Education on 9 March 1957 about Hattingshope school, 'many farmers are not eager to take care and responsibility for Bantu schools'. The mission, he said, was reluctant to develop a contract for buildings used for both church and mission purposes, and so 'there has been some hesitating on our side'.[31]

Given this fact, Scriba requested that the mission be permitted to retain farm schools, if the farmers were in favour of it. He wished to know whether it was possible to propose a lease contract for buildings and sites, used for both church and school purposes, which protected the vital interests of church work.[32] His requests were turned down, as the department insisted on compliance. In his response of 7 October, Scriba stated that the farmer he had approached was not prepared to take over ownership 'as he feared complications later on'. Even though he had told the farmer he would take the matter to the department, the farmer refused. Many farmers, Scriba explained, were unwilling to take over the ownership of farm schools, wishing simply to go on as before, and complaining to him: 'We are not against your work but we do not like to be troubled with it'. The department was unmoved by Scriba's pleas. Eventually a farmer was located and a lease prepared but this also created difficulties. The mission wanted to ensure it retained influence over the behaviour of people on its property, whereas the department did not want to grant the mission that right. Finally the mission was forced to agree to the terms of the contract, with the understanding that the department would terminate it at once 'in the event of the conduct of its servants being unseemly'.[33]

The Hermannsburg Mission did not get much support from fellow Lutherans in contesting the departmental conditions. Ongoing problems included the classification of schools for subsidy; the subsequent withdrawal thereof; and departmental insistence on forms and permissions by farmers for children from neighbouring farms to go to the farm schools run by missionaries as managers. This led Scriba to take the matter to a meeting of the Cooperating Lutherans. This meeting set up a committee consisting of Fritz Scriba, Gunter Krause from the BMS, and Ingolf Hodne of the Swedish Lutherans, to investigate the matter.[34] A difference of opinion clearly existed between at least the Hermannsburg Mission and the BMS. For Scriba, the encroachment of the authority of the state on that of the missions to conduct educational work overall was of great concern. For him, numerous questions remained unanswered. Krause's response, however, was simply to see no wrong and advise compliance. Scriba's approach generally was to appeal for humanity and understanding of the difficulties in which people found themselves. But this had little impact on the department, intent on strict application of its rules and regulations prescribing who could run a school, where, and under what conditions. One example suffices. Scriba had written to the secretary of Native Affairs[35] about the sudden withdrawal of subsidy from Müden Farm School because it was on land smaller than the requisite 400 acres. In his letter, he enquired:

> What will the fate be of the 179 children who cannot go to other schools, of the teachers, who will hardly find another post in the end of the year, of the Natives who were urged by the Department to build a school and to promote the education of their children? What is the reason of such a haste in this matter . . . .. 36 of the children are coming from other European farms, 129 are on the Mission farm, 14 are coming from the very near Native reserve. Most of the inhabitants of Müden Mission are squatters and have been squatters for decades. Their fate will be decided in the near future and the Mission will have to decide what to do with the farm . . . .. Whatever the decision, the future of the squatters and of the school would be automatically settled in connection with that decision. It will be a very hard blow for the Natives, if they have to leave the Mission Station, which was their home for a very long time. Will it be in the interest of the country to cause more bitter feelings of frustration?

He went on to request reconsideration of the decision and the delay of any action or change in schools on the bigger mission farms until such time as their future had been decided: 'it would be heart-breaking to close the school and to expel the children. I trust that the department will consider the welfare of the children and the teachers as well as of the Bantu community'.

In the long term, however, there was no interest on the part of the state in the control of farm schools by missions. That the interests of the children were now subordinated to the needs of the farmers for labour, and that labour rather than the education of the children on the farms was central, became clear in a circular sent to all managers and owners of farm schools on 28 June 1958 regarding the 'performance of farm work by school children during school hours'.[36] The circular noted that as there appeared to be some uncertainty on the part of certain managers or owners of farm schools regarding the extent to which they might utilise the services of schoolchildren for farm work during school hours, the department drew their attention on the one hand to pupils in farm schools having to 'receive their rightful share of tuition in the ordinary school subjects', but also indicated that 'during the periods of handwork and practical gardening . . . scholars may be employed on one or another [type] of farm work as practical training. The performance of farm work by scholars OUTSIDE school hours is a matter for private arrangement between the manager/owner and his employees' (emphases in original). This was music to the ears of many farmers who were in any case not well disposed to mission schools, believing that children should be occupied with labour and that 'if the kids have some education they will be lost'.[37]

There was thus no prohibition on the use of child labour on these farms; indeed, it was authorised as a part of the school curriculum. Twenty years later it was still common practice for farmers in the area to resort to such child labour, even drawing children from schools in neighbouring reserves for seasonal work during the harvesting period.[38]

The bureaucratic harassment relating to the leasing of land to farmers[39] and permissions from farmers for children to attend schools continued throughout the 1960s.[40] Schools were arbitrarily closed if they did not comply.[41] In the case of Hebron, which was being managed by Rev. Bodenstein, the school's status depended on the farm's status as a farm, which in turn depended on the sugar quota it produced. The school itself was attended by children from neighbouring farms. As the status of the farm hung in the balance, Bodenstein was informed by the inspector that a lease should be concluded with the neighbouring farmer by June of that year (1959). After discussing the matter with the inspector, Bodenstein was under the impression he could continue as before. When a telegram arrived instructing him to close the school until such time as he received the necessary authority, a distraught Bodenstein wrote to Scriba requesting that the mission at least pay the salaries of the teachers for a possible two-month period. Scriba replied immediately, advising him to request an extension of time. The department refused, simply berating Bodenstein for continuing with an illegal school. Scriba then visited the school, as there was some disquiet among the school community. But he made no promises, and the misgivings continued. A concerned Bodenstein wrote again to Scriba about the teachers' salaries, fearing especially the loss of one Gwala, who had remained with the school even when he had better offers, and who was in danger of going over 'to the Communists or a similar direction'. Scriba promptly advised

Bodenstein to inform the teachers of the reality of the situation – they would lose their posts as the school was closing, and the mission could not afford to carry the costs.[42]

Compliance was also ensured by the requirement that managers of farm, mine and factory schools should sign an undertaking to manage their school 'in accordance with the Bantu Education Act . . . and the regulations promulgated thereunder as amended, and future amendments thereof, as well as Departmental instructions issued from time to time in connection with the duties of managers of farm, mine and factory schools'. As a sop to the missionaries, the managers were also required to 'permit all state-recognised churches that wish to give religious instruction to their followers in the school adequate time to do so in accordance with departmental regulations'.[43]

By the mid-1960s, however, apartheid policies for the removal and resettlement of people were taking their toll on those who lived in mission areas. Increasingly, missionaries were fighting a losing battle as they and the people living on their farms and attending the schools over which they still had some influence faced eviction and removal. In one incident, a labour department official, Mr Aucamp, arrived on the mission farm Entombe on 23 June 1964 and told the people living there that 45 kraals had to quit the farm by 31 July, simply because there were too many children in the school. While the Hermannsburg Mission, and Scriba in particular, were enraged, the people themselves were thrown into confusion and fear for their future. Scriba wrote a long letter to the Bantu Affairs commissioner in Piet Retief, under which the farm fell, notifying him of what had happened. He provided a history of the farm, including written undertakings from the department that no one would be removed from mission farms without written notice, as well as reasons as to why the people should not be moved; the letter also contained an appeal, a statement of disapproval of the action of Mr Aucamp, 'a district labour officer attached to your office', and a threat of non-cooperation unless the removal proposition was withdrawn.[44]

This was not the first time something like this had happened, and Scriba was angry that correct procedures had not been followed. In characteristic fashion, he then engaged the department so as to win time and consulted with his superiors as well as the local community. Then he arrived at a conclusion which attempted to reconcile acting within the framework of the law and protecting mission interests as well as those of the people in their schools. Consultation with government revealed that Mr Aucamp had acted independently – there was no official notice for the removal of people, and no site to which the people could be moved. Meetings were not held with the people on the farm, who were repeatedly referred to as 'squatters' rather than as 'labour tenants'. With the approval of the tenants, Scriba made his position to government clear: he would work with government to resettle people on Entombe on condition that the people affected were informed timeously, that they were compensated for their loss and for the land they had lost, that they should be resettled as a group, and that there was a place for a church at the new site.[45] Privately, he expressed the view that everyone should work together and 'keep a firm order that respects the lives of the natives. Then there will be trust again . . .. The native is looking for help and support'.[46] As a result of all this, particularly the insecurity and threats to their lives, people began migrating from farming areas.[47]

The Property Management Company (PMC) was founded in 1968 to manage mission property in white areas. It soon came to serve all regional Lutheran churches, and in 1979 the mission handed over all its properties to the PMC for administration.[48] In the late 1980s the PMC commissioned a report on farm schools on properties it managed; it described the system as 'feudal'.[49] Farmers had in effect become not only the owners but also the managers of schools. But they were on the whole completely uninterested in or, worse, actively opposed to the schools.[50] With a few exceptions, they 'were stunning by their absence . . .. One of the problems was that school managers managed the teachers as if they were their farm labour'.[51] The schools themselves by law did not go beyond Standard 5.

Private schools

Every school had to be registered, regardless of whether it was eligible for a subsidy.[52] The only schools that remained entirely private were the Sunday schools, baptism and communion schools.

Continuities

By 1965 the Hermannsburg Mission still had influence over a number of schools. This included 42 farm schools with 4,072 schoolchildren and 80 teachers.[53] Of the 42 farm schools, 14 were on mission farms where the mission was the owner of the farm and school and the missionary the manager, 5 schools were not on mission property but on farms where the missionary as private person was the manager, and 23 schools that were on mission holdings smaller than 400 acres and therefore under the ownership of neighbouring farmers and under the management of the missionary. Not included in this number were 5 small private schools each with about 20 to 40 children and one teacher, and 21 Bantu community schools on mission farms, glebes, sites and land which they had permission to occupy. In such cases, buildings were mission property but the management was in the hands of the school board.

By 1969 the number of schools had not changed substantially, but the overall context had changed, and with it the role and position of the missionaries.[54] The challenges were spelt out by Scriba in a report in 1969. By this stage there were altogether about 67 schools in the former Hermannsburg territories. This number included 22 Bantu community schools (compared with 21 in 1965), 45 farm schools (compared with 42 in 1965) – 12 belonging to the mission because they were the owners, 5 belonging wholly to farmers, and 22 to farmers who leased land and buildings from the missionaries – and 6 private schools (compared with 5 in 1965). Either the number had increased, or the keeping of statistics had improved. Whatever the case, the mission attributed its growing number of farm schools to the fact that many farmers were German immigrants. In these schools the missionary as manager was still able to exercise considerable influence, and could also do youth work and hire teachers. But Scriba's report acknowledged that the schools were 'far back, because there is a shortage of educational aids'. The schools on the 12 farms larger than 400 acres and so engaged in 'bona fide agricultural work' were threatened and eviscerated by resettlements. Entombe, for example, had less than half the children it had before the resettlement took place. And in Ekhombela there were so few children left it was doubtful that the school would remain at all.[55]

In conclusion, then, the Hermannsburg Mission continued to exercise influence over the schools it had previously controlled. It had entered into arrangements in the Bantu community schools where communities rented buildings from it, and it had rights of representation on school boards as well as access to buildings such that religious instruction could still take place. In the case of farm schools, the mission retained control as owners or managers. What had been achieved had been effected through persistent negotiation coupled with formal compliance. The situation was, however, not to last.

Missions, school principals and the Department of Bantu Education

Schooling and principalship in the Hermannsburg Mission Society was a gendered phenomenon: the principals were generally men, while the teachers tended to be women. A lively correspondence exists between school principals and missionaries during the period under discussion. It gives insight into the issues that confronted the principals, how they dealt with these, how the missionaries mediated and responded to various concerns, and the role the department played. The letters express the power relations that existed between the white male missionary and the black male principal, as well as between missionary, department and school principal. More than this, they also provide insight into the manner in which textual production assembled a new set of identities among non-elites in colonial Africa. In these letters from principals, it is possible to discern an identity being crafted – authoritative beings taking their work seriously and intervening to ensure improvement. As Karin Barber has noted, such literary expressions 'were constituted under the shadow of colonial officialdom'.[56] These were writers who engaged with the colonial state (or missionaries as its representatives), hoping to harness it to their own ends, albeit from a position of vulnerability and insecurity.

Much of the correspondence revolves around requests, demands or interventions – for improvements in school buildings as well as maintenance and the provision of furniture.[57] In demanding improvements to either their own or the teachers' quarters, principals often made the case that they were forced to pay rent for unbearable living conditions: 'Come and see for yourself when you have time what I say and what I want'.[58] Principal Robert Kuzwayo complained bitterly that the previous missionary had not responded to his requests for improvements: 'My family as it is attacked by the fly the house is simply unhygienic and brings a lot of drought, and everyone coughs terribly'.[59] He was forced to consider pulling down the teachers' cottage, it was in such a terrible state, and he felt that the agreement that teachers be responsible for their own repairs was 'out of order'. Firmly and strongly, he contended: 'All teachers pay for rent. No teacher can stay like this . . . .. I pay more rent than all these people. This is unfair'. Another teacher complained of the 'roof allowing rain to pour in the house' with 'the gap between the wall and the house being open . . . allowing wind to enter the house and blow off the lamp or the primus stove at any time, which disturbs me with my evening work'. He also felt that he was 'an open target to colds because of cold night winds'.[60]

In one case, the school principal sought intervention by the mission to ensure that parents on reserves send their children to school. He was concerned that the lack of enrolment would result in the loss of a teacher. Principal H.M.D. Mbhele implored Rev. Scriba to do all he could, including writing to the local magistrate, to ensure that the children went to school. 'I am not concerned with the religious side,' he wrote, 'but with education'. Hinting at his legal bent, he said that 'this will even less [*sic*] these menacing faction fights, which are a nuisance due to the ignorance and illiteracy. It is high time that the law takes its side'.[61] In a strong appeal to Scriba's vanity, the principal ended his letter with the flourish: 'The whole truth is, should you like and be willing in June we can enrol a thousand in Keates Drift but only your word is necessary'.[62] Of course, this was 1958, and by now missions had been forced to abdicate authority and control. And yet the mission seems still to be in a position that enables it to exercise a modicum of control. To this letter, Scriba responded in a manner that encouraged Mbhele to act within the framework of the law: to take the issue to the school committee and even to Home Affairs in Tugela Ferry to advise unwilling parents to allow their children to attend school.[63] His letter ended with a moral injunction: the important thing was to teach 'the Faith', an especially important matter in his area, 'in order to stop all this crime, and killing of people'.[64]

The missionaries' own correspondence reveals a degree of patronising racism among some of them. An example is Rev. Herbert Franz Seinwill, who declined an invitation by the principal of Keates Drift to a quarterly meeting of the Natal African Teachers' Union (NATU) by first thanking and then cautioning him: 'The Bantu community will have to work in earnest if it wishes to overcome the obstacles of irresponsibility and laziness still being so strong among the Bantu, especially in heathen areas like Keates Drift and Tugela Ferry. Still all the faction fights have to be stopped and the heathen have to be preached the gospel of Christ. I hope that your meeting will set an example'.[65]

Such paternalism and racism was complemented by an intolerance of and control over sexual relations among teachers. Missionaries required that teachers be married or engaged to be married, frowning upon sexual relations outside these boundaries. Women's voices are seldom heard in the correspondence, and it is difficult to ascertain what exactly missionary opprobrium was aimed at: the control of sexuality, male as well as female, or the protection of women? Whatever the case, what does come across is the struggle over women's bodies, with women's voices remaining silent. Zebulon Dlamini, a teacher at Oebisfelde Mission Station, was, for example, found to have 'committed misconduct with a woman' in December 1938. He promised to marry the woman but failed to do so, thereby risking suspension. He saved the situation and avoided a forced marriage by paying a fine to the parents of the woman concerned.[66] In a more confusing case at Zendelingspost, Joseph Mdlalose pounced on a couple in the dead of night, accusing the 'assistant male teacher' whom he found in bed with his sister, of being there illegally and of having 'pregnated' his sister.

A meeting called to take statements and address the matter failed to resolve the conflict between the two men. Both the accused, Mr Dladla and Miss Gertrude Mdlalose, were dismissed from teaching.[67] In another case, Frank Cindi, a principal, also at Zendelingspost, was found guilty in the Piet Retief courts 'in a case of immorality with a young girl' and was also dismissed from service.[68] A telling case is that of Tokozile Dingile, who was suspended from teaching each time she gave birth to a child, four times in total, and each time at a different mission station. Each time, she returned to teaching. The expectations of moral conduct based on Christian sexual norms were apparently not so different for women teachers at Wesleyan and American Board mission schools.[69]

The subsequent conditions of service drawn up for teachers by the department provided for 13 areas of misconduct, which amounted to tight control over teachers' sexual, political and everyday lives. Activities for which teachers could be dismissed included 'impropriety', 'disobedience', 'incompetence', 'immorality and habitual use of drugs', 'being found guilty of a criminal offence', 'illegally appropriating funds', 'encouraging disobedience or resistance to the laws of the state', 'identifying actively with a political party', 'engag[ing] for remuneration outside work', 'knowingly mak[ing] an incorrect or false statement', 'mak[ing] critical reports via the press of the Department of Bantu Education or any other Department, school committee, school board or any Bantu Authority', and 'behav[ing] or act[ing] in a manner deleterious to his [sic] position as a teacher'.[70]

In the overall colonial scheme of things, missionaries remained among the powerful. But power relations between the department and mission were shifting. Missionaries were sometimes at a loss about how to deal with the new situation and requested intervention by the department. This happened in the case of Seinwill, who had not been long in South Africa and was still adjusting to the local culture. Outraged by concerts that were being held, he wrote a strong note to the principal: 'It is not allowed to have a concert in the buildings . . . after 6 o'clock'.[71] The principal promptly responded, parodying Seinwill as 'the Lawfull Attorney of the Hermannsburg Mission Society', and asking for precise information, including the exact official paragraphs concerning the holding of school concerts, 'for my files', since, according to information from the government, he was permitted to raise funds in that way. With barely disguised annoyance, he said: 'If such amendments were made, may I pleas [sic] have one copy for my files'.[72]

The matter was not resolved, and a year later Seinwill wrote to the inspector of Bantu Education in Pietermaritzburg asking him what the exact situation was as far as school concerts were concerned. He could see little sense in people making this 'terrible noise so that it is near-impossible to rest in the night'. He wished to know whether he had the right to forbid the concerts.[73] The inspector responded by providing homespun wisdom intended, no doubt, to enlighten the newcomer: 'the Bantu like entertainments as they so seldom get together' and so 'they naturally like to make the best of it . . . and prolong the function as long as they possibly can . . .. They simply cannot be punctual and they are always late in getting their functions started'. He ended his note by indicating that the missionary had every right to lay down conditions, and recommending that he place the matter before the school committee.[74] The reverend thereupon drafted a list of conditions, which were sent to the school, as well as an effusive letter of thanks to the inspector for his advice.[75]

There were many incidents that found their way into and through letters and correspondence testifying to the ways in which principals and teachers made use of missionaries for different purposes, and how the missionaries themselves responded – often appealing to the department for help. In the process they asserted their authority as principals and teachers vis-à-vis the mission, which had become a weakened institution. The missionaries still had considerable power over the mission school principals and teachers – signing their passbooks, and being the recipients and distributors of salary cheques, for example. But the shifting relations between mission and state were all too clear to those at the bottom of the racial pecking order. Room for manoeuvre was limited, and their appeals were often unsuccessful. Yet the letters are a clear demonstration that African principals as well as teachers sought to challenge and to use missionary power and authority in every way possible to improve the situation in which they found themselves. Power relations were continually negotiated and contested, albeit very differently from the Western Transvaal.

Conclusion

The transfer of schools from mission to state control was, thus, not as quickly and easily, nor nearly as neatly achieved as is often presented in the literature. Missionaries retained an overall symbolic control through the position they occupied in the racial hierarchy. And in practice they continued to have influence over schools by virtue of both their symbolic and historical position. The fact that their position was shifting in the hierarchy, however, opened spaces for Africans to seek improvement of their own position. Given the ambiguous position that principals occupied, their correspondence with missionaries during this period reveals a striking assertiveness as well as a strong sense of rights and justice.

CHAPTER 5

CURRICULUM, LANGUAGE, TEXTBOOKS AND TEACHERS

How did Bantu Education change what was taught in the Hermannsburg schools? In theory, colonial curricula had emphasised manual and industrial education, and teaching in the mother tongue, long before the advent of Bantu Education. In practice, what was taught in schools depended on the official curriculum, but especially on the teachers and whatever textbooks and resources were available. Industrial education, for example, could only be provided if the mission was able to buy the necessary equipment and tools for the boys' activities and the cleaning and sewing materials for the girls. Earlier chapters have suggested that, although Hermannsburg Mission schools had to comply with provincial curricula in order to qualify for a state grant and therefore taught English as well as the mother tongue, the missionaries' main emphasis lay in the schools' religious purpose.[1] The latter was evident in the schoolbooks that the Hermannsburg Mission Press continued to produce in Tswana until the 1960s. Primers or readers consisting of the alphabet and basics of sentence construction, as well as stories, always had a religious content. Religious verses were part and parcel of learning the alphabet, and religious stories and hymns were interspersed with tales of animals and local ethnic history.[2]

At the beginning of the 1950s, the vast majority of African children received a rudimentary schooling, with no education beyond the primary, and others had no education at all.[3] This meant that those who became teachers generally qualified with a Lower Primary Certificate or eight years of schooling. Before apartheid, teachers were generally white missionaries and mission recruits. In line with its overall approach, the Department of Bantu Education sought to dispense with the services of teachers from Europe in mission schools and to employ only African teachers for African schools. In particular, they wanted only women teachers in the early grades, in part because expansion depended on paying more teachers less, and female teachers were not only less qualified but also earned less than their male counterparts. Black teachers were generally not well trained. The situation did not improve with the implementation of apartheid policies, as qualifications of teachers fell rather than rose during the 1960s.[4] And by 1968, 40.71% still had only the Lower Primary Certificate.[5] The degree, rapidity and suddenness of the change led to significant dislocation, and this affected teachers who were now required to teach in the mother tongue in the early phase, and in English later on, with some subjects being taught in Afrikaans.

In this context, it could be argued that the availability of textbooks was crucial to assist teachers in their task. Contemporary school improvement approaches emphasise their importance in contexts where teachers may be insufficiently prepared to teach the curriculum, but this view has been criticised on the grounds that, without mediation by teachers, students seldom spontaneously use textbooks. Critical historical and comparative approaches, by contrast, highlight their significance as the embodiment of the official curriculum in the classroom, and therefore also as the official selection of legitimate knowledge.[6] As such, they analyse the messages that textbooks convey, their broader role in production and distribution, their reception by teachers, and the meanings they attribute to them.[7]

In the South African context, there is a substantial body of work on the overt and covert messages conveyed in history textbooks of the apartheid period.[8] There is also significant work on literacy and learning outside the formal classroom.[9] But there is a dearth of literature on how one period led into and shaped its successor, and which schoolbooks were actually available and used in schools. This chapter will therefore focus on the textbooks available and in use in Hermannsburg schools and show how they were taken up by the Bantu Education department. This will require some discussion of the wider context of production of textbooks, and the centrality of the mother tongue in the debate. In the process, the chapter will attempt to explore the extent to which the Hermannsburg approach to mother-tongue instruction was shared with other missions. The question is whether in fact a radical break existed between the mission education and Bantu Education period. The chapter will argue that, at least in the first decade, there was some continuity. While policy might have clarified and tightened, adding another language (Afrikaans) and a greater focus on agricultural and manual labour, the tendency was the consolidation of existing practice, at least in so far as textbooks were concerned. As before, despite policy, constrained resources determined their actual availability in schools, which remained limited.

Indigenous languages as languages of instruction

Textbooks in indigenous languages depended on the standardisation of African languages, which is understood to have occurred along two main lines. The first is the enabling of a process of colonisation through 'a process of symbolic domination'.[10] John and Jean Comaroff, writing about Tswana, contend that missionaries 'reduced the uniqueness of seTswana, making it into one of several similar "native tongues" brought under foreign linguistic control. And eventually they re-presented it back to its speakers, in its new orthodox form, as the gift of civilisation'.[11] Second, as Leroy Vail argues, the very process of production of the standardised language has been seen as creating and inventing the 'tribe'.[12] The reduction of 'hitherto unwritten language to written forms' had important consequences. In the first instance, they 'assembled' and 'created cultural identities through [the] specification of "custom" and "tradition" and by writing "tribal" histories'.[13] Consequently, the 'lesson . . . that Africans properly belonged to "tribes" was incorporated into the curricula of their mission schools', with the curricula themselves being 'backed up by studies of language and "tribal custom" in the vernacular'. Local Africans, educated by missionaries in these curricula, subsequently 'served as the most important force in shaping the new ethnic ideologies'.[14]

An important German linguist working in this way in the 1930s was Berlin-based Carl Meinhof. Sarah Pugach has argued that Meinhof's 'notions of linguistic and cultural differentiation became part of German mission and segregationist thinking'.[15] Language became a marker of racial and ethnic difference and led to 'the acceptance of separate development to solve problems'.[16] Meinhof, who was close to Eiselen, who studied under him,[17] worked in South Africa, became a member of the Nazi Party in Germany, and was an ardent defender of colonialism. The standardisation of languages became the base upon which was built an entire edifice of colonial control. The symbolic power of these initiatives contrasted radically, however, with the 'thin narratives' embodied in the schoolbooks that missionaries produced. These 'spare, childlike stories in which language itself was portrayed . . . as an instrument of naming, knowing, speaking and specifying' was a defect that would persist for many decades.[18] It is to these and their context of production and use that we now turn.

From the beginning, Hermannsburg missionaries were keen to teach in indigenous languages, and they went on to play a role in shaping the languages and producing the textbooks that would be used in their schools. Georg Scriba and Gunnar Lislerud argued that German missionaries' interest in vernacular languages had its root in Luther's translation of the Latin Bible.[19] As Lutherans, the role of the printing press and publication in the vernacular was vital, having been central to the rise of Martin Luther and the Protestant Reformation in the sixteenth century, some five hundred years ago. Much as in the early German context, instruction in local languages was considered crucial if conversion was to take place. But until such time as orthographies were developed for African languages, books and newspapers could not be written in local languages. Missionaries throughout Africa, assisted by colonial societies, undertook initiatives to turn African languages into a written form throughout the early part of the twentieth century.

In all languages, the first 'textbook' was the Bible. Its translation was always the first task, from which followed translations of hymns, catechisms and other religious texts. The Hermannsburg Mission founded book commissions in the early 1900s for its Zulu and Tswana missions, but constrained financial circumstances circumscribed its activities.[20] In 1909 it opened a Mission Press at its headquarters in Empangweni, Moorleigh, near Estcourt in Natal. During the First World War, it published church histories, a Zulu grammar, reading charts, and an ABC relating to the charts.[21] It was only gradually that the Hermannsburg Mission recognised the need for readers and primers beyond the elementary level. As discussed in Chapter 2 above, Hermannsburg missionaries seemed to borrow freely from other missionary societies until they eventually produced their own readers. Both schoolbook and Bible translation into Zulu and Tswana proceeded throughout the first half of the twentieth century, with a new Zulu translation of the Old Testament and a revised translation of Robert Moffat's Tswana Bible appearing in the 1950s.[22] The Mission Press at Moorleigh produced several iterations of schoolbooks in Tswana and Zulu between 1916 and the mid-1960s, co-publishing with the Mission Book Depot in Rustenburg from the 1950s.[23]

Within the schooling system, and from the perspective of its administration and control by government, another dimension of coloniality, the production of texts in African languages, was considered hopelessly inadequate for its needs. By 1936, four language groupings were considered partially or sufficiently standardised for use in schools: Sotho (Southern Sotho, Northern Sotho and Western Sotho), Nguni (Xhosa and Zulu), Thonga and Venda. All were fully standardised, except for Northern Sotho. Each language grouping was mapped onto a particular region.[24] The extent of textual production for schools in each language grouping differed. In Tswana there were only grammars, readers, poetry and prose books. History and Hygiene textbooks were available, in addition to the grammars, readers, poetry and prose books for Northern Sotho. For Zulu-speakers, there were textbooks for Physiology and Hygiene, as well as grammars and readers. The range of textbooks in Southern Sotho and Xhosa broadened from grammars, readers, poetry and prose books, to include textbooks for History, Geography, Hygiene and Agriculture. Venda had only grammars and readers, and Thonga only grammar, Science and a General Studies book. Overall, the number and range of texts varied across language groupings. Texts were also uneven in depth and quality, depending on the mission society that produced them.

The most extensive texts were those produced by the Berlin Mission Society (Sotho) and the London Missionary Society (Xhosa). Mission-produced texts were authored by missionaries as well as native-language speakers, in all cases male. Among the mission-based authors were inspectors of education such as G.H. Franz, son of a Berlin missionary. The native-language authors included Sol T. Plaatje, whose translation of Shakespeare's *Comedy of Errors* was among the texts available for use in schools using Tswana as medium of instruction. Several African writers, including Azariele M. Sekese, Edward Motsamai and Thomas Mofolo were available in Southern Sotho. The poetry of H.M. Ndawo, S. Mqayi and W.B. Rubusana was available in Xhosa, as were prose works by Mqayi, J.H. Soga, G. Sinxo and J.J.R. Jolobe, S.F. Zibi and J.T. Jabavu, as well as B.J.P. Tyamzashe. C. M. Doke wrote a textbook of Zulu grammar, R.R.R. Dhlomo and J.L. Dube school readers, and school inspector D. McMalcolm authored a Zulu manual. Other Zulu textbook writers included B.W. Vilakazi, H. Molife, M.J. Mpanza, F.L. Ntuli and P. Lamula. A.T. Bryant's textbooks for Physiology and Hygiene as well as Agriculture were used, and J.W. Colenso's Zulu-English Dictionary was also on the list. In Venda, the work of P.E. Schwellnus and E. Giesekke, and in Thonga of H.A. Junod and A.A. Jacques were listed.[25]

Despite the limitations of the books available, it appears that Sotho, Xhosa and Zulu were best served by texts for use in schools. Language books and readers were most widespread, and while there was a fair spread of History, Geography, Hygiene and Agriculture textbooks, there were virtually no Mathematics or Science books. It is possible that these were available in English, but they were not available in the standardised African languages. Almost all the books written in Sotho, Xhosa and Zulu were either used or available for use in schools. But even the school inspectors of the time were of the view that the texts available presented a 'grave difficulty' for 'the application of the principle of mother-tongue education'.[26] The first problem to which they drew attention in 1936 was 'the difficulties arising from the matter of medium in multi-vernacular areas'. They described these as 'very serious'. Second, the available literature was considered 'of the slightest': complete sets of readers did not exist for some languages, such as Venda, Thonga, Tswana and Northern Sotho. Third, textbooks in African languages in subjects such as Arithmetic, History, Geography, Hygiene and Nature Study were 'practically non-existent'.[27] And last but not least, agreed terminologies did not exist in any of the languages that had been identified in the official report.

For these reasons, and because they felt that extension of mother-tongue education would disadvantage them in gaining access to the official language, English, many Africans did not favour their mother tongue as a medium of instruction.[28] The Interdepartmental Committee on Native Education, made up of the chief inspectors of Native Education of the four provinces, therefore recommended that the use of the mother tongue be restricted to the first four years of schooling. The committee suggested that any extension of mother-tongue education would depend on the development of the literature available in each language, and on the provision of suitable textbooks and fixed terminologies in each, as required for school subjects.[29] It accordingly recommended that funds be set aside for such development.

In practice, the majority of mission schools during the first half of the twentieth century used English as the medium of instruction – the Cape Colony and Natal had been British colonies, so this was to be expected. In the Transvaal and the Orange Free State, for reasons that included the fact that the Dutch taught in schools for colonists' children was not a spoken language and Afrikaans was not yet recognised, English was accorded the same significance as in the Cape and Natal after the defeat of the Boers in the South African War in 1902. Apart from Natal, which prescribed the vernacular from 1885, 'comparatively little attention was in general devoted . . . to the teaching of the mother tongue as a subject'.[30]

As more mission schools accessed state aid through the provinces throughout the early part of the century, provinces started to demand that missionaries teach not only the mother tongue in the early grades, but also one of the two official languages. The age when a switch was made to English or Afrikaans varied from province to province. In all provinces, however, it was left to the missionary in charge to decide which official language to use. In practice, missionaries generally opted for English. In post-primary education, all provinces insisted on the study of an African language, but the decision as to which one, and whether to use one or both official languages, differed across provinces. The Junior Certificate exam, which also served as a teacher qualification, required that six subjects be taken, one of which had to be the mother tongue.

Missionaries did not oppose this development and indeed participated in promoting it. Keenly aware of existing limitations, they were eager to develop writing and reading in African literature.

Textbook development as a transnational, colonial activity

What kind of textbooks did the missions have to assist them in their task prior to and after Bantu Education, especially for teaching the mother tongue, which in many cases was only recently orthographised and with a very limited literature? The question may be approached by looking at Isabel Hofmeyr's work on Bunyan's *Pilgrim's Progress*, which provides useful insight into how such a book travelled across the colonial world, was translated into multiple languages, and was used in different ways for different purposes by missionaries and students at Lovedale in the 1930s and 1940s.[31] Following the translation of the Bible into African languages, mission societies were keen to develop standardised orthographies of African languages and to promote writing and reading of African literature. Right from the start, the production and publication of materials and texts in African languages was a transnational activity that involved colonial and also local writers, publishers and distributors.

A particularly important role was played by the London-based International Missionary Council's Committee for Christian Literature for Africa as well as the London Missionary Society through the Lovedale Press and principal of Lovedale, R.W. Shepherd, in stimulating discussion on how to develop literature in the vernacular. With the support of the Carnegie Corporation, Shepherd held two conferences in 1936. The second conference for African authors included known African writers such as D.D.T. Jabavu, R.T. Caluza, B.W. Vilakazi, J.J.R. Jolobe and R.R.R. Dhlomo.[32] The conference lamented the 'small reading public in the Bantu languages'. Authors were suspicious of the links between segregationist legislation on the table at that time and the development of 'tribal literatures' and the philosophy that Africans should 'develop along their own lines'. But the conference resolved to find 'possible ways of ensuring further development of a vernacular literature, including bringing Departments of Education on board'.[33] Far from mother-tongue education being the brainchild of Bantu Education, it was the step-child of mission and mission-educated elites across national, denominational and language divides.

It is probable that Bunyan, together with contemporary African writers listed as available for use in schools by the Welsh Report of 1936, was used in the elite mission schools of the Eastern Cape during the 1930s and 1940s. But there is no record of such use in the small Hermannsburg Mission schools. Records of the Hermannsburg Mission indicate that there were shortages of all books, especially of books in the mother tongue, in all schools during the late 1930s.[34] School inspection reports show that a decade later, many schools, especially smaller ones in the Transvaal, had neither slates nor books in either the local African language or in either of the official languages, English and Afrikaans.[35] From 1948, book grants made the purchase of some books possible; only readers and supplementary readers for use by pupils could be bought with the grants as they were not adequate to cover all the books required in all languages.[36] Typically, the books that missionaries ordered were readers in Zulu or Tswana and the two official languages, as well as a map, and a Geography and History book. These were usually authored by mission societies, with the Tswana ones being written by the Hermannsburg Mission. Limited by the grant, the numbers ordered were very small, with the books and resources intended to be shared. School expenditures for five mission schools in the Natal-Zululand area from 1947 to 1954 show that as a rule more was spent on sewing materials and gardening tools than on books. Only gradually did the amount spent on books increase.[37]

Curriculum policy and African responses: 1955

The Eiselen Commission on Native Education, upon which the Bantu Education Act was based, recommended that the mother tongue be used as the medium of instruction for the duration of the primary school period. Both official languages should be taught as subjects from the early grades.[38] A draft syllabus was published towards the end of 1954, and introduced in 1956 after comments and suggestions had been made.[39] An African child was thus required to learn three languages. Although the South African Institute of Race Relations welcomed the syllabus as 'educationally sound and an improvement on previous syllabuses',[40] the main criticism levelled was in regard to the use of the mother tongue throughout the primary school. Indeed, strenuous opposition was expressed by Africans themselves regarding the use of the mother tongue in African schools.[41]

The views of Africans on the mother tongue were vividly expressed in a memorandum prepared by the Edendale Joint Schools Committee on the aims of education a decade earlier.[42] The starting point of the memorandum was opposition to separationism in education, and the view that 'the basic aim of education must be to develop the latent intellectual powers of the individual so that he may get out of the quagmire of illiteracy and reach up to the highest pinnacles of human attainments . . . untrammelled by the inferiority complex and powerlessness'.[43] It argued against the use of the mother tongue, citing the 'non-existence of suitable and proper literature', and claiming that that which did exist was 'extremely poor and inferior'.[44] This situation ensured that 'teaching through the mother tongue is made the means of arresting and retarding educational progress'. The memorandum provided an analysis of the syllabi for various classes and concluded that the way in which the mother tongue was taught led to stagnation, with repetition in higher classes of material that had already been covered in lower classes. The author argued for scrapping the entire syllabus:

> The Zulu medium of instruction can only be acceptable to us on the expressed and unqualified condition that it is on par with the official languages . . .. In the event of the foregoing conditions not being fully and wholly satisfied, we have no option but to insist that the medium of instruction be English, and that the second official language should be introduced at Standard III. The Zulu language should be taken as a subject from the Infants classes upwards.[45]

The new syllabus for lower primary schools included Religious Instruction, Reading, Writing, Arithmetic, Hygiene, Handicrafts, Gardening, Physical Training and Singing. History, Geography and Nature Study were grouped together under 'environmental studies', and were 'intended to relate more closely than previously to the child's circumstances and surroundings'.[46] The syllabus introduced for higher primary classes 'included all the subjects taught in primary schools for white children'.[47] Teaching was to be in the mother tongue. This change was too sudden for many schools, however, and so the requirement was adapted: up until 1959, half the subjects not taught in the mother tongue had to be taught in English, and the other half in Afrikaans. From 1959 on, all subjects had to be taught through the mother tongue. One problem with this was the availability of suitable textbooks.

1955 Bantu Education textbook and syllabus policy

The Bantu Education Act intended to make readers available to all schools.[48] This policy did not change for over thirty years. In 1955 the Department of Bantu Education's prescribed list of textbooks included books written for the previous syllabi of the various provinces, which also conformed to the new syllabi.[49] Each list contained more than one series of readers. Principals were required to select two series of readers from the prescribed list: thus, a Tswana-speaking school could choose readers from the Lovedale as well as the Hermannsburg Mission Press. These readers were to be provided free of charge. But all stationery and other books for pupils' use had to be bought by the pupils themselves.[50] These included Arithmetic, Geography, History, Health Education, Nature Study and Gardening, Handwork, Homecraft and Needlework books, the large majority of which were in English. It was anticipated that books would be shared. This policy persisted right through to the 1990s. If additional texts were bought, as in Bophuthatswana in the 1980s, this was done on the basis of donor funding. Detailed in-triplicate procedures for requisitioning books were spelt out.[51] Of course, not all principals read or applied the rules; also, without adequate stocktaking, shortages continued.[52]

Readers and grammars previously developed by the missions were taken over by the Bantu Education department. These included readers published by Lovedale Press, the Christian Literature Depot, Morija Press and Hermannsburg Mission Press, and were often authored by or written in collaboration with African writers. They were supplemented with readers developed and published by Afrikaans publishers, most notably Afrikaanse Pers Beperk, Nasionale Pers, Juta & Kie, Via Afrika and Van Schaik, and by the established presses, namely Oxford University Press, University of the Witwatersrand Press, Shuter & Shooter, and Longman. Inspectors played a powerful role in assisting with content determination, serving as 'editors' or even authors of several books, which seems not to have been regarded as a conflict of interest at the time.[53] The Hermannsburg Mission books were used throughout the 1960s, but because of growing competition from Afrikaans publishers and the larger publishing houses, publication was eventually ceased.[54] By 1990, Ryôta Nishino argues, the South African textbook market was dominated by English- and Afrikaans-language presses that included on the one hand Juta, Shuter & Shooter and Maskew Miller and on the other Educum, De Jager-Haum and Via Afrika. Afrikaans publishing houses dominated the industry and a particularly 'cosy relationship' had developed between publishers and education departments, obscuring these companies' growing multinational character.[55] Nasionale Pers, for example, expanded its business interests into the 'independent' homelands through its subsidiary, Via Afrika. Alongside other multinationals such as Pearson, Maskew Miller Longman, Oxford University Press and a number of smaller local publishers that have come to dominate the market, it retains a powerful footprint in schoolbook publishing.

Content of readers

An enquiry into the content of readers used before and during the Bantu Education period yields interesting results. One set of English readers used in Hermannsburg schools in the Transvaal was the Sadie Merber series. It was written specifically for African schools, and, according to the author's introduction, 'in close co-operation with Dr W.W.M. Eiselen, Chief Inspector of Native Education in the Transvaal, and Mr J.N. de Jager, Inspector of Native Education in Johannesburg'. The series included three books, each containing a number of stories.[56] Each story is a simple moral tale. In most of the stories, the main character's bad behaviour is pointed out and corrected in an instructive incident that illustrates the error or vice. Bad behaviours include greed, laziness, rudeness, uncleanliness, dishonesty, thieving, and not caring for domestic animals. In one such story, 'Lazy Jim', a young black gardener who works for a white family, learns to mend his slothful ways through the intervention of a 'queer character' that comes to taunt, haunt and confuse him.[57] The illustrations are notable for locating African children in rural areas, in nature, among animals, or as servants in homes. Moreover, black people are represented with indistinguishable, featureless faces.[58] The stories are, in short, offensive and racist. A few years later, these books no longer appeared on the prescribed list of the Bantu Education department.

The Mission Press readers contained moral tales based on African myths and legends, but they were less overtly racist. The Hermannsburg Mission Press readers, for example, consisted mainly of fairytales relating to local animals and people, in addition to Christian history. One author of an English reader for African schools was particularly proud of the fact that content had been selected by asking a number of African schools and colleges to submit essays on 'My favourite story as a child', and on characteristics of 'liveliness, conversation, animalness, plot, humour, surprise, the grotesque, phantasy, the supernatural and adventure'.[59] Stories were gendered in so far as boys' and girls' activities were differentiated according to perceived roles within the domestic and public spheres. Local, 'tribal' history also featured in later textbooks. In keeping with the mission's overall approach, the histories were generally a patriarchal history of the chiefs within a broader colonial narrative, with little change as new editions appeared.[60]

Readers in use in African schools, whether in the mother tongue, English or Afrikaans, thus localised the content by linking it to the perceived beliefs, values and environment of the African child. This environment was framed in ethnic terms. In this sense, textbooks aimed to expunge the alleged Eurocentrism of earlier curricula and texts, and used content to 'reconcile' rather than 'estrange' African children from their 'cultures' – something in which Hermannsburgers such as Heinz Dehnke, for example, had a firm belief. These efforts raise questions about the difference between the periods before, during and after apartheid. It is something of a paradox that each period has sought, in its own way, to address the perceived difficulties brought about by the 'estrangement' from local culture and context occasioned by a colonial or 'Western' education by attempting to make educational content 'relevant' to local context and culture. In this sense, the past and the present appear to cast shadows over one another.

Principles of reading instruction

It is important to address the question as to how the readers that were used in schools envisaged that reading should be taught – in the pupil's first, second and often third language. As in earlier decades, contemporary debates still centre on the relative advantages of phonics-based versus whole-language approaches in teaching literacy. Whereas the former follows a skills-based approach, moving from the parts to the whole, the latter emphasises the importance of meaning in learning to read, and moving from the whole to the parts. Whereas a phonics approach would focus on grammar, for example, a whole-language approach focuses on reading for meaning and adopts a more holistic approach to learning reading.

Although the principle of a phonics approach, and the inclusion of local content, was applied across the board in South African schools, there were differences in how this was presented, not only between vernacular and official language (i.e. English and Afrikaans) readers, but also between different vernacular readers. Having examined more than 40 readers for English, Afrikaans, Zulu and Tswana on the prescribed list, it is clear that all took a phonics-based approach. But the Tswana and Zulu readers were slight in comparison with those in the second (i.e. official) languages.[61] This is not surprising, given that the readers were developed by missionaries and Africans, with neither group having much formal educational background. There were differences between the Zulu and Tswana readers,[62] but in both the main emphasis, increasingly in the higher grades, is on stories (or a whole-language approach) rather than the principles of language, grammar and spelling (a phonics-based approach) – as in second- and third-language readers.

The books in the two official languages taught reading according to what were then considered scientific principles of second-language teaching: they were based on what were variously called the direct method, sound method, or whole or sentence method. The direct method focused on using the target language during the lesson, and forbidding the use of the home language, and mixing or switching of languages. Textbooks consisted of lists of words to develop vocabulary, insistence on spoken language, and techniques such as reading aloud, question-and-answer, and filling-in-the-blanks exercises. Whether this is what happened in classrooms or not is another matter and depended on the teachers. About this we know very little, and not even the Hermannsburg records provide insight into this issue. What is clear, however, is that 'code-switching' is today common practice in schools.[63]

Conclusion

Then as now, there were no neat, simple divisions between past and present, mission and department, local and international – educational endeavours crossed borders of all kinds, particularly in relation to the development of textbooks in indigenous languages. Given the way in which the languages were standardised, the process was fraught with difficulty. They were standardised nonetheless, with efforts being made to produce readers and textbooks.

Whereas missionaries of various European nationalities could see the value in developing indigenous South African languages, there was considerable misgiving among Africans themselves. The provincial departments of education were aware of the limitations, but nonetheless saw fit to promote the languages. The Bantu Education department not only made this highly contested area a central tenet in its policy, but it also added another official language, Afrikaans, to the list of languages. The department took over the textbooks and readers that the missionaries, who were themselves neither trained teachers nor writers, had produced in earlier decades. These were based on linguistic maps and orthographies that effectively invented the ethnicities upon which the policy of separate development was based. These constructs were reinforced by stories of the ethnic origins and family histories of chiefs. Over the years, many generations of children were exposed to the same or only slightly varying iterations of such textbooks, despite persistent textbook shortages both pre- and post-apartheid.

While there were continuities with the pre-apartheid period, this chapter reveals the complexities that existed, showing that differences were present from the start as to how reading and grammar were taught in the mother tongue, not only to English- and Afrikaans-speakers, but also to speakers of African languages. Some textbooks carried overtly racist and gendered messages, and these messages were often embedded not only in content that placed Africans in romanticised rural settings but also in the way in which the principles of language itself were taught, whether as first, second or third language. In the main, though, the distinguishing feature was their emphasis on the inclusion of local content that constructed an African identity in terms of the 'tribe'.

Whereas mission publishing houses originally published African language texts in concert with international mission endeavour, or shared texts across missions of different persuasions, by the 1960s these were rapidly being displaced by the larger, more established publishing houses with a closer ear to government.

Figure 5.1: The first house built in South Africa by Hermannsburg missionaries, at a site named after the place of origin of the mission in Hermannsburg, Germany (courtesy Georg Scriba).

Figure 5.2: Burnt-out buildings at Bethel Training Institute, 1953 (courtesy Heinrich Voges).

Figure 5.3: Winfried Wickert, co-director of the Hermannsburg Mission South Africa, 1932–1934 and 1937–1957 (courtesy Georg Scriba).

Figure 5.4: Fritz Scriba, superintendent of the Zulu Mission, Ehlanzeni, Natal, 1954–1970 (courtesy Georg Scriba).

Figure 5.5: L to R: Wolfram Kistner (general superintendent of the Hermannsburg Mission, South Africa, 1965–1969), Fritz Scriba (superintendent of the Zulu Mission, Natal, 1954–1970), congregants, and mission sisters (courtesy Georg Scriba).

Figure 5.6: Ehlanzeni Church and Seminary (courtesy Georg Scriba).

Figure 5.7: Male and female students with mission staff, Ehlanzeni Seminary (courtesy Georg Scriba).

Figure 5.8: L to R: Missionaries Hans-Jürgen Becken, Wilhelm Kaiser, Fritz Scriba, Heini Fedderke (courtesy Georg Scriba).

Figure 5.9: Students participate in sports day at Moorleigh Farm School, near Estcourt (courtesy Georg Scriba).

Figure 5.10: Teacher using a poster to give a lesson on the Ten Commandments (courtesy Georg Scriba).

Figure 5.11: Hermannsburg missionaries, 1966 (courtesy Georg Scriba):
Back, L to R: Wolfgang Weissbach, Richard Otto, Friedrich Kuesel, Friedhold Dehnke.
Middle, L to R: Heinrich Voges, Johannes von Fintel, Christoph Meyer, Bernhard Rutkies, Hinrich Pape, Heinrich Holsten, Bernhard van Scharrel, Detlev Morfeld, Hinrich Rathje, Richard Schlueter, Fritz Scriba, Martin Schweizer, Fritz Otte, Siegfried Lemke, Karlheinz Schmale.
Front, L to R: Hermann Greve, Gebhard Dehnke, Hermann Wohlberg, Karl Bühr, Hans-Robert Wesenick, Wolfram Kistner, Reinhard Drews, Heini Fedderke, Georg Albrecht, Otto Rathe, Heinz Dehnke.

Figure 5.12: The Primary Education Upgrade Programme team (courtesy Christel Bodenstein):
Back, L to R: Dorothy Montwedi, Evelyn Mogalane, Christel Bodenstein, Valerie Loabile, Sylvia Seate, Nora Lebhebhe, Saphira Monare.
Front, L to R: Maggie Sedumedi, Philda Modjadji, Mollie Mosimane, Rosina Moalusi, Nancy Motlala, Johanna Morule.

Figure 5.13: Members of the Primary Education Upgrade Programme team (courtesy Christel Bodenstein):
Top, L to R: Sylvia Seate, Valerie Loabile, Lebogang Sedumedi.
Middle, L to R: Saphira Monare, Nancy Motlala, Rosina Moalusi.
Bottom, L to R: Evelyn Mogalane, Mollie Mosimane, Johanna Morule

CHAPTER 6

UMPUMULO: FROM TEACHER TRAINING COLLEGE TO THEOLOGICAL SEMINARY

Histories of mission education and schooling seldom acknowledge that, alongside primary schooling and teacher training, the training of pastors was an integral component of mission educational endeavours. This history is often simply excised from accounts of the role of the missions in education prior to the takeover by the state. On the other hand, it is acknowledged that during apartheid few positions were open to African people who had some form of higher education, other than teaching, preaching and positions within the Bantustan bureaucracies. Countless studies of the mounting student, civic and worker resistance to apartheid from the 1970s onwards document the leadership role played by clerics such as Archbishop Desmond Tutu, Father Smangaliso Mkhatshwa, Bishop Manas Buthelezi, and Professor Barney Pityana, to mention but a few. Indeed, Daniel Magaziner's recent study of Black Consciousness has shown that 'religious and primarily Christian ways of thinking' underpinned the emergence and development of the Black Consciousness Movement in the 1960s and 1970s.[1] He goes on to argue that, in 1976, 'as with the broader movement, a particular religiosity informed high school political rhetoric'.[2] Studies such as this begin to prise open the links between apartheid, the rise of Black Consciousness, and religion – or the persistent influence of missions in education during the apartheid era.

The next two chapters show how the rise of theological education and Black Consciousness were intimately connected to the responses of mission societies to apartheid and the takeover of their schools and teacher training colleges. This is to some extent argued by Philippe Denis and Graham Duncan in their history of the tragic fate of Fedsem, the Federal Theological Seminary established in Alice by Presbyterians, Anglicans, Methodists and Congregationalists in 1963. They show that the establishment of the seminary was a direct response to the closure of educational institutions at Tiger Kloof, Adams College, Rosettenville, Fort Hare and Modderpoort, as well as a report by the International Missionary Council (IMC) recommending a united seminary to address previous failures to train pastors and the proposal by the Department of Bantu Education in 1961 to relocate the theological education of Africans to the University of South Africa (Unisa). Fedsem's subsequent history was deeply marked by an 'abhorrence for the racist policies of the state' and the conflict that developed between the seminary and Fort Hare, the seminary and the state, and also among students and staff over questions such as whether to participate in the degree programmes of the University of Fort Hare, Rhodes, and the University of Natal's Pietermaritzburg campus, all seen as too closely linked to the apartheid state.[3] A radical community self-consciously establishing cross-race social and educational practices that were oppositional to the direction of social policy, the seminary was a thorn in the flesh of the apartheid government, which harassed its staff and students. Expropriated from its buildings adjacent to Fort Hare in 1975, Fedsem first moved to Umtata, (now Mthatha) then to Edendale, and finally to Imbali in Natal. There, under the impact of the resuscitation of non-racial politics in the United Democratic Front (UDF), and the rise of the labour movement, Black Consciousness politics went into decline, as did seminary enrolments and commitments by its founding members.

The relationship of Fedsem with the Lutherans was an uneasy one, reflected in Denis and Duncan's assessments as to why the latter declined to join this initiative when first approached. The reason for the Lutherans' 'lack of interest in ecumenical cooperation was the fact that they hardly felt the impact of the apartheid legislation on their institutions'.[4] When approached again in 1976, their failure to join up was ascribed to the fact that, for the Lutherans, Fedsem was 'too radical'.[5] Despite the Lutherans' repeated rebuff, this assessment reflects a perception that does not adequately appreciate the problems and options that the Lutherans themselves faced in the transition to Bantu Education, nor their own struggles with the state, and conflicts among themselves. The history and experience of Umpumulo and nearby Eshowe contradict the assessment that the

Lutherans hardly felt the impact of apartheid. Indeed, their experience at the linked institutions at Eshowe and Umpumulo was precisely what prompted the establishment of the Umpumulo Theological Seminary. Umpumulo was one of nine constituent organisations that formed the United Christian Movement in 1967 and which in turn gave birth to the South African Students' Organisation (SASO) in 1968. Along with Fedsem, Umpumulo was one of SASO's fourteen branches, four of which were theological seminaries.[6]

Umpumulo hosted key Black Consciousness thinkers such as Manas Buthelezi who had lectured there, and Dean Farisani, a former student at the seminary. It also developed a relationship between research and curriculum change that was innovative and, in its context, radical, as the next chapter will show. Umpumulo brought Hermannsburgers into a common relationship with other Lutherans in an educational experiment that was as non-racial as that in Fedsem, compromised only by the unfortunate fact that neither had white students. But the radicalism of Umpumulo was primarily intellectual, and this is perhaps what distinguishes it from Fedsem. The writings of Bengt Sundkler, Axel-Ivar Berglund and Hans-Jürgen Becken were all produced in the climate of research, debate and discussion that the institution promoted.

This was the period when Umpumulo, founded by the Norwegian Mission Society, consisted of a teacher training college, a feeder high school, and schools where students did their practice teaching. Established by Bishop Schreuder in 1850, in 1912 Umpumulo became a joint Lutheran teacher training college, with government support and using the state syllabus. From 1929 the Hermannsburg Mission began to send students there, whom it wished to train as teachers. By 1932, thanks to the judicious use of a surplus derived from mission reserve taxes for education building purposes, Umpumulo had become one of the best, if not *the* best, equipped colleges in Natal.[7] The new buildings were formally opened in 1933. Its spacious quarters now included a new college building which comprised five classrooms, a science room, head teachers' office, staffroom, map room and a verandah, a hostel for girls consisting of three cottage dormitories and a hostel building with separate dormitories of 17 beds each, one teacher's room, one common room, and a storeroom and quarters for European female teachers.[8] In 1938 a preparatory class was started, leading to high school, but this was moved to Eshowe in 1948. From 1933 to 1947 Umpumulo was run by the principal, W.O. Rindahl, until he left for Eshowe Zulu Lutheran High School, which he led from 1949.[9]

After Rindahl's departure, Rev. Løken was appointed principal of Umpumulo College. Reporting to him were head teachers for the college, high school and practising schools. The girls' and boys' boarding establishments each had a matron and housemaster. While the institutional head and principal of the teacher training college was generally a missionary, the high school, practising schools and boarding establishments for boys were headed by Africans.[10] The institution grew considerably, both during the war years and after. By 1952 the 11 staff members of the teacher training college – 3 from the high school and 8 from the practising schools of 1939 – had been augmented to 18, with an additional 15 for the training college and practising schools respectively. In other words, teaching staff had grown in number from 22 in 1939 to 33 in 1952. In the short term, Umpumulo's fate was similar to that of Bethel's. In 1955, the principal was replaced by a man who fulfilled the educational criteria of the department, and the mission head was demoted to superintendent of hostels. This chapter thus deals with Umpumulo as a teacher training institution and the difficulties of transfer to a Bantu Education regime.

In order to understand how the institution changed, it is necessary to know what it was before 1953, how the transfer affected it, how and why it became a seminary, and what kind of seminary it eventually became. Two major sources provide insight into the kind of teacher training institution Umpumulo was prior to 1953. The first is the curriculum and expectations of teachers, as expressed in the Natal Education Department's examination papers that student teachers wrote. The curriculum was broad, preparing students for leadership roles; it also incorporated practical, professional and religious elements. The second source is *Inkanyezi*, the annual school magazine published from 1936 to 1960;[11] it provides insight into the social and educational regime that prevailed at the institution and shows that, through its extra-curricular activities, the school also socialised students into activities that prepared them for participation in a wider world. Although the conflict between the curriculum of mission institutions and the reality that awaited students outside has often been remarked upon, few studies have examined the actual curricula of mission teacher training institutions in any depth. This chapter confronts the contradictory elements in the curricula.

Changes in the teacher training curriculum: 1945-1955

Assuming control over the preparation of teachers was a major priority for the National Party when it came into power in 1948. The infamous parliamentary statement of Minister of Native Affairs, Hendrik Verwoerd, about the need for central control in order to direct the aspirations and expectations of 'the Bantu' away from equal rights and inclusion in a common society and towards development 'within his own sphere', separate from a common society, applied as much to teacher education colleges as it did to schools.[12] Before Bantu Education came into being, teacher preparation for Africans was under provincial control, with relevant sections in provincial departments of education responsible for African education. Thereafter, teacher preparation was transferred to the Bantu Education division of the Native Affairs department, a national department. Effectively under state control, there remained however a degree of provincial involvement in the administration of training colleges.

Before the transition to state control by the national department, teacher education colleges were run by missionaries, though curriculum and assessments were determined by the provincial departments of the Union government, which administered a segregated system for different racial groups. Thus the Cape, Natal, Orange Free State and Transvaal provincial departments ran teacher training before 1948. Curricula and exams for teachers were set on a provincial basis, and were racially divided. Accordingly, the Natal Education Department's division for African education determined the curriculum and set the exams for student teachers at Umpumulo. This changed in the mid-1950s, when teacher training was transferred to the Bantu Education department of the national Department of Native Affairs. A closer look at the curricula of teacher training colleges under provincial control, and how these changed under the Bantu Education department, provides further insight into the nature of the perceived threat presented by mission education to teacher training. The curriculum paradoxically encouraged independence of thought and participation in a wider world at the same time as it instilled notions of the 'scientificity' of racial difference, while also promoting keen attention to school and classroom management and religious observance. The 'moralising' purposes of the curriculum are evident in all aspects of the preparation of teachers.

The formal curriculum at Umpumulo can be accessed through its examination papers. The college offered the so-called T3 and T4 certificates, each taking two years to complete. The entrance qualification for the T4 was a Standard 7 pass, and for the T3 a Junior Certificate (Standard 8).[13] At the same time, a matric certificate was the entrance qualification for a white student – an indication of the inequalities in the system. An analysis of the T3 and T4 exam questions set for African teacher training colleges in Natal between 1945 and 1955 is revealing. The official curriculum included elements of a classical curriculum but also subjects intended to ensure a 'practical' and professional orientation, and religious knowledge and observance. Thus it included not only English, Zulu, Latin, Biology, Mathematics, History and Geography, but also Health, Arithmetic, 'Elementary' Science and Agriculture, with the latter two subjects reflecting the 'adapted education' aims of the Loram era.[14] In addition, all students studied Church History and Scripture, which conformed to the syllabus of the Cooperating Lutheran Mission.[15] Professional training was covered by subjects such as Principles and Management of Teaching, as well as Methods of Teaching. This is true also of Psychology of Education, whose dubious content is discussed below.

The table below provides an indication based on exam papers of the teacher training curriculum that was followed before Bantu Education and during the transition.[16] Names of subjects changed over time, depending on the year and the teacher who taught the subject. If this was a full set of exam papers, then there are continuities and discontinuities over time in the subjects taught. Thus Physiology and Hygiene/Health continues through from 1945 to 1955, as does Agriculture, Organisation and Management of Schools and Scripture. Music as well as Arts and Crafts are apparently added in 1955, while extensive English Language requirements are dropped. The table below gives an idea of the breadth of the curriculum.[17]

The analysis of examinations as a window into the enacted curriculum has been explored both by Jane Starfield in her study of Healdtown in the 1870s and 1880s, and by Jeanne Prinsloo, who examined language curricula of the apartheid era.[18] In order to reconstruct changes in the expectations of student-teachers at Umpumulo, T3 and T4 exam questions administered from 1945 to 1954 have been analysed below,[19] guided by Prinsloo's methodology and approach.[20] The approach preceding the advent of Bantu Education seems to have shared some similarities with what Prinsloo found in English First Language papers in the white schools of Natal in 1990, where familiarity with a wide body of literature was considered essential. Students were expected to display a range of literary skills, including understanding of a text's meaning as well as interpretive and analytical competences. All the sources were from English literature, assuming a familiarity with a world beyond the immediate, but nonetheless a specifically British colonial world. Until 1954, the papers position students in leadership roles and ensure that they rehearse identities as teachers and citizens. Essay topics included contemporary themes such as race, water, and industries of Natal.[21]

In 1954, the English Composition and English Literature papers, as now set by the Natal branch of the Bantu Education division of the Department of Native Affairs, showed distinct changes from what had gone before, but also some continuities. The 1949 essay question in Composition required mainly narratives of personal or imagined experiences grounded in local experiences

Table 6.1: T3 and T4 Exam Papers at Umpumulo Teacher Training Institute 1945–1954

	1945 T3	1945 T4	1949 T3	1949 T4	1954 T3	1954/5 T4
English Comprehension & Reproduction	■	■	■	■	■	
English Literature	■		■	■	■	
English Reading	■	■	■	■		
English Reproduction	■			■		
English Language	■					■
Physiology & Hygiene/Health (1954)	■			■		
Geography	■					
Physical Science/Elementary Science (1949) Elementary General Science (1954)	■			■		
Agriculture					■	■
Science & Agriculture	■					■
Biology	■			■		
Bantu Studies (Anthropology & History)	■			■		
Organisation & Management of Schools	■			■	■	■
Methods of Teaching	■					
Principles & Psychology of Education			■			
Methods of Teaching & Fundamental Principles of Education Paper 1 and 2			■	■		
Educational Psychology	■		■			
Theory of Needlework	■					
Domestic Science		■		■		
Zulu History & Literature				■		
Scripture		■		■	■	■
Script Arithmetic		■		■		
Mental Arithmetic		■		■		
Arithmetic (Problems & Method)						
Arithmetic (Mechanical)					■	
Music			■			■
Arts & Crafts (Theory)						■

concerning animals, fire, superstition and rescue. The paper contained a letter section, which required requests for correction or assistance; the telegram that needed to be written was about travel. There was also a précis, and the topic was time. Unlike the 1949 paper, which included challenging topics such as 'Race Problems in South Africa', the 1954 paper ends with a written task based on an extract that ends with the admonition, 'Ask No Questions and You'll Hear No Lies'.[22] A law-abiding, obedient person keeping to regular rules and routines is identified and called forth, rather than the universal citizen pronouncing on injustice. Compared to that of 1945, the English Literature paper of 1954 requires more limited competencies: description, understanding of meaning, and knowledge of how to teach reading according to the Oxford Method (a phonics method for teaching reading). Religious notions remain evident in questions requiring students to identify the theme in lines such as 'Dear God! The very houses seem asleep' as well as 'And was the holy Lamb of God on England's pleasant pastures seen?'[23] For Verwoerd, the idea that African students should have knowledge of any such 'pastures' was anathema.

From a Foucauldian perspective, the kind of teacher envisaged in departmental exam papers was one fully engaged in the rigours and rituals of producing disciplined subjects through daily school routines. This is evident in the 1945 paper on the Organisation and Management of Schools. It examines students on issues such as the value of regularity, punctuality and hygiene, punishment, promoting school libraries, doing intelligence tests, as well as holding teachers' meetings, implementing marking scales, and focusing on the relationship between class and teacher.

This 'professional' emphasis continued through to the 1950s. In 1954 the importance of planning through lesson plans, schemes of work and records of completed work was equal to the importance of maintaining records of attendance; ensuring adequate lighting, ventilation and furnishing of the classroom; attending staff meetings; membership of school committees; and regular examinations. Teaching activities included reading the official *Bantu Teachers' Journal*; attending morning assembly; maintaining the school garden; cleaning the school premises; ensuring and practising punctuality; attending to students' homework; interacting with school prefects and monitors; and daily filling in of the log book.

The pedagogy underpinning the Methods of Teaching paper was generally a progressive one, emphasising children's activity, and sources such as pictures, charts and visits to museums in the teaching of History, as well as the project method, the inductive lesson, and nature study. Definition, illustration, experimentation and demonstration all present a teacher who performs in front of the class, and uses a variety of methods in teaching content. In 1949 the paper on Methods of Teaching suggests that teachers were expected to: play a role in education beyond the school walls, in the community; display a historical and geographical understanding of the Bible; understand the implications of the direct method for the teaching of the new primary syllabus;[24] use methods of improving English phrasing, intonation and pronunciation among Zulu-speakers; use materials, questioning and blackboard work in Mathematics teaching; maintain playground cleanliness; keep a school garden; ensure visualisation in Geography; and teach music notation in schools. The following were normalised: community education, cleanliness, learning English with no code switching, and the use of visual materials. The 1949 Principles of Education examination validated inclusivity, play and memory work; it also trained teachers in different methods for dealing with behavioural, intellectual, physical and other differences between children in classrooms.

But this seeming educational progressivism had a darker side. The Educational Psychology and Principles of Education exams reveal the extent to which the mental testing of students, the bedrock of biologically-based scientific racism in South Africa, was normalised in mission school teacher training.[25] The exams were set provincially and so would have been taken by all African teacher training students in Natal. In 1947, for example, the T3 exam (not included in the Table) examined knowledge of tests that differentiated between various types of tests, such as knowledge and intelligence tests, and standardised tests; it also considered the suitability of tests for African children, various definitions and characteristics of intelligence, as well as methods of testing intelligence. The T3 Principles of Education exam included a discussion question on the problem of 'retardation' under the following headings: classification of sub-normal children; causes of retardation; treatment and curriculum, as well as methods for such children. The 1949 paper included a question that tested the ability to distinguish between different types of tests; conduct and do a statistical analysis of tests; define prevailing notions of intelligence; describe the value of intelligence tests for school organisation; distinguish between knowledge and intelligence tests, group tests and individual tests, and describe the advantages and disadvantages of each. The incorporation of this kind of 'knowledge' into the provincial teacher training programme in mission schools is an indicator of the prevalence of social Darwinist thought in teacher training prior to Bantu Education. The mental testing movement, with its origins in the late nineteenth and early twentieth century in the United States and United Kingdom, was indigenised in South Africa via educationists such as E.G. Malherbe and C.T. Loram, both of whom had studied at the Teachers' College, Columbia University, in New York. Having adopted its key approaches, these men occupied influential positions in the Union government, enabling them to spread the ideas and methodologies throughout the educational system.[26]

Gendered social institutional practices

To what extent do the extra-curricular activities at the school reinforce the picture emerging from the curriculum then in use at the school? As the official magazine of the institution, *Inkanyezi* is typical of the school magazine genre, celebrating the school's achievements rather than revealing its tensions and conflicts. It presents the positive image of itself and the students that the institution wished to project to the world. Nevertheless, the lists of names of staff members and chairs of student committees, the prize-giving honours and short articles by students and photographs of sports teams, tell us something about those who controlled and participated in the life of the institution.

As a training college and high school, Umpumulo included both boys and girls. *Inkanyezi* is revealing about student activities at the school, and in particular the gendered participation of boys and girls. Between 1939 and 1960, *Inkanyezi* included many female contributors, though it is hard to determine whether there was equal representation since authors were sometimes named and sometimes identified by initials only. Nevertheless, there is twice the number of males among those whose first names indicate gender, showing that boys and/or male teachers contributed double the number of articles written by girls and/or female teachers. One possible reason is that at no time during this period did a female occupy the position of editor-in-chief of the institutional magazine – or indeed that of chair of the literary society, which organised debates and various educational activities. As a rule, girls were in supportive roles such as deputy or associate editor, secretary or vice-secretary. The fact that boys held titular authority does not mean that they did all the work, and it is probable that most of it was done by deputies and associates, who were generally girls.

The contributions were probably a selection of class essays or written specifically for the magazine, so the topics do not really provide a window into the political consciousness of the students. Rather, they might point to that of the teachers, who would have guided the topics and selection of articles. Female contributors wrote about a variety of social, professional and personal themes, including 'The Teaching of Arithmetic in the Standards' (1939);

'On the Duty of Loving One's Country'; 'Progress' (1940); 'The Difficulties of Young Teachers' (1941); 'The Show at Mapumulo' (1948); 'Loneliness' (1950); 'The Blackboard tells its Story' (1950); 'My Soul' (1950).

Mostly, however, the magazine reported on the activities in the school. Reflecting the students' lives, these were gender-segregated, with gender-specific subjects offered in the curriculum, the division of the college into a Boys' Department, Girls' Department and Normal (Teaching) Department, and separate sports and youth movements. Within the gender-segregated divisions, females were probably able to exercise leadership, but this was not the case when they participated in joint activities. Thus, males penned pieces on 'Democracy' and 'Peacebuilding' (1939), but also on 'The Carpentry Shop' (1940), the Bluebirds Football Club, the Boys' Department, Scouts and Pathfinders. They also reported on the activities of the students' representative council (SRC), high school debates, and outings. Female contributors, by contrast, concentrated on the activities of Sunrise (the girls' boarding division), Domestic Science, netball, the college choir, and the Wayfarers youth movement for girls.

As already indicated, leadership positions in societies were by and large occupied by boys. A case in point is the magazine committee, which consisted of elected office bearers and reporters on student activities such as the Students' Christian Association (SCA), the SRC, the evangelical band, the literary society, and so on. The committee produced a bi-monthly newsletter, based on such reports.

Girls participated in all activities, but not as equals. Whether girls should be educated at all was the topic of a magazine contribution in 1948, and a topic for debate in the literary society in 1953. Busisiwe Sangweni argued that girls should be educated because they are 'just as capable as men of forming an opinion', that it was a question of justice and of broader development: educating girls, she said, was tantamount to educating 'the whole race', as it was women who made the nation, being the mothers of tomorrow. In a 1950 edition of *Inkanyezi* Catherine Gumede (T4) decried the growing tendency to use facial creams and powders instead of the traditional 'ubulawu', while Irene Danibe extolled the virtues of 'Good Manners', which were expected of African children but also a sign 'that a person who possesses them, is educated in the true sense of the word'.[27] Grappling with contemporary issues as well as the relationship between African and Western behaviours, the magazine thus gave expression to the girls' sense of womanhood: this was achievement oriented, though within a separate sphere; it was also deferential towards, and supportive of, male authority and decision making, and emphatic about what constitutes 'good' womanhood. Prize-giving ceremonies were shown to celebrate boys as well as girls as leaders, as class achievers, and as hard workers, though within their separate spheres. Through these articles the school expressed its own sense of what it was trying to achieve. *Res non Verba* was the school motto – Deeds not Words. It was not so much in the words of the journal as in the deeds described in the articles that one can read the nature of the gender regime that prevailed at Umpumulo.

Once again, the picture is one of students being introduced to a wider world in which it is expected they will participate as equals, albeit one in which males will take the lead over females. Both were socialised through their involvement in school clubs and societies to become active members of the broader society in which they lived, across a range of walks of life. They were invited to think about and engage with topical issues of the day, to reconcile African and Western habits and ideas, and to become 'responsible' citizens in a society which excluded them – and would do so increasingly after 1955.

From cautious uncertainty to misgiving

The stance of the CLM in Natal and Zululand with respect to the impending transfer at Umpumulo and Eshowe from provincial to national control under the Department of Bantu Education was at first cautious and uncertain. While encouraged by the fact that the Education department had expressed satisfaction with Umpumulo as an institution, the principal of Umpumulo was nonetheless aware of the 'far-reaching consequences' of the Bantu Education Bill read in 1953, and doubtful of the department's bona fides as regards the institution.[28] When presented with the hard fact of a 50% reduction in the government grant, or a government takeover in whole or part, the CLM executive committee in Natal and Zululand met in Eshowe from 27 to 29 April 1954. There was ongoing discussion about how to retain control, and in the first instance, the discussion revolved around continued ownership of buildings. In November 1954 the committee resolved to inform government that, while the mission did not wish to relinquish control, it was prepared to rent the buildings to government under certain conditions.[29] But government was slow to respond, and no contract was entered into.

Though neither Eshowe nor Umpumulo were immediately affected by the new policy in their daily practice, both were eventually taken over by the Native Affairs Department in 1956. Government had appointed a missionary, Rev. Monstad, to the post of principal at Umpumulo, and this reassured the mission community. Rev. Ofstad remained as superintendent for hostels. There were no changes to the staff. But as the year dragged on without any contract or pay-ments for rent of buildings, boarding subsidy, or students' bursaries, misgivings grew. It was only when a special delegation was sent to the undersecretary of Bantu Education in November 1956 that a contract was signed and an advance of £900 sent.[30] Other pressures were also mounting. The new requirement that all principals and staff of educational institutions be South African citizens meant that Rev. Monstad would have to step down as principal until such time as he was awarded citizenship. In January 1959 he was duly forced to step down, and was replaced by a white South African.[31] In the same year, the Bantu Education department had reduced the funding by limiting the intake of boys to 44, well short of the original 81; it also proposed that a series of 3-week courses be held in Afrikaans, for 25 teachers at a time. This enraged the CLM, which voted to reject the proposed courses, since this would entail extra supervision; also, the reduction of students would mean reduced income.[32] The executive committee resolved, furthermore, to terminate its agreement with the department to continue running the hostels.

Disillusion and departure

By the beginning of 1960, disillusion at Umpumulo was palpable. The CLM stated its position clearly:

> Umpumulo Institution and Eshowe Training College . . . can no longer truthfully [be called] "our schools" . . . even if the buildings still belong to the Cooperating Lutheran Missions. We have come to the end of the journey as far as our direct Christian contribution to these schools is concerned. The final stage of conversion from being Mission Schools to being Government Institutions has been reached.[33]

At Eshowe, in particular, there had been marked changes. A matric class was started at the beginning of 1959, signalling the new status as a teacher training college; and while the number of boys declined, the number of girls increased.[34] Importantly, changes were made to the staff. When Rev. Rindahl left Eshowe in 1959, he was replaced by a government appointee, a Mr du Toit. All the signs indicated that departing mission staff would not be replaced by missionary personnel.

The end of the road had been reached, 'a sad day' indeed, but the planned alternative now came into being: the conversion of Umpumulo into a theolog-ical seminary fully controlled by the CLM in Zululand and Natal. This move was precipitated not only by events at Eshowe, but also by occurrences at the joint Lutheran Theological Seminary (LTS) at Oscarsberg. Here, a commission of enquiry conducted by the CLM into 'The Situation of the Oscarsberg Theological Seminary' highlighted a number of issues. These included, firstly, the implications for the seminary of the application of the various Group Areas Acts. The seminary grounds were in what was designated a 'European area', whereas the mission reserve lay on the other side of the Buffalo River. Those Africans living on the mission farm at Oscarsberg were faced with the prospect of forced removal to the reserve. By now, the CLM had learnt not to trust the authorities. Although the secretary for Bantu Affairs and Development had given the assurance that the work of the seminary could continue, the removal of people from the farm to the reserve would mean that 'the local congregation would cease to exist [and] that also the primary school will be closed so that the married students' children would be affected as well as the seminary with regard to practical instruction'. The report secondly indicated that if Oscarsberg were to remain a theological centre, major capital investments were needed.[35] Its recommendation 'to develop a central theological college on a high level discouraging local or regional training' was in line with the widely discussed IMC survey of the state of theological education in South Africa. The report explicitly recommended that the site for a theological seminary be Umpumulo, that entrance qualifications be raised accordingly, and that all Lutheran churches be involved in all aspects of the undertaking – which presented an exciting new prospect for the CLM.

Although the report's recommendation to move Oscarsberg to Umpumulo as a centre for the training of Lutheran pastors for all denominations was adopted, it displeased some within the Lutheran fold – not least those Hermannsburgers who had already begun a similar initiative, though one that was more regionally restricted and denominationally limited. A training institution for pastors had been built in Rustenburg in 1958 with the aid of the Lutheran World Federation and the Hanoverian Lutheran Church in Germany. The subsidy was granted on condition that it be used as a joint effort of Lutheran churches in the Transvaal.[36] Greve, who was now head of Marang, put the case for the college in terms of the need for continued training of Batswana pastors at a regional seminary, since Marang itself was in the process of development through funding from the Lutheran World Federation. He was equivocal about Umpumulo, hinting that a more suitable location should be found.[37] The matter was eventually settled at a conference of the Cooperating World Mission in Berlin in 1961. There, with the intervention of Fritz Scriba, himself a

Hermannsburger devoted to the CLM cause, it was agreed that 'Marang would be a centre for training of evangelists at a lower level, while Oscarsberg would be the main Seminary for training of pastors for the entire South African Lutheran community'.[38] This succeeded in clearing the way for Umpumulo to become the main Lutheran theological training centre.

At its April meeting in 1960, the CLM decided to relocate the theological seminary from Oscarsberg to Umpumulo at the end of 1962, and to sell the Eshowe High School buildings to the Bantu Education department. The department was prepared to hand over Umpumulo in exchange for Eshowe. At the end of 1960 it took over the running of the hostels at Eshowe. In September 1962 Oscarsberg celebrated its fiftieth anniversary. A month later, the Lutheran Theological College was moved from Rorke's Drift to Umpumulo, where the institution then occupied the campus of the Umpumulo Teachers' Training College. The complicated and complex nature of the changes and transactions discussed above brought to an end a period in which Umpumulo had been a teacher training college for the Lutherans. A new phase would begin in 1963 with its establishment as a seminary for the training of pastors.

Conclusion

Fedsem was created as a theological seminary in 1963, a result of the state takeover of key mission educational institutions, as well as pressures from within the international mission world for greater attention to theological education, in particular the training of black pastors. The policy of Bantu Education provided the spur and opportunity to do this. The same applied to Umpumulo. Its creation as a theological seminary was similarly a response to the experience of loss of institutions which, despite their weaknesses, had been built up over many years. As argued in Chapter 1, however, strengthening a Lutheran identity was also a strategy that developed against the threat of secularisation and other external challenges from the state. Cooperation with government had not meant a smooth transition, and agreement with some of its goals did not result in a painless transfer of institutions. The compensation for the loss, in the case of both Fedsem and Umpumulo, was to create new and more focused institutions aligned with the mission's religious purposes.

The era of mission-based teacher education had come to an end, though as this chapter and the previous one reveal, it was neither extensive nor highly developed. Teachers were not trained to a high level. And yet the curriculum expectations of teachers, as can be gleaned from insights provided by exam papers and the Umpumulo magazine, did induct teachers into a broader world in which it was expected they would occupy leadership positions, and would think and write independently about critical issues of the day. Although activities in the school were gender segregated, and the curriculum included practical and gender-defined subjects such as Agriculture and Needlework, with leadership positions generally occupied by males, expectations regarding students' gender roles in the wider society were typical of other mission schools – and vastly different from what loomed on the horizon. Whereas the curriculum could thus be described as having been broadly liberal and 'practical', albeit gender differentiated, it is noteworthy that it also included the socialisation of teachers into the principles and practices of scientific racism, as manifested in the mental testing movement of the day.

CHAPTER 7

TRANSNATIONALISM AND BLACK CONSCIOUSNESS AT UMPUMULO SEMINARY

In 1960 the Swedish missiologist Bengt Sundkler published a book that addressed the position of the pastor in Africa, and the question as to what a theological college should be.[1] This was a year of great change in Africa. Even as apartheid was being consolidated, no less than 17 states gained independence during the course of that year, 'and the cry "Africa for the Africans" [could] be heard everywhere'.[2] A professor at the University of Uppsala, Sundkler was married to a South African woman, and had spent time teaching at the Lutheran Theological College at Oscarsberg in Rorke's Drift in the early 1940s. In 1948 his book *Bantu Prophets in South Africa* secured Sundkler's 'international reputation as an Africanist'.[3] His appointment as research secretary of the International Missionary Council enabled him to conduct the survey for the IMC Commission on Theological Education in Africa in 1953, 1955 and 1957, which also provided the basis for the book published in 1960. The IMC survey results were widely disseminated and discussed in South Africa, and formed an important part of the background to the establishment of both Fedsem and Umpumulo.

As suggested in the previous chapter, this provided missionaries who were losing their schools to the state with a substitute, enabling them to re-direct their energies. Sundkler sketched a vision of an alternative educational project[4] which aimed at raising the standards of a hitherto neglected theological education. He argued that this could be achieved by addressing both the Eurocentric content and also the dull and uninteresting teaching methodologies of existing educational approaches. To succeed, it was necessary to create an atmosphere in which education was experienced as 'the enjoyment of good company',[5] and to teach African Church History in a way that would bring out the creative tension between national and universal dimensions of education. Rather than this history being taught as 'a catalogue of names and dates', it should bring out 'the main trends, the great ideas and movements'.[6] The tendency to treat Church History as a catalogue of unrelated data, or 'historical facts' was, he argued, a reason why students found Theology so difficult to learn.[7] For this reason, too, thorough research and the study of local history needed to be a central element of the new theological college.[8] Sundkler's vision inspired, and was also visible, in Umpumulo's approach to the curriculum.

The IMC's recommendation that theological education in Africa should be coordinated was eagerly taken up by the Protestant churches in South Africa. In order to provide financial support, the IMC established the Theological Education Fund in 1958.[9] Among its first beneficiaries was Marang, which had been established by the Hermannsburg Mission at Rustenburg in response to Bethel being turned into a high school, with theological and teacher education no longer being permitted. The IMC also supported the establishment of both Fedsem and Umpumulo. From the very beginning, Umpumulo was conceived within the framework of transnational debate and discussion about the nature of education that missionaries were providing, though not so much to schoolchildren or teachers as to African pastors. The IMC's Commission provoked a wider recognition of the restrictions on broader African participation within the church, in different national contexts, that were imposed by the limitations of the education which the missionaries provided. Even as apartheid was closing down opportunities and possibilities for Africans, missionaries re-opened them, doing so within a space that was both a logical development within their own history, and also permissible within the broader apartheid context. In the process, mission identities were recalibrated, as will be shown through a discussion of Hermannsburgers at Umpumulo. The notions of education developed within this broader framework were, however, deeply subversive, contradicting not only all that apartheid stood for, but also giving rise to deeper challenges from among African staff and students to the role and place of missionaries in Africa. Unlike the picture presented by Philippe Denis and Graham Duncan of a community united in the face of external threats, the one presented here reveals a community riven by continuing racial tensions in addition to facing external challenges. In order to understand how this process took shape within the institutional context of Umpumulo, it is necessary to understand the contradictory nature of its educational project in practice. This chapter does this by examining the funding model of the institution; the way in which Hermannsburger identities began to undergo change in a new context; the formal and informal curriculum in the institution; student resistance in the form of Black Consciousness; and continuous efforts to assert moral authority through regulating and controlling students' sexuality. In this respect, African and especially Zulu masculine identities were 'troublesome', the 'antithesis' of the notion of masculinity constructed by the mission.[10]

Finance, governance and staffing

Umpumulo's independence from government control was secured mainly through its funding model. Though chiefly self-supporting, it also raised funds and received grants from a host of Lutheran agencies, churches and individuals.[11] The main source of support, however, was the constituent churches and missions. These included the American Lutheran Mission, the Berlin Mission Society, Church of Sweden Mission, Hermannsburg Mission Society[12] as well as the Norwegian Mission Society and churches and synods from across South Africa, including Southern Rhodesia and Botswana.[13] Together these constituted first an Advisory Board, and then from 1964, once a Constitution had been drawn up, the Board of Governors of the College.

Discussions about the model to be used in order to be self-supporting began as early as 1960. It was decided that each of the four churches would contribute proportionally to the capital and running expenses, and that each would cover the cost of their students. Supporting members paid block grants and salaries of seconded teachers.[14] Costs per student were calculated on the basis of specified amounts for allowances for married and single students respectively plus children, and expenditures such as paraffin, upkeep, toiletries, medicines, textbooks, teaching materials, use of the seminary car, and fuel.[15] Eventually the churches also paid a fee per student. Although the Hermannsburgers found this a heavy burden to bear, they wished to participate 'fully', particularly 'in view of the necessary greater unity' that would be achieved. Their participation was facilitated by the sale of Eshowe High School, which repaid basic shares of £5,000 to each of the missions that had contributed. The mission would use this money to fund its participation in the seminary. Since this funding had originally been granted by a donor in Berlin, permission needed to be granted if it was to be used in this way.[16]

This model eventually created racial tensions, as the salaries paid to the white mission-seconded teachers were substantially higher than those paid to African lecturers. In 1959, Oscarsberg had had not one African staff member. Since many missionaries extruded from schools taken over by the state applied for and were given positions at Umpumulo, the majority there were white. In 1962, there was one African man and one white woman on a staff that comprised seven teachers. Diversification and increasing the number of African staff members was a constant preoccupation of the Umpumulo Board. The rector, Gunnar Lislerud, noted despairingly in 1966 that the number of African lecturers had not only declined that year, but also that there were too many from the south-eastern region, making for a 'rather strong "Zulu" impact upon our institution'.[17] His main concern was that '[n]o European Professor would have the possibility to relate his theology to a class of African students as [sic] an African professor' would. Ten years later, and a year after Axel-Ivar Berglund had replaced Gunnar Lislerud, white missionaries at Umpumulo still comprised two thirds of the staff; Africans remained a minority.[18]

With growing pressure to indigenise staff and to equalise salaries, it became necessary to change the existing structure. How to change it became a subject of considerable discussion: should all salaries be pooled and redistributed among members, should churches be called upon to contribute more, or should funds be raised for the additional amount? A memorandum on the subject was produced in 1971: the redistribution option was rejected on the grounds that it would not work because of the commitments of the foreigners to their children's schooling abroad. And so, African and white churches would instead be called upon to increase their contributions proportionally.[19]

The 'foreign' and more privileged status of many of the white staff members created internal tensions, but it also brought unwelcome, external attention to the institution. In 1971 a Dr Lochmann returned to Germany because the state refused an extension for his residence permit.[20] But others, such as Berglund and Hans-Jürgen Becken, shaped a different identity for themselves through their scholarship on African indigenous churches. Berglund's *Zulu Thought Patterns and Symbolism*,[21] and various other articles on, for example, baptism among African Zionist Movements and cattle riding among the Zulu were published in reputable journals and are cited to this day.[22] Becken's work on oral history and the Nazareth Baptist Church also survives as a significant contribution to the history and sociology of African independent churches in South Africa.[23]

This work and interest in African independent churches resulted in applications from both Mr Shembe, 'leader of the Shembe sect', and Mr Mthiyane of the Nazareth Baptist group, to be admitted to Umpumulo in 1966.[24]

Changing identities

Hans-Jürgen Becken was a Hermannsburger who became rector of Umpumulo. His Annual Reports to the mission from 1964 to 1973 provide insight into how the changed context and participation in this CLM educational project had begun to alter the Hermannsburger identity.[25] In Becken's reports we see representations of a more cosmopolitan, non-racial and liberal identity than that which existed in earlier decades. It may not have been an identity shared across the mission, but it shows what became possible through transnational interactions. Key to this identity were recognition of the value of coopera-tion and unity,[26] the significance of higher education for Africans, the role of English as a unifying language rather than a threat, and the importance of the Africanisation of content within a broader intellectual project. Unconcerned with promoting narrower segregationist and ethnic identifications, and more open to a wider world, Becken's approach differed greatly from that proposed by Heinz Dehnke, for example. Nevertheless, as rector, Becken supported the policing of sexual behaviours that transgressed Christian norms of heterosexual monogamy.

Despite this anomaly, Becken saw himself not only as a Hermannsburger and Lutheran, but also as an internationalist. This was reflected in his reports to the mission. Here he advanced an approach to educational content that was in line with Sundkler's vision: content should be at once international – without racial, geographical or national boundaries – and local, i.e. rooted in context.[27] Becken recognised that the content of texts was the product of a European or American context, and did not fit the local situation. But he wished to localise content without breaking contact with the rest of the world.[28] He expressed pleasure at the fact that the Lutheran Church was increasingly reaching out across racial boundaries, and disappointment about the general absence of white students.[29] Becken was proud of the fact that students were drawn not only from different ethnic groups, but also from the coloured community in the Cape, and the Indian community,[30] and continually celebrated the non-racial and cross-national composition of staff and students. Furthermore, he reported favourably on cooperation with the Association of Southern African Theological Institutions and related inter-denominations conferences and discussions.[31] Above all, he took pleasure from the fact that 'one could no longer think of oneself in terms of the smaller units of Lutheran Churches, but only as a worker in the greater mass of God's Children'.[32] He was not alone in holding these views. A temporary successor, Karl Bunjer, expressed a sense of pride that Hermannsburgers, with proven international interdependence, were no longer isolated, particularly with the frequent conferences held at Umpumulo.[33] Becken was able to perceive that there were closer relationships among Africans than between Europeans and Africans, and he saw the resentment of students towards white paternalism. The roots of this, he saw, was the treatment of a middle class community as second-class citizens, and the understanding that white people were free to leave the country, whereas Africans could not, or would face more difficulties if they attempted to do so. Such observations enabled an awareness and understanding of growing signals of hostility towards missionaries.[34]

Hermannsburgers at the Marang Theological College may not have shared in this new vision in all respects. Notwithstanding the quest for relevance in texts being studied, the context should not, according to Heinrich Voges, 'eat the text'.[35] For this long-serving staff member, the main difference between Marang and Umpumulo was the fact that teaching and learning took a more political direction at Umpumulo. Black Theology did not find the same home at Marang as at Umpumulo. Also, teaching at Marang was in Tswana rather than English. Voges noted ruefully that by the 1980s he was the only one left teaching in Tswana – all the black teachers at Marang were teaching in English at that time. By this stage, too, politicisation of staff and lecturers had become unavoidable: some students supported the ANC, others the Pan Africanist Congress (PAC), and yet others were pro-Bantustan.

Students, the curriculum and relations with the state

The Umpumulo curriculum was multi-faceted, gendered, and included both formal and informal, as well as visible and hidden elements. Even though the institution had created a curriculum in opposition to apartheid, state policy continued to structure who could participate in the institution and on what terms. Moreover, while the curriculum was oriented towards the training of male pastors, the participation of their wives was confined to the religious and domestic spheres.

Student numbers were never very high, reaching a maximum of 48 in 1965.[36] The students were male, often accompanied by their wives. Thirty-three women attended the institution in 1964. They not only 'showed great interest in the lessons' but also played an active role in Umpumulo and the wider community.[37] While their male partners attended various theology classes at the college, or followed a curriculum in English, Zulu, Afrikaans, Geography, History, Arithmetic, Bookkeeping and Music in the pre-seminary school, the women had Bible Study, Hygiene, Needlework and Cookery classes. They attended guest lectures at the college, organised their own prayer groups,[38] and also conducted prayers at the local hospital, where they visited the sick. As the College authorities saw it, the students' wives were being provided with 'courses to equip them for their future duties as pastors' wives'.[39] By contrast, the activities of male students were organised by means of various associations and organisations, including a Students' Representative Council, Students' Literary and Theological Society, Students' Christian Association, class choirs, brass bands, a sports' committee, and work in neighbouring schools and communities.[40] As a space for single people and married couples, the college provided a context for gendered interactions and tensions which, as will be shown later, sometimes resulted in friction with the college authorities. But first it is necessary to turn to the formal and informal curriculum.

The formal curriculum

Students could go to Umpumulo and take a Joint Matriculation Board (JMB) exam at the end of three years, or they could follow a general theological course qualifying them for ordination and resulting in a 'Candidate of Theology' certificate; alternatively, they could take a theological course leading to a BA (Theology) through the University of South Africa (Unisa). As at Fedsem, the discussions around this Theology degree had been controversial, as it meant working through a state institution linked to the apartheid project. The Lutherans had not reacted positively to the government's proposal that they join the Bantu University Colleges when this was first raised with them in 1961.[41] The Extension of University Education Act no 45 of 1959 in effect extended racial separation and exclusion to the sphere of higher education. It became a criminal offence for black students to attend a white university without permission of the Minister of Internal Affairs, and four new institutions, the so-called Bantu University Colleges, were established on an ethnic basis: at Bellville on the outskirts of Cape Town (for coloured students), Ngoye in Zululand (for Zulu-speakers), Durban-Westville (for Indians), and Turfloop in the Transvaal (for Sotho-speakers). Fort Hare was restricted to Xhosa speakers.[42] At a meeting in Pretoria to discuss the proposed BA Theology with representatives from Unisa, the Bantu University Colleges, and the Government Commission investigating Theological Studies at Bantu University Colleges, the CLM of Zululand and Natal 'pointed to the fact that we are afraid of tribal churches and the aim of the Lutheran Church was to have one Lutheran Church of Southern Africa'.[43] But unlike Fedsem, they were prepared to enter into negotiations and discussions with Unisa, and these began immediately. They were thus not as radical as Fedsem in their rejection of working with any state institution, and were more willing to compromise in order to achieve their goal of a theology qualification at tertiary level.

Limitations on access

As at Fedsem, Umpumulo required 'pigment permits' from coloured students and students from then-Rhodesia.[44] Here too, the approach of the authorities at Umpumulo was far more accommodating than at Fedsem. Whereas Fedsem at first showed its opposition by simply ignoring the permit requirement, Umpumulo attempted to negotiate conditions – much as Scriba had done during the transition from mission to Bantu Education in Zululand and Natal – by sending polite appeals that were apparent demonstrations of compliance. Their first appeal to the Minister of Bantu Education, in 1963, justified coloured students' attendance at Umpumulo on the grounds that they came from such 'small synods [that] cannot possibly establish nor run a theological school of their own'. Moreover, there were only four coloured students, and of course 'they have always been given their own dormitories, and this shall also be our policy in the future'. The mission went on to request permission to run a boarding establishment which would include a 'limited number of coloured students with the understanding that they be given separate dormitories from the Bantu students'.[45]

Umpumulo was informed, however, that its application for a permit for coloured students should be submitted to the Group Areas Board. Also, since the Umpumulo Mission Glebe was not 'within a scheduled Bantu area', the location of the boarding school required a permit for the African students, to be requested from the Department of Bantu Administration and Development through the local Chief Bantu Affairs Commission.[46] The necessary letters were written and permission obtained, albeit for only a two-year period in respect of the coloured students. Using their government contact, Werner Eiselen, to intercede on their behalf, an extension was granted for two Indian students up to the end of 1970, and six coloured students up until 31 December 1971.[47] Thereafter the permits had to be renewed on an annual basis. The period of extension was so short that, no sooner was one extension granted, than the process of making the next request began. This continued until 1980. Students from the then-Rhodesia required not only permission, but also visas. African students who did not carry their passes on them at all times were at constant risk of arrest as soon as they set foot outside the institution – as happened to a student who was arrested en route to a conference in Caledon.[48]

Despite its compliance and accommodation, Umpumulo soon fell under a cloud of suspicion. Towards the end of December 1967, the Secretary of Bantu Education wrote to the Chairman of the Governing Body and the Rector of the Institute indicating that an inspection report of the pre-seminary school in October had drawn certain matters to his attention, and he therefore requested a meeting. A delegation duly met with the secretary and minister on 8 January 1968. It transpired that, besides the routine inspection pronouncement, a record of events had previously been sent to the Minister of Bantu Education in which reference was made to a 'newspaper report lesson' and subsequent discussions between Chief Inspector de Waal and the teacher concerned, namely Rev. Lindberg. During the meeting, the minister voiced concerns about the pre-seminary school, including indications of student opposition to the policy of separate development, and political discussions in the classroom 'leading to active propaganda against the government'. He took the opportunity to remind the delegation that it employed staff members 'from Overseas without any orientation as to the history, languages, customs, etc., of the peoples living in South Africa – both White and Black'. He was, moreover, keen to be assured of the governing body's willingness to cooperate with the department on this matter.[49]

The delegation responded not by promising obedience, but by saying that 'it had made no ruling as to political propaganda' in the school, and reaffirming the board's policy of orienting new members of staff to the local environment. In exchange, they requested 'the privilege of admitting six single Rhodesian students annually', and extending the two-year permit of coloured students. The threats of expulsion were real – members of staff, being foreign, could and did have their visas revoked at the whim of the government, and students could just as easily have their permits withdrawn.

In the meantime, at Umpumulo, a committee was established to determine the future of the pre-seminary school. Its deliberations focused on ways of improving the school rather than on instilling obedience. The school had been opened in 1963 to help prepare students for the BA Theology course, but because of its high matric failure rate, there was difficulty in registering the school with the department. The committee recommended that the school should continue, though only admitting students with a First or Second Class Junior Certificate, which should be completed within the usual two-year period. A letter was sent to the Association of Southern African Theological Institutions, inviting it to send students to the school. Significantly, Berglund underlined the importance of secular education for Theology students, who were now younger and less experienced than before.[50]

Limitations and restrictions on access of coloured, Indian and non-South African students to the institution was a constant source of irritation, gradually hardening CLM opposition towards government policy even as the CLM itself was forced to comply in order to continue and survive.

The informal curriculum

The formal curriculum at Umpumulo was supplemented and enriched by a range of lectures and cultural activities that helped to break the physical isolation of the institution. Indeed, Umpumulo was connected to – and exposed staff and students to – the main currents of thought in a radicalising social and political environment. Understandably, these were perceived mainly through the lens of church-based organisations. In 1965 alone, Umpumulo received visitors not only from sister institutions in South Africa, but also from Sweden and Germany. Women did not feature, however. A musical evening for students was arranged by Hans Bodenstein, who brought the Broadcasting Choir of the nearby Hermannsburg School, and also R. Woodcock from Australia, who gave a violin concert. In addition, numerous academics, including radical theologian Beyers Naudé, attended conferences at Umpumulo.[51] In 1966 the institution was graced not only with a visit by Pastor Niemöller from Germany, but also with visitors from the Lutheran World Federation, the Christian Institute, and sister churches in South Africa, America and Europe – all of whom called at Umpumulo.[52]

The Missiological Institute

One of Umpumulo's main attractions for visitors was the work of its Missiological Institute. Stimulated by the Lutheran World Federation, the Missiological Institute was conceived as an essential dimension of the work at Umpumulo as early as 1960.[53] The aim was to serve as a centre for research and as a central archive for the Lutheran Church in South Africa. Its spheres of interest encompassed topics such as Mission Theology and Approach, Indigenisation, African Church History, Contemporary Church Problems, Ecumenical Relations, Sociology, African Religion, and Linguistics.[54] From 1965 on, the college held regular annual conferences on topics that crystallised the political issues of the day. The conferences drew scholars from across the country – 'politicians, sociologists and philosophers', both inside and out-side the church – who reflected on such issues, thereby enabling the college to develop its own position on important matters of the day. Conference themes included 'The Approach to the Independent Church Movement' (1965), 'Migrant Labour' (1969/70), 'The Church and Development' (1971), 'A Relevant Ideology for Africa' (1972), 'The Church and Nationalism' (1973/74), 'Affluence and Poverty'(1976), and 'Ideologies of Change' (1978).[55] Gender inequality as a theme was unrecognised and therefore absent.

Conferences were not only academic but helped to express and shape broader attitudes towards apartheid. In 1974, for example, the following was concluded:

> We find that no black (i.e. African, coloured or Indian) member of the consultation feels that he is free, and that from the heart of every black Christian goes up a deep and passionate cry for liberation. No only so, the white members of the consultation feel that they too are entangled in the servitude of their black brethren . . .. We have felt ourselves drawn to . . . the conclusion that a peaceful future for South Africa is to be found nowhere else than in the formation of one single nation under God . . . in which, by the enjoyment of a common citizenship, every single human creature will have the certainty of freedom, of human integrity, and of equality of opportunity.[56]

In its findings, the Missiological Institute expressed opposition to Afrikaner nationalism and the notion of separate development based on the ethnic nationalism embodied in concepts such as *volksnasionalisme* (people's nationalism) and *volksidentiteit* (national identity).[57] The Missiological Institute proposed a different model for understanding South Africa, namely that of pluralism. In this regard the document sought a model of consultation between the leaders of different groups, with the aim of moving towards an open society and away from the imposition of *volksnasionalisme* on society, urging that steps be taken towards achieving an inclusive South Africa without delay, 'if institutionalised violence or armed conflict are not to make all efforts at peaceful change impossible'.[58]

In the realm of politics, the findings affirmed the human dignity of all, and warned of the consequences of discrimination. The following recommendations were made: ensuring legal recognition of trade unions; free, compulsory education up to the age of 16; English as medium of instruction; opportunities for young people of different races to get to know one another; textbooks that instruct rather than indoctrinate; freedom of choice on which university to attend; the requirement that all children should learn an indigenous language; minimum restrictions on freedom of movement; closing the racial salary gap; reducing racial disparity in social welfare and pension grants.

By now Umpumulo was fully supportive of the movement opposing apartheid. Black Consciousness and Contextual Theology – an approach that linked the study of theology to the historical and contemporary context – complemented broader debates on nationalism, socialism and Marxism. The Missiological Institute addressed these debates through its interdisciplinary study programme on capitalism, socialism and Marxism. This resulted in a major conference being held, with speakers representing positions across the political spectrum: from Anglo-American's C.M. O'Dowd to a group of young economists and political scientists that included Johan Degenaar, Norman Bromberger and Raphael de Kadt, also radical Catholic socialists like Albert Nolan, African socialists like S.R. Motshologane, and a variety of Black Consciousness perspectives represented by, among others, Manas Buthelezi and Father Seoka, who was at the time organiser of the Black Allied Workers Union (BAWU). The papers, discussion and final assessments appeared in 1979[59] in a publication that included rigorous conceptual analyses as well as purposeful discussions of action to be taken. Klaus Nürnberger's study[60] provides a strong sense of the intensity of debate at the time, which included discussion on the nature of South African society, the direction change should take, and the role of the church in achieving that change.

Student resistance

The role of men at Umpumulo in developing Black Consciousness ideas, particularly as these related to Black Theology, or Black Liberation Theology, has been well documented.[61] Black Consciousness was clearly an assertion of a masculinity that was oppositional to mission masculinity. Its adherents, whether activists or thinkers, sought to affirm the value, humanity, dignity and identity of black men – Indian, coloured and African – who were oppressed by the South African racial regime. Black Consciousness thought developed in phases, from a critique of liberalism and the assertion of African humanism to African and Black Theology, and finally the idea of a black Messiah. Ideas around Black Theology were informed by the secular theology approach that developed in response to the 1968 'Message to the People of South Africa' of the Theological Commission of the South African Council of Churches which not only 'offered a scriptural critique of apartheid'[62] but also promoted the idea of faith in the secular world.

Black Theology called for the Africanisation of the Christian message and bringing the experience of African oppression into the church (though with no explicit reference to the oppression of women). With its leadership firmly committed to the idea of Africanisation of curriculum content, as part of a wider project to improve theological education, Umpumulo provided a natural base for the development of many of these ideas among Africans. As rector of Umpumulo, Becken promoted what became known as Secular Theology, while Simon Maimela and Chris Mzoneli developed Black Theology; though T.S. Farisani had by 1975 left Umpumulo, he became a firm advocate of the notion of a Black messiah. Magaziner provides a powerful sense of how theology and notions of equality and social justice were combined in Farisani's visionary thought, expressed in the form of dreams envisaging a new world, beyond apartheid:

> In his final address to the Black People's Convention, T.S. Farisani employed his training at the Lutheran Church's Mapumulo Seminary to great effect. He recalled a recent morning when, on the cusp of waking, he had had a vision in which, while soaring far above the earth he had seen 'a pale man, holding the sun in his hand'. The light-skinned demon had captured the source of light and turned its rays to his advantage. There were thirteen rays, and each bore a resonant word or phrase: 'apartheid, oppression, suppression, torture, bannings, Robben Island, Central Prison, Security Branch, Bureau of State Security, discrimination, injustice, inequality of man and Homelands'. Farisani watched, transfixed, when a great storm rose up and swept away both the pale man and the 'thirteen abominables'. One can easily imagine the passion with which he described what came next: 'On the horizon I saw a Blackman with his legs apart, his mouth wide open, the sun in his hand, with sheaths of rays folded, shouting . . . Sas (the) sunray sheaths unfolded. JUSTICE, EQUALITY, FAIRNESS, UNITE, LIBERATION . . .. The man grew taller, the sun rose higher and higher and the shouts grew louder and louder as the golden words (became) clearer and clearer'. Farisani recognised the 'Blackman' and greeted him on behalf of BPC [Black People's Convention]: 'SIYABONGA. (We thank you). BLACK MESSIAH!' Returning to earth – and his audience – Farisani explained what the vision meant. It was the Black Messiah's turn to hold the sun, and the rays told the tale: the specific horrors of apartheid would 'soon' be replaced with the worthy promises of political liberation. He wished

his audience the 'POWER, SOLIDARITY, PERSISTANCE AND FORTITUDE' to make it so . . .

As Magaziner points out in his discussion of Farisani, 'the faith implicit in the talk of a messianic age was there, as was the prophecy and vision of things as yet unseen'.[63]

Farisani's passionate commitment to liberation was not learnt in a passive manner at Umpumulo. In 1972 he and fellow student at Umpumulo, J.M. Ramashapa, were engaged in a major conflict with the institution in which they mobilised the support of the president of the Black Consciousness-aligned South African Students' Organisation (SASO) and the Lutheran publication, *Isithunywa*. Although Umpumulo was among the founding members of both SASO, in 1967, and the University Christian Movement (UCM), in 1968, the Governing Board refused to recognise either the UCM or SASO branch until 1971, when it held meetings first with the students and then SASO to discuss the new student movement. These meetings were reportedly open and constructive.[64] But in 1972 a simmering conflict between staff and the two students, Farisani and Ramashapa, blew wide open.

The events were as follows: in April 1972 Farisani and Ramashapa were reported absent from manual labour duties. The rector referred the matter to the faculty, who took a tough position and recommended that the two should proceed with correspondence studies and not return to the college. From the perspective of the authorities, the students had been a disruptive presence: 'While these students were with us there was mounting unrest and intimidation of students which prevented many of them from studying freely. After their departure, most of the students are relaxed and a spirit of eagerness and study has returned'.[65] From their perspective, manual labour was 'meaningful and to the benefit of the community' and 'part of the preparation of responsibility'. It included student projects such as 'building tennis courts and upkeep of the College Campus for one and a half hours each week'. Their discussions about the students' 'lack of experience in life', and their apparent reluctance to join the ministry with its requirement to work in the parish for a least a year, serving a period of probation before they could reapply for readmission, were communicated to the two students. They were suspended on the understanding that they would continue with their studies at Unisa, and once these were completed, they could return for the Theology course. Their fees and books would be continued to be paid for, but they were not permitted board and lodging at the college.

On 8 May 1972, Maimela attempted to intercede on the students' behalf, and a week later, Ramashapa wrote a letter contesting the allegation that he did not want to be a pastor. To no avail, however. Farisani seems then to have approached *Isithunywa*, which in September published an article '*Amanyvesithi Ezinhlaya*' ('Universities of the Insane') decrying the 'expulsion' of the students. This enraged the authorities, and Becken immediately wrote to correct the information that the students had been expelled, expressing displeasure that the conditions under which they had been asked to leave had not been accurately described. Ramashapa was by this stage anxious to return, and he approached Bishop Pakendorf in Pretoria with a letter that amounted, in his view, to an apology.

Later that year, the SASO drew up a resolution on the matter. The president, Barney Pityana, noted in his covering letter to the college: 'we have reason to believe that the action was more ominous than just "discipline"; it was a veiled threat aimed at frustrating student initiative and independent thinking. We regard it as extremely expedient that the two students be reinstated to college next year'.[66] The resolution itself noted 'the unprecedented and fascist actions of the rector and the staff'; that the two students were SASO members; that 'confirmed reports have been received to the effect that these two black brothers were expelled because their SASO ideologies conflicted with the whole teaching of the Lutheran Church'; and that the college administration was 'determined to kill the effectiveness of SASO on that campus'. Furthermore, SASO 'condemn[ed] in the strongest fashion the action of the authorities', and 'instructed the Executive to thoroughly investigate the matter' and to 'communicate the contents of this Resolution to all the parties concerned including the highest authority of the Lutheran Church'.

The letter was returned to SASO forthwith, but the pressure had had an effect. College authorities made it clear that what was required was a formal apology from each of the students. Ramashapa, communicating through Bishop Pakendorf, appears to have been anxious to return, seeming more receptive to this request than Farisani. In early 1973, his formal letter of apology resulted in a letter advising him to apply for the General Course. And so, Ramashapa was readmitted to the college. In the case of Farisani, after his apology was accepted by the bishop, he 'finished his degree by correspondence and then went into the ministry'.[67]

Umpumulo's educational philosophy and practice provided the intellectual and social framework within which ideas connected with Black Consciousness could develop at the college. However, the creative tension that developed between universalising and African nationalist principles, as promoted by Sundkler, appears at times to have collapsed, with either-or positions being taken by the students. It was inevitable perhaps that a more radical, a more activist form of Black Consciousness within the college would find opposition among its faculty, committed as they were, in the first instance, to an intellectual project. But this conflict was unusual, being the only 'disciplinary' case of a political nature in the college files.

Asserting moral authority and regulating sexuality

In the 1960s, the strict religious sexual mores of an earlier era began to weaken throughout the Western world. At the same time, the ruling National Party in South Africa enforced a strict code through its Christian National Education policy which segregated on the basis of race while enforcing patriarchal control and authority.[68] The Umpumulo Lutherans were closer to the ruling party on this matter than their more liberal political philosophy might have suggested. They policed the students' sexuality in a manner that confirmed both the authority and the rectitude of the mission's white, male version of masculinity. Disciplinary cases, with the one exception cited above, all concerned sexual transgressions, i. e. transgressions of the 'Sixth Commandment'.[69] These almost always entailed violations of the code forbidding sex before marriage and adultery.[70] Such sexual practices were cast as 'sinful', especially for pastors in training. The effect was to create an atmosphere in which sexuality itself was strictly regulated and controlled. The cases that resulted in suspensions reveal that the missionaries did not expect a total abandonment of traditional marriage practices, such as the payment of *lobola*. Rather, they negotiated these within a Christian framework that forbade sex outside the framework of marriage. Thus, once it was discovered that students were engaged in a sexual relationship, the man was duty-bound to pay *lobola* and marry the woman. The intellectual orientation of the missionaries was syncretic and inclusive, but their moral code as far as sexuality was concerned was rigid and unforgiving.

Most of the incidents appear to have occurred during the period when Rev. Peter Beyerhaus was rector. A climate of sexual intolerance seems to have prevailed: there were unpleasant incidents in which it was clear that students were being spied upon and pounced on. 'Guilty' parties were subjected to intense rituals of confessional interrogation in which the 'truth' was wrung from them. This becomes apparent when reading between the lines of the stories themselves, as extracted from often lengthy correspondence and reports. The 'truth' of what happened in each case is difficult to discern, as each is laden with attribution of guilt, and enacts performances of repentance. Opprobrium was sharply expressed to induce shame, but what the reported cases suggest instead is a shameful invasion of privacy and voyeurism on the part of the authorities. Punishment usually entailed suspension for a period. Only in a few cases were students expelled. The object of suspension seems to have been to impress upon the student a sense of guilt, shame and wrongdoing which, ironically, was equally applicable to the actions of the missionaries. In most cases, the women involved were workers in the homes or kitchens of the college.

The fear of being found out is evident in the case of Eriksen Mthiyane. When in 1962 he was found hiding under the bed of Rev. Beyerhaus's 'servant girl', he explained that he was 'proposing marriage'. He was duly sent home to make *lobola* arrangements. The wedding date was set, and it would take place at Umpumulo. Mthiyane returned to the college, but his fiancée failed to turn up for the wedding, arriving some days later at the college. Afterwards, it was discovered that she had in fact arrived there two weeks earlier, together with her new born baby. Once the woman was found with the baby, Mthiyane was forced to confess, admitting that he had frequently visited her in the past. She had fallen pregnant some time before, but he had been too afraid to admit this, knowing full well what the consequences would be. Instead, he had taken her to Empangeni, where she had given birth, and where he settled her with relatives. In a letter to the principal, he 'firmly' stated that he had 'never committed any sin', begging for pardon and permission to return. However, he was expelled on the grounds that he had 'committed sin against the 6th Commandment' and 'had made false statements and written false letters'.[71]

That Mthiyane had been found 'hiding under the bed' of a woman suggests that a surprise visit was sprung upon the couple.[72] The following story suggests the nature of the interrogation that occurred in the hours between 10:30 p.m. when another couple was discovered, and their release at 2:30 a.m. the next morning. Rev. Beyerhaus and the rector caught one Mabaso in the act one evening with the 'kitchen girl' known only as Sylvia. He was brought before the rector and interrogated in the presence of Rev. Monstad, Rev. Dlamini, Rev. Makhatini and Rev. Beyerhaus. Mabaso denied responsibility and claimed Sylvia had come to him unbidden. He confessed that he had been 'in love with her for the whole past year'. He also admitted to having had relations with another woman whom he left when he discovered her with another man. He had bought the nightdress Sylvia was wearing when they were caught together. She admitted to their relationship and he grew angry with her for so doing. He had no intention of marrying her even though she was pregnant. Lecturers voted unanimously for Mabaso's expulsion. Sylvia immediately packed her bags and left.

In some cases, African pastors were called on to intervene. Thus, when Busisiwe Buthelezi fell pregnant and claimed that Sipho Nyandeni was the father, Dean Luthuli was mandated to go to her family kraal to find out the truth, as Sipho had denied paternity. It was discovered that the child's father was indeed another man, and Sipho was cleared of blame.[73]

Christopher Hlongwane, a married man, was not so lucky, however. An unsent love letter to Mirriam Nzimande, a nurse aid from Stanger, was found in Hlongwane's Dogmatics term paper. He 'admitted his sin' before Rev. Scalf, Rev. Makhatini and the rector. His wife continued to support him and was willing to stand by him. Nonetheless, he was expelled and forbidden to write final exams, despite a petition from his fellow students that he be permitted to do so. The authorities reasoned that this was not his first disciplinary case – he had previously been suspended for drunk driving.[74]

A more difficult case for the institution was one of adultery involving a student and the wife of one of the coloured students. According to the authorities, the affair had been visible and also upsetting to the student body. The woman as well as the two students, known only as Matthews and A. Farao, were sent back to Cape Town. The married couple appeared to have reconciled, and their main concern was to return to the college. Both wrote letters to Beyerhaus, explaining their situation and requesting permission to return. Beyerhaus's reply to Matthews, the husband, expresses a self-righteousness that seemed to take pleasure in its power to control:

> It is impossible to let your wife come back to the College . . .. [I]t is evident that she and Farao broke the 6th Commandment . . .. Your fellow Coloured students feel that the presence of your wife would be such a serious embarrassment to their staying here that they could hardly tolerate it. This does not mean that the guilt of your wife is proved with absolute certainty [but] we must be concerned with the spiritually healthy climate within our student body . . .. [We] renounce the privilege of having you in the student community.

The College Board was apparently less extreme in its attitude. A month later, in June 1965, the College Board held a special meeting where it was decided that Matthews should be suspended from March to August, and thereafter be readmitted with a warning to his wife. On 1 December 1966, Farao was also permitted to return to complete his studies the following year, by which time the Matthews' would have left.[75]

Conclusion

The transformation of Umpumulo from a teacher training college to a seminary for the training of pastors was a response to the implications of new apartheid education policy for the educational projects at Eshowe, Umpumulo and Oscarsberg. Umpumulo was an institution with many positive and proactive dimensions. In the first instance, it was inspired by the work of the IMC on improving theological education in Africa and increasing the number of Africans playing leadership roles in the church. The vision for a different type of college, as set out in Sundkler's *The Christian Ministry in Africa*, was enthusiastically taken up and followed. Umpumulo's connections with the World Council of Churches and international Lutheran organisations were strong, and they were further strengthened by the many visits people made to the college. In addition to this, the college brought Europeans and Africans together in one space. Importantly, its students cut across the ethnic boundaries that the apartheid state defined in its attempt to separate people into different 'nations'. Indeed, any such narrow identifications were self-consciously abjured. Instead, a broader, more fluid and liberal sense of self began to emerge as a result of the connections and interactions experienced at Umpumulo, changing significantly the character not only of those Hermannsburgers who were drawn into the work at Umpumulo, but also of its staff and its students. Finally, however, the 'alternative' nature of the project was fundamentally limited by the secondary status of women, whether as teachers or wives of students at the institution, and with regard to the seemingly obsessive regulation of mores and sexual behaviour among students.

There were, moreover, multiple transitions in the formation of Umpumulo. These included the shift from a focus on secular schooling and teacher training to theological education, a move away from a conservative to an alternative, more critical educational project within the framework of theological education, and a leap from the lowly form of pastoral training for extremely small numbers of students for whom the future held few prospects, to one which aspired to higher education and the promise of meaningful social participation. It saw a change from narrower to broader educational approaches that placed social knowledge at the centre of an educational project that was conceived as a 'conversation' between equals, a dialogue based on research and study. From approaches which sought to conserve the status quo, or simply convert Africans to Christianity, the Umpumulo project sought to challenge racial inequality and promote a Sundklerian vision of a theological college that was open to the world and to secular forms of knowledge.

Transitions thus occurred on a social, institutional, structural and individual level. Umpumulo's transnational dimensions and corresponding transitions played a significant role in reshaping the nature of the educational initiatives and interventions of at least one set of mission societies in South Africa. Ultimately, however, Umpumulo was limited by the structuring framework of a deeply conservative regime with regard not only to gender but also to sexual discipline: it profoundly characterised, and also constructed, the social relationships within the institution.

CHAPTER 8

BOPHUTHATSWANA'S EDUCATIONAL HISTORY AND THE HERMANNSBURGERS

Between 1979 and 1988, a child-centred Primary Education Upgrade Programme (PEUP) was initiated in the most unlikely of contexts: a Bantustan. The programme expanded dramatically: from 7 schools in 1980, it grew to 114 in 1981, and 625 in 1983. Two years later, 760 out of a total of 840 schools, i.e. more than 90%, were involved. A decade after it was first introduced, the PEUP was described as having 'infused primary education in Bophuthatswana with a new spirit and orientation'; it was also perceived to be responsible for this particular Bantustan's superior educational results.[1] This, despite the fact that unemployment was higher in this area than in other rural provinces, and that it had the highest proportion of people without schooling in the agricultural sector.

Hermannsburgers were deeply involved in both the development and provision of education in Bophuthatswana. Central to the implementation of PEUP was Christel Bodenstein, connected by marriage to the Bodensteins of the Hermannsburg Mission, one of whom, Wolfgang, became advisor to Lucas Mangope. Wolfgang Bodenstein had been a doctor at the mission hospital at Appelsbosch in Zululand, and was a close associate of Mangosuthu 'Gatsha' Buthelezi, who had recommended him to Mangope.[2] I interviewed Christel Bodenstein and her husband, Hans, in the German Old Age Home in

Johannesburg, in 2009. Hans was born into a missionary family, while Christel became a Hermannsburger through marriage. Her public role in education in the Bantustan demonstrates the changing position of women and the possibilities that opened up from the early 1970s onwards.

The driving force behind PEUP, Bodenstein was a self-effacing but energetic and charismatic teacher trainer at nursery and primary school levels in Rustenburg. Born Christel Bokelman in 1926 in East London, she attended the German school in Hermannsburg, where she first met her husband-to-be. She left to do her training at the Pretoria Teacher Training College, which offered a course of study she found inadequate, and from there she went to Barkly House in Cape Town. In 1948, while teaching at a nursery school in Durban, she married Hans Bodenstein. Within the space of ten years, she gave birth to five children. At the same time, during the 1960s, while moving 'from place to place', she taught at various nursery and primary schools in Philippi in Cape Town, where she became principal, and also at Hermannsburg and in Johannesburg.[3]

Pietermaritzburg followed in 1971: there, she was a nursery school teacher and then principal of Sunny Lea (1973–1974), after which she joined the teacher training college as a lecturer. There, she developed early childhood courses from scratch while her husband taught Mathematics and Science at the Edendale Technical College. Given her German-influenced schooling, it was perhaps not surprising that Christel Bodenstein would turn to German thinkers on early childhood and primary education when she was preparing her courses. She herself cites the influence of Johann Pestalozzi (1746–1827) and Friedrich Froebel (1782–1852). Both Pestalozzi, who laboured among working people and their children for most of his life and Froebel, influenced by Pestalozzi's ideas, were deeply affected by Jean-Jacques Rousseau's educational treatise, *Emile*. Both thought the task of education was to develop what was inherent in the child. At first inspired by the work of Pestalozzi, Froebel and Maria Montessori, among others, and later by work being conducted at Leeds University in the United Kingdom, Christel Bodenstein brought a mix of European and British child-centred educational traditions to bear on the PEUP experiment.[4]

The Bodensteins moved to Rustenburg in 1976, where Hans headed up the Thlabane Technical College. Christel taught at the neighbouring teacher training college for African teachers, which was close to the Marang Theological College. Both the teacher training college, now state controlled, and the theological college had been located at Bethel before the state take-over in 1955.[5]

Christel Bodenstein was based in Rustenburg, located in 'white' South Africa, while the PEUP project was conducted in the Bantustan. Feeling isolated and alienated in Rustenburg, she soon established networks associated with the Bophuthatswana government, the Popagano Commission of Inquiry into Education[6] instituted by Mangope, as well as Christian networks linked to the newly established university and teacher training college. Ken Hartshorne, a Popagano Commission member, was 'a firm supporter' of PEUP, while his co-member, Nancy Motlala, was a key co-organiser with Christel.[7] Many of the mediators of the new ideas, with whom Bodenstein worked, were themselves schooled in ideas that were child-centred. Bill Holderness, who worked closely with Christel Bodenstein, used the University of Bophuthatswana as a base for the development and distribution of materials. Born into a Grahamstown mission family, Holderness had studied Language and Literature in Education at the University of London's Institute of Education from 1974 to 1975. Thereafter, from 1976 to 1980, he lectured at the Johannesburg College of Education where he worked with the English Language Teaching and Information Centre, a non-governmental organisation (NGO) working to improve literacy in black schools. In 1980, in the midst of discussions on the findings of the Popagano Commission, and the establishment of the PEUP, Holderness was inspired to join Unibo.

Although Christel Bodenstein worked closely with African teachers at Unibo, local teacher training colleges, anti-apartheid NGOs based in urban centres, as well as with teachers in schools, she was no radical. At a time when 'collaboration' with Bantustan authorities was frowned upon by those opposing the apartheid system, she chose to work closely with these authorities. But Bodenstein also interacted with, and had close social and cultural links with the liberal educational establishment in South Africa. She was an advocate of racial equality as well as African agency and leadership, albeit within a framework that did not actively oppose the Bantustan system.

In describing her life to me, Christel professes: 'my husband was always the most important person'. As a wife, she followed where he went, carving out her own space between his priorities and the needs of her children, in a manner typical of Hermannsburg families. Neither she nor her husband were, however, missionaries. Hans was born in 1924 and grew up in the impoverished circumstances of the mission station Empangweni at Moorleigh, where his father was the missionary.[8] In Stäcker's book of reminiscences, Hans recalls the deprivations of the Depression years, when he wore clothes made from maize-sacking, and he and his siblings worked hard digging and composting the vegetable gardens. He recalls his early schooling with its dreary rote learning and recitation, and evenings of family readings and analyses of pro-Nazi books such as Hitler's *Mein Kampf* – a situation that changed for the better when he was sent to the secondary school for the children of missionaries at Hermannsburg.

Unable to attend the nearby University of Natal in Pietermaritzburg, which had dismissed all German-speaking students in the period after the Second World War, he enrolled instead at the University of Pretoria. With the news from post-war Germany having shattered any 'illusion of a strong, proud Reich',[9] under the guidance of Heinz Dehnke, he and other young South Africans of German origin tried to stimulate and share a vision of hope and renewal among their communities through travelling theatre and song groups. Outside of his teaching responsibilities in Cape Town at St Martin's School, and later at the German school at Hermannsburg, Bodenstein developed a deep and lifelong interest in organising musical events. He was later able to further his studies at the University of Natal's Pietermaritzburg campus, and he went on to teach and study in Germany, in Hermannsburg and Göttingen. In 1967 he became active in a South African branch of the Lutheran World Federation-funded Christian Academy, an organisation of pastors and students, and was given the task of forging contacts between black and white churches, associations and organisations. He describes as a 'high point' the research at Umpumulo for the Missiological Institute around the themes of migrant labour in 1970 and church and development in 1971.[10]

From the early 1970s, Hans Bodenstein's interest moved to the education of black South Africans. He became principal of Edendale Technical High School in Pietermaritzburg where, in his final year, 27 out of 35 matriculants, he claimed, gained an A for Mathematics. At the same time, though, he had earned the wrath of the Bantu Education authorities for his anti-government perspectives.[11] In 1976 he received an invitation from Lucas Mangope, chief minister of the Bantustan that would become Bophuthatswana in 1977. Mangope, whom he had met as a student, asked him to develop and lead a higher technical school, to be funded by Johannesburg Consolidated Investments, in Thlabane near Rustenburg. The Bodensteins then moved to the nearby Hermannsburg community of Kroondal, described by Marcus Melck as a diasporic German community in South Africa.[12] Both Bodensteins were involved in the first Bophuthatswana Education Commission Report, 'Education for Popagano', in which Ken Hartshorne, an official in the national Department of Bantu Education, played a leading role.[13] Hans Bodenstein was made chairperson of the second commission in 1986, and thereafter became director of planning, assuming responsibility for the building of new schools. During this period, Christel Bodenstein ran the PEUP, and through his position Hans was able to make schools available to the programme.

The activities of the Bodensteins raise many questions regarding their involvement in the education system that they helped to create, as well as its nature and underlying principles. Also, as part of a community beginning to broaden its perspectives on education and society, what networks did the Bodensteins draw on? Christel Bodenstein clearly drew on current trends in international and development education, and the PEUP project consequently mimicked regional and international development education models.[14] Unlike early twentieth-century Hermannsburg approaches to education, the PEUP was firmly located in a progressivist, child-centred educational framework. However, budgets were not large enough to sustain the educational programme in the longer term, and Bantustan politics did not permit its broader realisation. While the failure of educational 'progressivism' (also known as child- or learner-centeredness) is not unique to South Africa, it is also the subject of histories of education in Botswana, where similar processes occurred in parallel.[15] This failure indicates that, however well received international educational ideas may be, they can also ultimately fail to indigenise as a consequence of context and history.

Bantu Education and Bantustan education

Until recently there has been little interest in the history of education in the Bantustans. But growing difficulties in provinces that incorporated former Bantustans have led to a renewed interest in their history and their legacies. A special issue of the *South African Historical Journal*, 'Let's Talk about the Bantustans', opens new approaches: while researchers recognise their functionality to the South African apartheid economy and the retribalisation and impoverishment that the Bantustans entailed, they also emphasise the need to move beyond the historiography of the 1970s and 1980s where they were viewed as 'simple instruments of control and repression', with responses to their creation dichotomised as collaboration versus resistance.[16] The Bantustan educational project should, however, be seen within the context of Bantu Education, which ultimately ensured its failure.

The introduction of Bantu Education in 1953 was a watershed, as it brought all mission schools in South Africa under full state control, operating on miserly budgets. Prior to this, the Bantu Authorities Act (No. 68 of 1951) inaugurated a new era of retribalisation, with education playing a key role in the eventual establishment of the Bantustans. But it was not plain sailing for the government. In 1957, the Bahurutse revolt in Zeerust revealed 'the depth of hostility to the Bantustan system in the northeast of the country'.[17] However, its defeat enabled the appointment of collaborationist chiefs two years later, in 1959. In terms of the Promotion of Bantu Self-Government Act (No. 46 of 1959), six territorial authorities were granted nominal independence between 1968 and 1969. Each was based on putative cultural and linguistic commonality. One such 'self-governing' state was established for the Tswana people in 1972; its chief minister was Lucas M. Mangope, a traditionalist in the battle between traditionalists and modernisers at the time of the Bahurutse revolt.[18] In 1977, Mangope became 'president' of the 'independent' Republic of Bophuthatswana. Promotion of ethnic nationalism was central to the existence of the Bantustan. 'Community' and 'culture' were key ideological themes. After a serious effort to promote Tswana ethnic nationhood earlier on, in the 1960s, Mangope briefly flirted with non-racial liberal democracy from the mid-1970s to the mid-1980s. This flirtation, which also saw the introduction of the PEUP, was, however, brought to a rapid close in 1988 when an attempted coup precipitated a drastic and repressive response with widespread arrests and a government purge. It was in this context that Bophuthatswana abandoned the chimera of non-racialism and reasserted ethnic nationalism.[19]

As Bernard Magubane points out, Bantustans created all the trappings of states: they built capitals, established parliaments and development boards, inaugurated presidents, designed flags, composed national anthems and, above all, devised mechanisms of control and coercion.[20] It went so far as histories being written for use in teacher training colleges and the new university, constructing a sense of a common Tswana history of education. One such, authored by African and Afrikaner academics, celebrated Bantu Education as heralding the expansion of education in the area, with the systematic introduction of mother-tongue instruction and a 'drive towards the indigenisation of education'.[21] At the same time, there were widespread removals of whole communities as the Bantustan became consolidated as a reservoir of labour for use in the cities. In this context, while a liberal, child-centred project was undoubtedly an anomaly, it might nevertheless be viewed as part of Mangope's effort, in the first phase of his rule, to legitimate the Bantustan through the assimilation of the trappings and symbols of a liberal democratic, non-racial state.[22]

In theory, each Bantustan could devise its own education system: it had its own minister of Education and secretary of Education, with professional and administrative staff that enabled it to draft its own legislation. In practice, Bantustan education departments largely operated under regulations that fell under the umbrella of the South African Bantu Education department; accordingly, Acts tended to be modelled on the parent Education and Training Act (No. 90 of 1979).[23] The goals and curricula of Bantu Education provided the overall framework for Bantustan education, and there was close cooperation between the Department of Bantu Education and Bantustan authorities. The intended curriculum and goals of Bantu Education were primarily to limit and reorient African political, economic and social aspirations away from a common political and economic life towards a separate, rurally focused existence. This would be achieved through separate funding – which was grossly unequal – for racially as well as ethnically distinct departments of education, and the location of teacher training in the Bantustans. The financing of schools – and consequently their material conditions – in the Bantustans always lagged behind that of schools that fell under the central Department of Education and Training (DET), which in turn were disadvantaged in comparison with the education delivered to the coloured, Indian and white sectors. Average pupil-teacher ratios, class size, and prevalence of double sessions were routinely higher in schools in Bantustan rural areas than in DET schools, most of which were urban based.[24]

Bantustan syllabi broadly followed the template of Bantu Education curricula for African schools in 'white' South Africa. The difference in the enacted curriculum was that the much poorer funding for Bantustan curricula enabled far less than in other schools. The graded readers available in some urban township schools were not available in countless Bantustan schools. A key difference between the white Transvaal Education Department syllabi and those of Bantu Education, and by extension those of Bantustans, was the fact that mother tongue was the compulsory medium of instruction throughout the eight years of primary schooling for all subjects. This meant that, while white schools taught only two languages in the primary grades, i.e. English and Afrikaans, African children had to take three languages from Grade 1: English, Afrikaans and the home language.[25]

While, on paper, subjects to be taken in white and African schools were broadly similar, there were differences of depth, time allocation, and resourcing. Primary school subjects included Religious Education, Afrikaans, English, Home Language (African schools), Arithmetic, Environment Studies (African schools), History and Geography (white schools), Health Education (African schools), Handwriting, Music, Arts and Crafts and Gardening (African schools), Art and Science (white schools). As Curtis Nkondo points out, Bantu Education pupils were three years behind white pupils, even when the age of school entry (five for white children; seven for African children) was taken into account.[26]

Curricula for African children were much narrower and more circumscribed, so that 'by the time the T.Edc. [Transvaal Education] Department children complete Standard 2 [Grade 4], they have been taken out of their home districts and have been introduced to a much larger area of their country and their world than the B.Edc. [Bantu Education] children, who have only learned briefly about the physical features of their province'.[27] In addition, resources for teaching purposes were virtually non-existent in Bantu Education schools. Teachers' guides were inferior to those produced for white schools. History teaching at primary level was limited, and at secondary level curricula became explicitly vocational and agriculturally oriented, to the extent that teachers resisted implementing them.[28] It needs to be borne in mind, furthermore, that the exit qualification for teachers at that stage was Standard 6, so that teachers themselves, especially in rural areas, were poorly equipped to teach an elaborated curriculum. Much of this 'education for servitude', as Nkondo describes it, would have prevailed in schools in Bophuthatswana had not the PEUP attempted a programme of reform.

The Primary Education Upgrade Programme (PEUP): educational progressivism, ethnic nationalism and transnationalism

The PEUP grew out of the recommendations of Bophuthatswana's 1978 commission of inquiry into education, also known as the 'Education for Popagano', report. It encompassed the entire spectrum of education, from early childhood to higher and adult education. Its recommendations were based on a combination of principles which simultaneously promoted progressivist educational principles and a narrow ethnic nationalism. Before examining the recommendations of the PEUP in greater depth, it may be necessary to spell out what progressivism in education has meant over time.

Educational progressivism has been the subject of considerable educational historical investigation. It has its roots in nineteenth-century European educational thinkers such as Froebel and Pestalozzi, mentioned above; in the early twentieth century it became entrenched in transatlantic educational thought through the work of John Dewey (1859–1952), with its emphasis on democracy. South Africa's New Era Fellowship of the 1930s owed much to these ideas.[29] As educational historian David F. Labaree has observed, educational progressivism today refers principally to 'pedagogical progressivism', which means:

> basing instruction on the needs, interests and developmental stage of the
> child; it means teaching students the skills they need in order to learn

any subject, instead of focusing on transmitting a particular subject; it means promoting discovery and self-directed learning by the student through active engagement; it means having students work on projects that express student purposes. . . . In the short-hand of educational jargon, this adds up to "child-centred instruction," "discovery learning" and "learning how to learn." And . . . there is a single label that captures this entire approach to education: constructivism.[30]

There are many variants of progressivism, with some educational historians, specifically in the United States of America, differentiating between administrative and pedagogical progressives, conservative and liberal progressives, while others focus on social efficiency, child development and social reconstruction progressives.[31] This is specific to the history of education in the United States, but given its influence internationally, and at various times also on South African educationists such as Malherbe (see Chapter 5 above), it is worth relating South African practices to the broad practice of progressivism. The PEUP may thus best be described as a type of conservative progressivism, given its affiliation with an apartheid project promoting ethnic nationalism. Historically, pedagogical progressivism has contrasted with the 'drill, discipline and didactic exercises' associated with Bantu Education.[32] In South Africa, pedagogical progressivism, in its more conservative as well as more liberal forms, found expression in approaches that had been developed among NGOs as an alternative to the narrow curriculum of Bantu Education and its emphasis on rote learning; it found expression too in the reformist post-apartheid outcomes-based educational approach, which was implemented in the period 1997 to 2009. Labaree's observation that progressivism, and its offshoot constructivism, has had a greater impact on educational rhetoric than on the actual structure and practice of education in schools is apposite in evaluating progressivism in South Africa.[33]

The 'Education for Popagano' report embraced four main philosophical elements: 'the creation of a new self-reliance and confidence', 'progress and development', 'building of a new nation', and 'cooperation and interdependence'.[34] Proposals for the restructuring into primary, middle and high school, already been made in the Bantu Education department, were taken up in the Popagano report under the influence of Hartshorne.[35] A position antithetical to Bantu Education was however taken in recommendations to change both the structure and pedagogy of the primary education curriculum. These included the introduction of an early childhood education programme, the phasing out of double sessions in Grades 1 and 2, the extension of the school day to include more Music, Drama and Physical Movement classes, the division of Social Studies into History and Geography in Standards 3 and 4, making religious education a non-examinable subject, and, from the first grades, the introduction of English alongside Tswana as preparation for the switch to English as the medium of instruction from Standard 3 (i.e. after four years).[36] Specific attention would be given to modernising the language curricula. Pedagogically, Popagano critiqued the dominant classroom norm in which there was 'still too great a passivity on the part of pupils'.[37] Instead, it advocated increased 'activity, participation, creativity, problem-solving, individual responsibility' – all the issues that are essential to progressivist thought in education, or, as its framers put it, 'modernization of the mind'.[38] The report argued that Bophuthatswana could not afford to educate 'only passive "followers" in its classrooms: individual drive and initiative were needed'.[39]

The Popagano goals thus differed in some respects from those underpinning Bantu Education as a whole. Popagano included goals for Grades 1 to Standard 4 (Grade 6) to develop not only 'functional, effective numeracy, and literacy in Tswana and English and to a lesser extent in Afrikaans' but also 'the child's creativity, capacity for problem-solving and awareness by participation in school'. The goals for 'creation of a degree of national pride and consciousness, good social attitudes and acceptable moral standards', along with a 'basic knowledge of the environment and positive attitudes to health' were, however, more in line with those of Bantu Education. The goals for middle school – Standard 5 to Standard 7 – were envisaged as developing both a 'broad general education' as well as a 'love of country, of Setswana language and literature, of the history and traditions of the people, and a broad unity of national purpose'.[40] Some of the pedagogical dimensions of the Popagano vision were thus broader than those in the Bantu Education syllabi.

The methodology that the members of the National Education Commission used to gather evidence and make recommendations helped to legitimise these and to give its members some authority. The commission was chaired by E.P. Lekhela, retired professor of Education from the University of the North, and consisted of ten Batswana and five white members. The Batswana included school principals, teacher trainers, chief inspectors, and members of the Bophuthatswana Education department. The white members all came from church or mission education backgrounds. They included 'social gospel' Methodist, Ken Hartshorne (a former principal of Kilnerton College who had recently retired as a planner in the Bantu Education department);

Hans Bodenstein, and his wife Christel; and two Roman Catholic nuns, Sr Louis Michael McDonagh and Sr Mary Margaret O'Brien.[41]

The commission's modus operandi involved receiving memoranda and evidence, though members also had 'regular discussions with small groups and large public meetings with parents, students, teachers and the traditional leaders'.[42] According to Hartshorne, criticisms of Bantu Education were soon overtaken by recommendations that considered 'the needs of Bophuthatswana'. What it meant to be a Motswana – a Tswana person – was 'of over-riding importance' to the Batswana members, he said, and this issue comprised a full chapter in the commission's report. The promotion of Tswana nationhood was not perceived as contradictory to the adoption of child-centred elements in schooling.

Popagano and PEUP were similar to the Kagisano Report and the Primary Education Improvement Project in neighbouring Botswana.[43] However, Botswana's initiative was a donor-funded USAID project, while the Bophuthatswana project was not. Botswana borrowed its ideas from the United States and the United Kingdom, but Christel Bodenstein and her colleagues had few links with the US; they took their ideas from European and British progressive educational theory and integrated these into a meliorative, liberal development approach. A visit to Israel, with which Mangope maintained close ties, had also introduced Bodenstein to decentralised models of school improvement.[44] Both programmes had state support, but the Bophuthatswana initiative differed from the Botswana project in that the latter enjoyed international legitimacy. Nonetheless, it developed from a local initiative and worked closely with local NGOs and non-departmental personnel, which gave a certain legitimacy to the overall project.

Essentially part and parcel of South Africa, the political entity of Bophuthatswana was a mirage to all but its creators; as such, its relationship was always first and foremost with South Africa, rather than with either Botswana, the United Kingdom or indeed other countries such as Israel. The consequences were tortuous grapplings with the meaning of the entity known as 'Bop', even as resources remained constrained. Trying to construct an alternative vision within this context, those intellectuals associated with the PEUP had to grapple with the ambiguities of (in)dependence bequeathed by Bop's relationship to South Africa. The motivation for change and search for room for manoeuvre came from within these ethnic enclaves, some argued, while the resistance came from above: 'always in the background Pretoria wielded its purse, showing clear disapproval and manipulating opposition when changes were envisaged that were contrary to South African education policy'.[45] Others argued that Bophuthatswana was simply 'a laboratory' in which South Africa experimented with 'new ways of modernising apartheid or moving away from the more dysfunctional aspects of apartheid'.[46]

The PEUP was funded by South African government allocations to the Bantustan, but this was always insufficient for its needs. Bodenstein, a tireless fundraiser, approached the private sector and external donors. Mining giant Johannesburg Consolidated Investment (JCI), whose wealth derived from local platinum mines, was an early supporter. The Development Bank and the Independent Development Trust (IDT) also contributed.[47] Additional funds were secured through the British Council for teacher exchanges with Leeds University, with whom the PEUP organisers maintained close contact.[48] Bodenstein's methods, as we shall see, even included asking hard-pressed parents for contributions. Key Britons involved in the programme included A.R. Thompson, director of the Overseas Education Unit at Bristol University, Jimmy Taylor of the Overseas Education Unit at Leeds, and Rick Collet, British Council trainer in Molteno Programmes and inspector for Multicultural Education in Kent. The project was successful in drawing additional funding from various sources outside the South African government, but the British link remained strong throughout.

The PEUP in practice

The objectives of the PEUP were both infrastructural and pedagogical.[49] The organisers aimed to turn the learning environment into a rich, stimulating environment for children by, for example, ensuring that classroom walls were painted, and that there was an adequate water supply, as well as improving school toilet facilities. But infrastructural improvement was generally quite basic and initially relied on parental contributions. Bodenstein states the following:

> [I]t took some time until I got to that point that I could do something. But I thought really one can do small things, and you can start with little things and just change those. We started with the programme that . . . got the teachers to collect money to buy. Because they didn't have any furniture. They were just sitting in the classroom. There was no furniture there. We took time and we collected furniture. . . . That was a major achievement when we started collecting money for furniture because I insisted on the furniture . . . the lay-out was important for learning. Something that always haunted me was child-centred education. I sort of hung onto that. Child-centred education. That for me was the operative word.[50]

But it was not an easy task, as she points out: 'We got to a stage where I managed to persuade the powers-that-be to buy furniture for these classrooms. That was quite a hard nut to crack. . . . I kept on talking to them. I went to them and talked to them and I said, "Look. The classroom must echo that child-centeredness. You must be able to look (after) your environment".[51]

In order to enter the programme, schools had to demonstrate their commitment to an upgrading process, and were required to fulfil five conditions. They had to commit themselves to single teaching sessions – at the time, double sessions where children received three hours' teaching were common in both urban townships and rural areas, such as those where she worked. Schools had to limit their class sizes to 50, as most were well in excess of this. Unlike other schools under Bantu Education, where pupils were admitted at the age of seven, Bophuthatswana schools were permitted to admit pupils from the age of five and a half years. They were also required to carry out certain classroom improvements, such as constructing shelves, at their own expense, and to contribute on a rand-for-rand basis towards the purchase of furniture. Though this cost was initially intended to be absorbed by parents, this is unlikely to have occurred, since Bodenstein sought additional funds and lobbied the education department for increased resources.

In 1980 Bodenstein worked with principals and teachers to upgrade and renovate Grade 1 classrooms, organise children into ability groups, and encourage teachers to introduce more child-centred and discovery-learning approaches. By the end of that year, seven schools had already became 'model schools' or 'satellites' for others. Each year, additional schools were linked to the programme as satellite schools, and began 'the upgrading journey moving from Grade 1 to Standard 4 which marks the end of primary education in Bophuthatswana'.[52] The programme expanded dramatically: from 7 schools in 1980, it grew to 114 in 1981 and 625 in 1983. Two years later, 760 out of a total 840 primary schools (i.e. over 90%) were involved.[53]

The implementation of classroom-based changes began with changing the understanding and approaches of teachers. Despite the existence of several teacher training colleges, primary schools were relatively badly served. In 1981, when a range of diplomas were introduced in Bophuthatswana for primary and secondary school teachers, the vast majority of black primary school teachers had no more qualification to teach than their own primary or junior-secondary schooling, at times with a three-year diploma that in most cases testified to a mere repetition of content taught at school.[54] Many teachers so qualified were also used at secondary school levels. Upgrading programmes were run by

NGOs and the Bophuthatswana government in the 1970s and 1980s, but with inconclusive success.[55]

Both the newly established University of Bophuthatswana and the teacher training college, where Christel Bodenstein was based, became centres for the implementation of the PEUP. Its teacher training programme was closely integrated into the school improvement programme. In addition to introducing new teacher education courses from 1980, which combined theory and practice, teacher training for the PEUP consisted of intensive one-week courses covering all the subjects in the primary school curriculum at any given level, as well as observations of teaching practice in model school classrooms, and coaching in the new methods by PEUP organisers.[56] The university also provided the central distribution point. In this regard, Francine de Clercq, an academic in Unibo's Education department at the time, and who was interested in but not directly connected with the project, recalls observing the 'huge operation of delivering the materials to the far remote areas'.[57]

Holderness has described the excitement of the early days of his involvement in the PEUP. The programme would begin with teachers and principals being introduced to the new ideas in a community hall in a village. Thereafter they would observe demonstration classes in nearby Grade 1 classrooms and return for discussions, having been 'inspired' in the classrooms.[58] Through discussion, participants would prepare for the next day, and also the next school, thus continuing the process of observation, reflection and preparation. This method appears to have had moderate success with respect to motivating teachers to do things differently. The involvement in the training by South African NGOs such as the South African Council for Higher Education (SACHED), which were committed to exploring educational alternatives to Bantu Education, may be explained by the persuasive powers of Bodenstein in presenting the PEUP as an authentic alternative to Bantu Education. Its 'alternative' character, she argued, was manifested in its pedagogical progressivism which was contrary to general practice in Bantu Education schools, and common to the anti-apartheid educational movement.[59] Hartshorne does however make the point that Transkei and Bophuthatswana developed school systems different from those in South Africa: they set up their own curricula and examinations – except at senior certificate level – with Bophuthatswana having a teacher education system that did not rely on Department of Education and Training courses and certification, but were linked instead to the University of Bophuthatswana.[60]

Part of the success of the project depended on its structured programme, its organisation, and the involvement of all key players in the provision

of education. As it grew, circuit teams consisting of local programme education officers, principals, teachers, and college lecturers were identified. They
ran the in-service courses, prepared reading and writing materials, and conducted follow-up school visits. Christel Bodenstein, Bill Holderness, Nancy
Motlala, Rosina Moalusi and Molly Mosimane worked with the 'Bop' department of education. But their relationship with the department and school
inspectors, despite official support from Mangope in the initial stages, was not
easy. Bodenstein stated bluntly in 2009: 'They were an absolute pain. That's
why when I showed you those pictures – there are pictures of inspectors
learning to read – I made them do that. They had to learn what it means to
read. Whatever we could lay our hands on. And the higher you got, the worse
they were'.[61]

The most significant aspects of the PEUP were however the pedagogical
changes effected inside the classroom. Pupils were divided into ability groups
so that each child could, at least in theory, learn at his/her own pace, become
an active learner, and fully participate in the learning process. In the early
grades, the Molteno Project's Breakthrough to Literacy method was a critical innovation to improve literacy. Bodenstein first encountered it through the
work of Victor Rodseth and Leonard Lanham at Rhodes University's Institute
for the Study of English in Africa. Breakthrough to Literacy was an integrated
approach of reading, writing, oral work and phonics, adapted from the British
Breakthrough to Literacy Programme prepared in the UK by the Schools
Council Programme in Linguistics and English Teaching. In 1990, some 30%
of children in the UK were taught to read with the same method.[62]

According to Rodseth, it was 'the crown of her [Bodenstein's] upgrading
scheme', representing 'a radical shift from teacher-centred to learner-centred
education'.[63] Instead of teaching literacy through teachers instructing children
to chant words by rote from chalkboards without any additional resources,
as was common practice, children were taught language through readers,
word-picture charts on walls, and word-cards, or 'flash cards'. In addition to
this, the use of 'sentence-makers' encouraged children to take individual letters,
and to arrange them to form words. This method was used in the first year of
Tswana language classes, and from the second year in English classes. In addition to the Breakthrough to Literacy innovation, an important aspect of the
PEUP was the elimination of end-of-year examinations up to and including
Standard 3, with automatic promotion of pupils at these levels. Released from
the constraints of formal testing and the consequent cramming, teachers were
free to institute child-centred methods at the lower end of the primary school.

In the overall context of Bantu Education, as will be demonstrated below, these elements of the PEUP altered the classroom experience, and they seem also to have influenced literacy levels in the early years.

Bodenstein retired in 1986, though by then relations with Mangope had already begun to cool, as he seemingly became less and less reliant on white liberals for his authority. In 1988, PEUP was effectively closed down as a consequence of the coup and Mangope's subsequent clampdown.

Academic assessments, programme evaluations and teacher responses

A decade after its introduction, the PEUP was acknowledged as having made an impact on teacher-pupil ratios, grade repetition, as well as throughput rates and matric results.[64] Despite significantly constrained resources, the matric pass rate was considered to be substantially higher than in the other Bantustans during the period 1987 to 1990.[65] These achievements were ascribed to the PEUP.

Hartshorne's assessment is that, while 'some changes were brought about in various homelands . . . the school systems in general continued to operate very much as in the rest of South Africa'.[66] Ultimately, the entire PEUP approach was undermined by the squeeze on resources at both secondary and post-school level. The broader apartheid policy impacted fundamentally upon it in terms of the population resettlement programme, the emphasis on ethnicity and traditionalism, as well as a host of issues related to household poverty.[67]

As a consequence, and notwithstanding this brief period of educational innovation, there was no long-term impact. The greater impact appears to have been the broader political and socio-economic trajectory of the region, which, though part of the grand apartheid design, showed distinct particularities. For example, at no point in the brief history of Bophuthatswana was the education budget allocated to it by Pretoria anything other than paltry. It was for many years well below that received by white, Indian, coloured or urban African schools in the rest of South Africa.[68] Additional resources allocated by national government and funds raised from external donors could not compensate for the deprivation and inequality imposed by national policy. Thus, the PEUP became embedded and was implemented for a brief period, but its long-term effects were more limited: it was not sustained beyond a ten-year period, if that.

Although the successes of PEUP did generate 'some national pride',[69] in that it was 'one of the best ventures ever to be introduced in the school system in black schools in the subregion',[70] programme evaluations have pointed to certain fundamental weaknesses in its approach. Detailed evaluations were conducted by Samuel Lehobye[71] and Carol Macdonald.[72] Lehobye's most significant finding was that, although the programme enjoyed substantial success in the grades and first two standards, its success declined after Standard 2 (Grade 4). Whereas the same teacher could teach the whole curriculum up to the end of Standard 2, the curriculum from Standard 3 (Grade 5) required specialised knowledge and different methods. It thus became increasingly difficult for the teacher to address the curriculum while simultaneously following a child-centred methodology. There was thus 'progressively less support for the aims and activities propagated for the programme by the senior classes'.[73] Although the first new corps of teachers had been trained at colleges now working in association with the University of Bophuthatswana, 'the new primary teachers' programme introduced in the colleges did not specifically cater for the needs of the primary schools in terms of relevance and content'.[74] Also, there were complaints about the lack of alignment regarding the training and the material to be taught, as well as neglect of the practical component of teaching experience.

Shortcomings in the programme as identified by Lehobye related mainly to the senior phase or lower secondary schooling. Above and beyond teacher competence, they included the incompatibility of textbooks in this phase with the new philosophy and practices of learner-centred education, teachers' English language proficiency, and the lack of departmental and in-service support. These phases appeared to require something more than the learner-centred methods of the earlier phases.

The focus of Macdonald's study was assessing the efficacy of the PEUP classroom in preparing children for Standard 3.[75] Like Lehobye, she had nothing but praise for the coordination and organisation of the PEUP. And similarly, she found that methods were more progressive in the early grades and 'almost wholly traditional by Standard 3'.[76] Teachers in Standard 3 had difficulty in using classic PEUP methods, mainly because the differentiation of children into three ability groups, and the need to design lessons and materials for all three simultaneously, imposed enormous demands on teachers.[77] The result was that teaching was simply not done on a regular basis. Macdonald did, however, find more mixed evidence on teachers using a child-centred approach, as well as on the scholastic achievement of pupils, the nature of learning experiences, and the use of a cooperative approach. The nature of testing and the accent on creative expression were found to be the only truly progressive educational elements in PEUP classrooms.[78]

Macdonald's most significant conclusion was that the particular style of differentiated learning adopted in the junior primary grades created a time management problem for teachers, who were thus unable to prepare children adequately for later standards in language skills and concepts. Much of what the PEUP set out to do it had achieved, she claims, with the exception of the development of the child as a problem-solver and learner of concepts.[79] A major additional problem she identified[80] was the transition from mother tongue to English in Standard 3: by the time children reached the end of Standard 2, they were inadequately prepared for suddenly learning ten subjects through the medium of English. Her proposal was not to adopt a 'straight for English' approach, but to ensure a 'gradual transition'.[81] Once again, given the constraints outlined above, there was no opportunity to build on the researcher's evaluative remarks.

And yet, despite these limitations, there is evidence that the PEUP became firmly embedded in institutional and cultural memory. As such, there were continuities between interpenetrations of pedagogical practice across successive historical phases. During interviews conducted in 2009, a group of teachers recalled a glorious past where teachers were trained properly and children learnt to read and write.[82] In contrast with current approaches, the PEUP provided a successful method as well as a process for teaching children to learn. 'When PEUP started,' one recalled, 'teachers were a bit negative'. However, this attitude 'changed when they saw the results. Those learners could read and write compared with students now. Something wrong is happening in the Foundation Phase now. At that time our learners were so good that we were able to send them to Batswana High School, the International school, Model C [former white] schools'.

Other teachers recalled the PEUP being introduced at a time when schools were massively overcrowded, classes were full of over-aged children, and teachers struggled with a lack of resources. The PEUP's success was associated with its strong coordination, its 'scripted' or detailed and explicit learning process, the teaching resources it provided (such as sentence makers, charts and teaching kits), as well as the systematic teacher training in PEUP methods provided in workshops. Not surprisingly, these teachers held that it was 'a good system because at the end of six months the learners could write'.

This all came to an end, however, in 1996 with the introduction of the new post-apartheid educational philosophy, outcomes-based education (OBE), when teachers were told that PEUP methods were 'a thing of the past'. For the teachers concerned, the switch to OBE was distressing, but they nevertheless adapted to it, 'mixing' the precepts of the new, at that stage ill-defined and jargon-filled OBE with their own known methods of teaching. Their descriptions suggest a 'mix of strategies',[83] and a complexity in the translation of ideas into practice. What Bodenstein has to say of her fellow coordinators is illustrative of the effects of the change in the regime:

> Rosina was a very independent sort of person and she very much went her own way. But once the flood of the new kind of education that was coming, which didn't come, was there, it just didn't work. Rosina died. Molly is still around. They were very isolated once the new regime had taken over.

Conclusion

The PEUP was an educational project brought into being by a long-standing alliance between Hermannsburgers and African chiefs. Although relations were often conflictual in the pre-apartheid period, alliances were forged during the early apartheid period through the schools the Hermannsburgers established, and the specific relationships that developed between Lucas Mangope and Hermannsburgers through the agency, inter alia, of Heinz Dehnke. Hans and Christel Bodenstein, although closely connected to the tradition, were not missionaries themselves. Nor was their approach primarily religious – or indeed ethnically based. And yet they had no difficulty accommodating either approach. Christel promoted a pedagogical progressivism with an international dimension that relied for its success on work with women. The PEUP thus combined seemingly contradictory principles: educational progressivism and ethnic nationalism. While not contradictory to the broad precepts of Bantu Education and how Bantustans were intended to realise these, there were certain aspects and innovations that ran counter to the goals and practices of Bantu Education. Apart from the effort to create attractive and child-friendly classrooms, the programme included principally the introduction of early-childhood education programmes; an emphasis on interactive teaching and learning methods using well-developed resources generally lacking in the resource-constrained Bantu Education classroom; the use of the Molteno Breakthrough to Literacy method; attempts to differentiate by ability inside the classroom; and the elimination of formal testing. Significantly, teacher training was central to the implementation of the programme. New teacher training qualifications were devised, and teachers were specifically trained and coached in new methods through active approaches based on demonstration and reflection on teaching activities and experiences. The vast majority of the new teachers were women.

To conclude, then, the past may be said to leave traces of strong yet fragile, forgotten and hidden legacies in an ever-changing present. South Africa now has a well-documented educational history. But little attention has been paid to the people who brought the systems into being. Such studies are necessary to better understand current conflicts and debates in the educational sphere. Conflict and contradiction have been integral to the complementary positioning of countries, ideas and practices in processes of adoption and indigenisation. In this story, the local and the global have been as intertwined and inseparable as are the past and the present. Educational progressivism has found local expression in the most unlikely corners, leaving 'deposits' that add to the richness and diversity of the history of the experience. Efforts to construct 'purified' histories or pedagogies, from whatever angle, are bound to caricature and conceal the complexity and diversity of educational practice. It is only through the recognition of this complexity and diversity, in the present as well as the past, that the full scope of historical change may be appreciated.

CHAPTER 9

INKATHA AND THE HERMANNSBURGERS

Like Bophuthatswana, the KwaZulu Bantustan made its own distinctive mark on the education system within its jurisdiction. It did so with the introduction in 1978 of its *Ubuntu-botho* (good citizenship) syllabus, and also by establishing Youth Brigades in all schools. Unlike their Popagano experience in Bophuthatswana, the Hermannsburgers did not play a significant role in educational developments at the official Bantustan level. And, unlike the Popagano Commission report which was generally praised by liberals and intellectuals, the 1978 syllabus devised by Mangosuthu Buthelezi's Inkatha party[1] invited much criticism. In the following decade, for example, Praisley Mdluli's study, 'Ubuntu-botho: Inkatha's People's Education', and Gerhard Maré's 'Education in a "Liberated Zone": Inkatha and education in KwaZulu-Natal' perceived it as an instrument of propaganda, intended to create loyal Inkatha followers, while Johan Graaff's 1994 report saw it quite simply as 'An Instrument of War'.[2] Inkatha, the party of Bantustan leader Gatsha Buthelezi, tried to cast it as a syllabus that focused on 'Education Now for Liberty Tomorrow' in opposition to the popular slogan 'Liberation Now, Education Later!' that had caught fire in the townships under the auspices of the United Democratic Front (UDF) campaign. As a compulsory, non-examinable subject introduced by Inkatha, and taught through a number of textbooks in all years for one hour a week, the opposition it provoked was symptomatic of the violent conflict in the region at the time. It is important to determine what role the Hermannsburgers played in developing this syllabus, and to attempt to understand their educational role during this period.

The 1970s and 1980s were critical years for the Hermannsburgers in Zululand and Natal. With their role in schooling diminishing, in Natal they started to play a larger part in broader cooperative Lutheran activities. During this period when Bantustan policy was put into practice, Hermannsburgers worked closely with the authorities in two areas where Bantustans came into being: the Western Transvaal and Natal/Zululand.[3] Whereas Mangope embraced the idea of self-determination as spelt out within the framework set by the National Party government, Buthelezi took every opportunity to participate in it while simultaneously presenting himself as being in opposition to the entire concept.[4] He was adept at working within the system while promoting the appearance of not doing so. Both Mangope and Buthelezi sought to create legitimacy for themselves through various symbolic initiatives, particularly in the sphere of education. Both leaders constantly played off a rhetoric of independence against the reality of their collaboration with the apartheid state through the Bantustan system. The initiatives of both came into being in the aftermath of the 1976 Soweto uprising and heightened resistance in schools throughout the 1980s. They self-consciously set their programmes up as alternatives to both apartheid and anti-apartheid proponents. As demonstrated above, Hermannsburgers played a distinct role as well as exercising influence in the education strategies of Mangope. In evaluating the situation in KwaZulu, this chapter considers the role of the Hermannsburgers in Inkatha's *Ubuntu-botho* syllabus, compares it with their role in Bophuthatswana, and then examines the Hermannsburgers' simultaneous support of and marginalisation as missionaries within Bantustan politics in KwaZulu. Here the development of the syllabus was dominated by males, within a highly patriarchal organisation. Part of this narrative also illustrates, as in the previous chapter, how Hermannsburg women increasingly played a role not only as wives but also as public figures.

Inkatha's *Ubuntu-botho* syllabus and the Hermannsburgers

There is no direct evidence of the involvement of Hermannsburgers in the development of the syllabus or textbooks in KwaZulu. Mdluli and Maré both maintain that the syllabus was developed by the Natal African Teachers' Union (NATU), the black Inspectors' Association, and University of Zululand academics who were also members of Inkatha.[5] The latter may have included P.C. Luthuli and E.P. Ndaba, educationists who were deeply influenced by Fundamental Pedagogics, which had in turn been inspired by the policy of

Christian National Education.[6] Fundamental Pedagogics was a 'particular style
of theorising education' that became hegemonic in institutions involved in
teacher training, in particular in the Afrikaans-speaking universities and their
satellites, institutions of higher education for Africans, the first of which were
established on an ethnic basis in 1959. Fundamental Pedagogics included a
number of sub-disciplines that made claims to universalism and scientificity.
According to its critics, Fundamental Pedagogics was the ideological underpinning in teacher education of apartheid education.[7]

Although the éminence grise of the notion of *Ubuntu-botho* within Inkatha
was J.K. Ngubane, Oscar Dhlomo, the minister of Education and Culture in
the KwaZulu Legislative Assembly who introduced the related syllabus in
1978, probably played a key role in consolidating it. Like Buthelezi, Dhlomo
had matriculated at Adams College before going on to study History and
Anthropology and gaining his post-graduate University Education Diploma at
the newly established University of Zululand under the tutelage of Afrikaner
academics who promoted ethnic and culturalist perspectives. In 1974 he was
appointed as a lecturer in Didactics at the university where he specialised in
teaching history. There, he completed his MEd in 1975. Having been awarded a
British Council Scholarship and the Ernest Oppenheimer University Travelling
Fellowship in 1977, Dhlomo travelled to Britain, the United States and various
African countries, researching current trends in teacher training.[8]

Dhlomo was heavily influenced not only by Afrikaner practitioners of
Fundamental Pedagogics such as H.J.S. Stone and R.M. Ruperti, but also by
the work of Babs Fafunwa, a Nigerian educationist who argued for the freeing
of African education from colonial influence and its adaptation to culturally
relevant, local community needs and goals.[9] In their call for local relevance,
there was some continuity with earlier 'adapted education' ideas developed by
Natal segregationists such as C.T. Loram.[10] But in Inkatha's educational thinking, the call was linked to notions of the pseudo-independence offered by the
Bantustans and traditional authorities. In 1980 Dhlomo completed his Doctor
of Education degree, which focused on teacher training.[11] It was an effort to
assess what was necessary for a system of teacher education in the KwaZulu
Bantustan, which he characterised as 'a developing country'.[12] Dhlomo was
particularly taken with ideas about the role of teachers as community devel-
opers and agents of social change. In 1978, a year after his return to South
Africa, Dhlomo became secretary general of Inkatha, and was appointed minister of Education and Culture. He introduced the *Ubuntu-botho* syllabus, which
sought local relevance through the assertion of an ethnic cultural nationalism:

it promoted Inkatha as the main source of unity, nationhood and liberation of and for Zulus, and for South Africans as a whole.[13]

Maré contends that Buthelezi and Inkatha had links with white people whose backgrounds were not so much religious as agricultural, industrial or academic.[14] Lawrence Schlemmer of the University of Natal was particularly influential, tasked as he was with running the Inkatha Institute, a think-tank whose main activity comprised the development of the Buthelezi Commission. In 1982 the commission published a set of policy analyses, prescriptions and recommendations,[15] and it grew into the KwaZulu-Natal Indaba which in turn created the KwaZulu-Natal Joint Executive Authority. Hermannsburg-educated men and women counted among the people who supported Inkatha and kept it in an 'uncritical focus'.[16] One such was Arthur Jacob Konigkramer who was a journalist with the *Natal Mercury* from 1964 to 1973, editorial director of *Ilanga Lase Natal* from 1973 to 1979, and general manager of the Mandla-Matla Publishing Corporation from 1980 to 1986.[17] While men such as these had been socialised through the Hermannsburg network, they themselves were not missionaries.

The Buthelezi Commission published its report a year after that of the De Lange Commission of Inquiry into education was published in 1981. Both were part of, as well as symptomatic of, the reformist thrust within apartheid at the time. They also shared the same limitations, working and making proposals for change within a framework that did not fundamentally challenge existing power relations between black and white. Both were major policy initiatives, the Buthelezi Commission ranging more broadly than education, and the De Lange Report, coordinated by the Human Sciences Research Council, specifically focusing on education. Within education, both provided information on finance, control and management of the system, curriculum-related matters, and so on. Both attempted to encompass the entire system, sketching its key features, what needed to change, and how change might be brought about. Both made tentative steps towards recommending integration of the educational systems – though within a broader political framework that did not permit this.

The commissions drew on similar people to develop their reports, none of whom were Hermannsburgers or particularly influenced by the Hermannsburgers. While more radical members of liberal universities eschewed these commissions, staff members from the University of Zululand who associated themselves with Inkatha participated freely. Oscar Dhlomo, for example, was a member of the management committee of the De Lange Commission. The education section of the Buthelezi Commission was chaired by Dennis Gower Fannin, a scion of the Natal English-speaking legal elite. Among the Buthelezi Commission sources were the writings of Inkatha stalwarts Dhlomo, P.C. Luthuli, Frank Mdlalose, C.L.S. Nyembezi and Ndaba Nene, as well as material from the KwaZulu legislature, Inkatha Institute and the Natal African Teachers' Union. A number of references cited white liberal educationists as well as the educational initiative in Bophuthatswana. There were no sources that could be traced to the Hermannsburgers, however.

Nonetheless, the philosophy that underpinned the *Ubuntu-botho* syllabus arose from the same ideas that shaped the thinking of Hermannsburgers such as Heinz Dehnke, and that saw a unity between language, ethnicity and nationhood. The draft syllabus committee of 1978, as cited by Maré, for example, wrote that the committee was influenced by:

> The need to develop among our youth the whole person within the ambit of the Inkatha Constitution. For this reason the study of the individual as a member of a family which family is part of the community and which community is part of the nation is essential. The rehabilitation of many people from social problems like drink, crime, poverty, continued illegitimacy is as important as the prevention of these social problems in the building up of a strong and united nation.[18]

The textbooks developed for *Ubuntu-botho* appear very similar to the early missionary textbooks in Zulu upon which the Bantu Education prescribed list relied, and which were used in schools up to the 1970s.[19] But in the curious blending of Black Consciousness with the celebration of ethnic history that was the hallmark of Inkatha, the syllabus and textbooks defined black history in terms of

> the concept of race; rulers and nation builders in building Black Africa before the advent of White rule; colonization; the struggle for liberation from white rule; liberation movements such as the OAU, pan-Africanism, African nationalism and the role of Zulu people; role of educational, religious and other organisations in the struggle for liberation; the significance of the Black American's struggle; the struggle in South Africa – the land question, riots, liberalism, racial discrimination, *the homelands and the future* [sic].[20]

Mdluli provides an extensive analysis of the textbooks that were produced by KwaZulu Booksellers, a publishing company in Pietermaritzburg. All were written in Zulu and promoted the history of Inkatha and of African peoples. They embodied themes which drew on cultural symbols such as *Ubuntu*, *ukuhlonipha* (the essence of *Ubuntu*, namely respect for elders, authority and the law) and *isizwe* (a concept incorporating race, nation and ethnic group). Images of Buthelezi predominated in this account, with the Zulus defined as the nation which, together with Buthelezi, would lead South Africa to liberation. Ordinary people did not feature in this Great Man approach to history. Moreover, in this view of the Zulus as a leading nation, there was a narrow selection of leaders: they either came from Natal, or were Zulus from other parties, such as Albert Luthuli from the ANC. The books were, however, mere tools to promote Inkatha. In one, the reader is presented with counter-arguments to perspectives critical of Inkatha, enabling statements such as the following to be challenged: 'Inkosi Buthelezi is a stooge of Pretoria and his position in KwaZulu was created by the South African Government'; 'Inkatha is a tribal movement of Zulus only and members of Inkatha are uneducated and illiterate'. Rebuttals included statements to the effect that Buthelezi had himself suffered at the hands of the South African government and rebuffed the offer of independence; his position and the Zulu nation had not been created by Pretoria but by history and tradition – in particular by Shaka; Inkatha was not a Zulu-specific movement but 'a movement of all black people'[21] – a contradiction, as Mdluli points out. Mdluli goes on to describe this kind of ethnic chauvinism as 'cultural populism'.[22]

In a later analysis of the same textbooks covering much the same ground as Mdluli and Maré, Daphna Golan similarly highlights the way in which the textbooks base the notion of Zulu nationhood on spurious accounts of the history of Shaka, so that 'biographies are presented as the only explanations in historical events'.[23] However, in contrast to Mdluli and Maré who present a unified image of the ideology under construction in the textbooks, Golan emphasises its confusions and incoherence, and in particular the 'reliance on white writings and its incorporation of racist ideas into its own ideology'.[24]

While it might therefore be argued that the basic ideas informing the *Ubunto-botho* syllabus shared something with Hermannsburger ideas on education celebrating ethnicity, as explored above, it seems that the set of influences on Inkatha in the development of the particularities of its syllabus were simultaneously far broader and narrower than missionary influence alone – with Hermannsburger influence not featuring at all. Key to this may be the fact that Mangope had been trained as a teacher at Bethel, a Hermannsburg Mission institution, in a region where the Hermannsburgers had historically played a significant role, while Buthelezi's exposure to the Hermannsburgers had been more distant. He attended school at Adams College in Natal, one of the bigger, more liberal missions run by the American Board of Commissioners for Foreign Missions. It counted among its principals, from 1933 to 1945, Edgar Brookes, a respected liberal in the region. Such connections created a different starting point for Buthelezi, who thereafter became a student at Fort Hare, a network which Mangope did not share. Though the origins and networks of the two leaders were very different, both seemed to reach into their earlier educational connections to develop their specific educational approaches within each region. By this stage, however, the role and influence of missionaries had been significantly reduced, and those who did have influence were the offspring of missionaries, educationists who had moved into more secular fields.

The *Ubuntu-botho* syllabus came into being by combining indigenous knowledge built upon traditional values with notions of citizenship or civic education then popular in the United States. It drew on essentialist notions of nationhood and ethnicity that were of a piece with Afrikaner cultural nationalism, but it also promoted ideas of connectedness with political parties such as the ANC, and used pan-Africanism to bolster its legitimacy. As in all cases involving the transfer of knowledge, ideas seem to have been translated, adapted, and suited to local circumstances by local actors who gave it their own stamp. In this sense it may be yet another classic case of a borrowed idea indigenised through repackaging in a local idiom.

Black Consciousness, independent churches and marginalisation

The increasing marginality of the Hermannsburgers as educationists within the region is exemplified by the history of Christian and Heidelore Kohn.[25] The lives they led in Zululand/Natal provide insight into the different ways in which Bantustan leaders such as Mangope and Buthelezi engaged with the Hermannsburgers.

The Kohns were in their mid-20s when they arrived in South Africa in 1963, part of Germany's post-war generation of emigrants. Christian had found his way into the Hermannsburg Mission by virtue of developments in Germany. A pastor's son born in 1938 in East Prussia, he was seven years old when the war ended and his family was forced to flee the advancing Russian troops. He arrived at Eversen near Hermannsburg as the child of refugees, a status he was acutely aware of throughout his schooling. When he left school, he trained as a missionary between the ages of 18 and 23, during which time he met his

wife-to-be, Heidelore, who came from neighbouring Celle. In 1962 she broke
off her studies in Sociology at the University of Frankfurt – home of Max
Horkheimer and Theodor Adorno – to marry Christian and travel with him
to South Africa.[26] In preparing for the trip, he was briefed on South Africa by
Heinz Dehnke, who was at the time visiting Hermannsburg in Germany; it is
likely that Dehnke also communicated his views on the relationship between
language, ethnicity, community and nation, thereby inducting him into how the
Hermannsburgers adapted themselves to the racial politics of South Africa.[27]

After their arrival at Hermannsburg in South Africa, the Kohns took up
the position of hostel parents at the boarding school, and Christian studied
Zulu with Heinrich Filter. He was ordained on 22 March 1964 at Moorleigh,
and his first posting was at Ehlanzeni, a dry, desolate and isolated area in
the Msinga district of the province of Natal. There, the school was next to
the church building, though at one of the outstations, Mfenebude, church and
school were housed in the same building. The African children suffered from
malnutrition, and a nutrition programme was put in place with the help of
the neighbouring clinic. Kohn's main duty was Religious Instruction. During
this time he learnt that, in order to achieve anything, such as the building
of a church, it was necessary to cultivate relationships with and seek permission from local chiefs. He quickly developed links, too, with Hermannsburgers
such as Becken at the Lutheran Theological College in Umpumulo, whom
he assisted with field work on independent African churches in Msinga, an
area then perceived as being 'famous for the strongly traditional attitudes of
its inhabitants'.[28] Kohn was also a friend of the Kistners and part of a wider
circle of younger Hermannsburgers grappling with the meaning and role of the
mission in a changing South Africa.[29]

During their time at Ehlanzeni, the Kohns had two sons, both born in
Greytown, one in 1967, the other in 1969. The family stayed at the mission until 1969, when they left for Hamburg where Christian spent a year
of study. Following this, they moved to Eshowe, a stronghold of Zulu traditionalists whose authority was bolstered and consolidated by legislative provisions in 1970 and 1971 to establish the Bantustans as 'self-governing' states.
Local chiefs and the reinforcement of traditional authority were central to
the Bantustan strategy. Although at this stage formally opposed to the homeland policy, Buthelezi began the process that led to the formation in 1975 of
Inkatha, which became his political base. This was also the moment when the
Hermannsburg connection with schooling in Natal was finally severed. Yet in
Kohn's view his relocation from Ehlanzeni to Eshowe was not so much the

result of this severance than of the formation of the Zulu Lutheran Church –
the Evangelical Lutheran Church of Southern Africa, South Eastern Diocese
(ELCSA-SED). Founded in 1963, this led to a transfer of buildings and property to the church and a reorganisation of the activities of missionaries. From
early on, Kohn had been concerned about the uncertain implications of this
development for the mission.

In 1967, three years after his arrival at Ehlanzeni, Kohn wrote an astute
analysis of the differences between the Tswana and Zulu Lutheran churches
formed, respectively, in the Transvaal and Natal/Zululand under the auspices
of the Hermannsburgers, and also of their current condition and the implications thereof for the mission. Although the Tswana church was far larger
numerically than the church in Zululand, the latter deployed more missionaries, evangelists and assistants, had an 'enormous' organisation with several
commissions to oversee its activities, and a budget whose expenditure for the
commissions was larger than that for the entire Tswana church. The reason for
the differences, according to Kohn, was that whereas Tswana people lived in
villages, the Zulus were spread out over far-flung rural areas. As a result, the
processes of conversion differed, and so too did the nature of organisational
activities. Kohn was concerned that 75% of the funding of the Zulu church
was external, raising questions about its independence.[30] In answer to concerns
as to whether the formation of the ELCSA-SER indicated that the time of
the Hermannsburgers in South Africa had come to an end, he pointed to the
many positions that former missionaries had taken up in the new Zulu church.
Nevertheless, this was a question that persisted.

In 1969, having furthered his studies in Hamburg, Kohn was ready
for a new challenge, and when the opportunity arose to become principal of Maqhamusela Lutheran Bible School at KwaMondi near Eshowe, he
took it up. At this stage, he also occupied the position of chairman of the
Mission and Evangelism Department of the Zululand Council of Churches.
The Bible school had been founded in 1944 at KwaMondi near Eshowe by a
Norwegian missionary with the purpose of training Christian laymen. Its curriculum included study of the Old and New Testament, and subjects such as
Introduction and Exegesis, Dogmatics, Catechism and Catechetics, History of
Israel, Church and Mission History, Homiletics, Bible Study, Youth and School
Work, Stewardship, Hygiene, and Singing. After 1963 vocational subjects had
been added: Typewriting and Bookkeeping as well as Woodwork. From 1972
onwards, the vocational side of the curriculum was further extended through
the introduction of Gardening and First Aid.[31] As Kohn regretfully admitted,

none of these subjects enabled people to find work, although that had been the intention. Much of the work of the Bible school was inspired by Kohn's view that the task of the church was to train people as laymen 'fully engaged in life' rather than merely ensuring that they attended church each Sunday. The role of Christians was to be in the world, evaluating social structures and social problems, and findings solutions.[32]

The social world of the Kohns, especially of Heidelore, was enlarged and invigorated by the move from Ehlanzeni. Through their children, their network within the white community broadened. Though at first the children were shunned and the parents falsely stigmatised as Nazis due to their origins, in due course they became active members of the local Rotary Club, initiating various projects and developing many friendships. On occasion they provoked the wrath of the conservative white community, for example when black staff members from the Bible school accompanied them to public events. At one such event, a public lecture, they were chased out of the hall and later pursued by the Bureau of State Security.[33] Kohn openly expressed his rejection of racial segregation, and did so in his writings too.[34]

During this period the Kohns had frequent contact with their neighbour at KwaMondi, Anglican Bishop Alpheus Zulu, who was also a member of the World Council of Churches. Through him, they developed friendships with Buthelezi – also an Anglican – as well as Gideon Zulu, Sibusiso Bengu, and various other members of Inkatha and the Zulu traditional and professional elite. Kohn notes that Buthelezi would have been unaware that he was a Hermannsburger, given his appointment to a Lutheran Bible school. The friendship with Buthelezi remains to this day; he has visited them at home in Hanover and they have visited him when they are in South Africa.

As a result of the Kohns' access to the upper echelons of local Zulu society, Heidi was invited by the *Zululand Times* to report on matters pertaining to the Zulu community, and soon became a 'prolific' correspondent.[35] As Vicky Kolbe later reported, 'very little news of this section of the people appeared in the *Zululand Times*, but when Heidi took on the job, there were not only articles, but they were often illustrated with appropriate photographs'.[36] Inkatha started sending her all their press releases, so that the *Times* became a conduit of information for white readers regarding news of the Zulu cultural organisation. She also translated a handbook, which was in fact propaganda for Inkatha, for distribution in Germany.[37] One of her last pieces for the *Zululand Times* – written anonymously in 1975 – was an article on Dr Sibusiso Bhengu, at that stage an Inkatha Freedom Party (IFP) member, but later to become democratic South Africa's first minister of Education.[38] Bhengu had just completed a PhD in Geneva, having graduated from the University of Zululand with a BA in English and History. Having joined the Eshowe Teacher Training College in 1966, Bhengu eventually went on to complete his BA Hons through Unisa, and upon returning from Geneva, became head of 'the biggest Zulu High School in Zululand, Dlangezwa with 700 pupils'. The article reports: 'What emanates from his studies was the deep insight that political liberation alone does not bring true freedom. To become truly liberated man as a whole must become free from fear, ignorance, hunger and sin'. Furthermore, Bhengu's commitment was to 'freedom for his fellow Africans through what he calls non-violent liberation activities' – thereby suggesting that he was affiliated to neither the ANC nor the PAC. Although there was substantial evidence of the involvement of Inkatha in political violence, it persistently cast itself as non-violent.

In 1975 the Kohns returned to Germany, mainly to avoid the prospect of their two sons being called up to do military service and to fight in the war against liberation movements based in Namibia and in Angola. However, the Kohns were also concerned about the quality of schooling – they had doubts about the quality of the German that was taught at the Hermannsburg school, as well as the standard of education in schools in Eshowe. A further concern was the implications of the formation of the ELCSA-SER. The documents, and in particular Kohn's farewell speech to a gathering of local clergy on 28 April 1975, reinforced this point. In it, he assessed not only his personal achievements and failures, but also South Africa, race relations in the country, and the role of the Hermannsburgers.

Kohn positions himself as an outsider who learnt a great deal during his time at KwaMondi, but was ultimately neither accepted nor considered useful by the community. He was grateful for the years he spent in South Africa because he had the opportunity to learn new languages and to share his life with other people 'to a certain extent'. He learnt 'something about their background, their culture, their attitudes towards other human beings, their hopes and frustrations', and this gave him 'a new understanding' of his own life and 'the responsibility which we have for each other' [*sic*]. However, Kohn goes on to regret his pastoral – and linguistic – shortcomings: 'the message I had was always given in poor Zulu, poor English or in an ununderstandable German'. He also acknowledges that his 'knowledge of the situation of the listeners was very limited. You can teach facts, that is easy, but to care spiritually for persons from another culture is an almost impossible task'.

There are hints that Kohn experienced the dilemma faced by many Lutheran missionaries at the time:[39] whether to stick to the 'spiritual' realm of mission work as prescribed by the Two Kingdoms notion within Lutheran theology, or to engage in the 'temporal' world and address the social problems presented there. Feeling compelled to take on the latter, Kohn was however unsupported by his colleagues – whether in the white church or the Zulu church (the ELCSA-SER). He took up the post of principal at KwaMondi because, he said, he saw his task as teaching 'facts and skills', which he felt more able to do than missionary work. His aim was to 'teach the young people to see problems and to find answers and to make their own decisions'. But he felt he had failed to get the necessary support for his views: 'as a white Minister I cannot tell the Church what to do and after the first proposal was rejected I did not try again'.[40]

Central to Kohn's predicament was an increasing sense of irrelevance as a missionary. The creation of the ELCSA-SER had integrated mission work so successfully, he said, that it was 'no integration but a take-over and the end of mission work':

> The remaining missionaries are not really necessary, but they provide some links to other countries from where all sorts of help come. Missionaries have done a lot of good for the peoples of SA but these times have passed. Mission as the work done by the white christians [sic] for the black brother . . . has had its time. Mission is always understood in terms of colonialism and is therefore no longer wanted. The necessity of reaching out to non-christian people is also no longer seen, because there are christians in all the streets of our towns and townships and in all the valleys of this country . . . .. [The view that] white christians should leave them alone in order to let black christians in their own churches make their own experiences and give them a chance to grow as mature is shared by me. I also feel that white christians in SA should not offer any help to black Christians. The blacks should approach the whites first.[41]

Kohn was not alone in being acutely conscious of the perception of missionaries as colonial and imperial agents, as expressed in Majeke's *The Role of the Missionaries in Conquest* (1952), and in the oft-repeated accusation: 'Before the missionaries came we had the land and they had the Bible. After they came, we had the Bible and they had the land'. Indeed, Wolfram Kistner himself requested Mission Director Hans-Robert Wesenick[42] not to send any more missionaries to South Arica.[43]

Rejecting the notion of separate development, Kohn contended: 'It is my impression that South Africans have much more to learn seeing in the partner from the other race another South African, in whom they have a vital interest for the sake of this country. Cultural, social and racial gaps must be bridged. This can only be done through information, dialogue and meeting each other'. He concluded that 'as long as the Gospel is not preached to mixed gatherings the Gospel cannot be understood in the South African situation . . . [and] Christian principles will play no role in the future'.

Christian and Heidi Kohn, the Hermannsburg Mission, as well as missionaries in general, had been defeated by new developments and political and ideological trends in South Africa during the 1970s, which had of course likewise manifested at Umpumulo. And yet the Kohns have maintained their links, albeit unofficial and in much attenuated form. Through the church in Hanover, Kohn established an official partnership between 11 parishes from Hanover's North East Circuit in Germany and 20 parishes from the Eshowe Church Circuit. Every two years a group of South African Lutherans goes to Hanover for a programme of activities. And every two years Hanoverian Lutherans come to South Africa to renovate a building, build a church, plant trees, or participate in a local project.[44]

Conclusion

There was a certain inevitability in the gravitation of the Kohns towards traditional authority, given the mission's modus operandi since its inception. It provided the basis for their work within communities, which was always geared to the local context. But their approach to traditional authority also meant that they were always on the side of the apartheid state, which allied itself with chiefs in its construction of the Bantustans. By the 1970s the missions' formal role in secular schooling, now taken over by the state, had ended, and their engagement operated solely at a social and religious level. Though the links between Hermannsburgers in the Transvaal and Bantustan leaders like Mangope were close, those between Hermannsburgers and the Bantustan authorities in Zululand appear to have been rather more tenuous: unlike the case of the Bodensteins, the Hermannsburgers were not integrated at the official level as advisors and education planners. Hermannsburgers played no direct role in the formulation and implementation of Inkatha's *Ubuntu-botho* syllabus.

In Hermann's account of the role of church and mission in the homelands,[45] he observes that Lutherans – black as well as white – took the situation in the Bantustans for granted, accepting the status quo on the basis that the mission should not involve itself with politics. As a result, there was silence in the synods on certain excesses of the Bantustan governments. Yet despite the conservatism that underpinned this acquiescence, Hermannsburgers soon found themselves in the firing line of the newly independent Zulu church they had striven so hard to establish. Despite the ELCSA-SER perceiving itself, as Hermann has shown, to be part and parcel of Inkatha, with which Hermannsburgers generally sympathised, the ELCSA-SER seemed also – ironically – to be hostile to the involvement of white missionaries in its work. Its opposition to the missionaries therefore had less to do with their conservatism than with their strategy to remain in South Africa to serve the newly established Zulu Lutheran Church. The antipathy of this new black church, Hermann argues, was aimed less at individual missionaries than at missionaries in general who represented white people and white domination. Unable to get rid of those in actual power on a political level, it directed its anger at missionaries instead.[46] From a gender perspective, hegemonic missionary masculinities had been overtaken by what, up to then, were previously subordinated versions of African masculinity.

CHAPTER 10

TRANSITIONS THROUGH THE MISSION

While the mission record provides some access to African voices, and also to the response of Africans to the Hermannsburgers, it is necessary to venture beyond the mission record to gain a clearer understanding of such voices. Here, autobiographies are a useful source, though of course, such writing is not unmediated. Conventional notions of authorship and the subject are challenged in an account which suggests that a 'host of people' are normally involved 'in the making of autobiographical accounts'.[1] The reasons for collaboration in autobiography are varied. Although such textual collaboration 'mirror[s] an intimacy in personal relationships', it is necessary to distinguish between 'advocatory texts, where the writing author speaks on behalf of the oral narrator', 'texts in which the writing author plays a mediating role' and 'truly collaborative texts in which the participants are on a comparatively equal footing'.[2] This chapter explores two autobiographies in the light of these considerations. Although these autobiographies are not direct reflections on the transition from mission education to Bantu Education, they nevertheless provide insights into, and a sense of, the experiences of Africans with regard to education by the Hermannsburg Mission. In a context where the formal archival records provide little in the way of such experiences, these autobiographies are very useful. In parts, they provide an interesting contrast with

Micah Kgasi's *Thutô ke eng?*, discussed in Chapter 1, which is only partly autobiographical.

In 1971, a London-based publisher, C. Hurst and Company, published Naboth Mokgatle's *Autobiography of an Unknown South African*, and in 1986 the Killie Campbell Africana Library together with Natal University Press published *Paulina Dlamini: Servant of Two Kings*, essentially a book of reminiscences, or a memoir, compiled by Heinrich Filter.[3] Kgasi was born in the late 1870s or early 1880s, in the Western Transvaal. Paulina Dlamini, a contemporary of Kgasi, was born near Babanango in Zululand. S. Bourquin, translator and editor of the reminiscences compiled by Filter, suggests that Dlamini was about 67 years old in 1925; thus, she was probably born around 1858, shortly after the arrival of the Hermannsburgers in Natal. Naboth Mokgatle was born in 1911 on the mission station Saron, at Phokeng, in the district of Rustenburg, half a century after their arrival in the Western Transvaal.

Crossing the genres of memoir, autobiography and reminiscence, each work is distinctive in its composition, its themes, and the light it casts on the life of the subject in relation to the broader context and the 'narrative identities of the collectives' with which each wished to or was 'forced to associate'.[4] Micah Kgasi's book is suffused with the conflict between two identities – one African and the other European. In Paulina Dlamini's reminiscences, refracted first through notes compiled by Hermannsburg missionary Filter and subsequently through the editorial intervention of Bourquin, the gendered experience of a woman who was part of Cetshwayo's *umuzi* (household) and then converted to Lutheranism, is recorded; in this process, the former identity is narrated as having been surrendered in preference to the latter. Naboth Mokgatle's story documents the politicisation of a young man caught up in the forces between industrialisation, urbanisation and growing political and trade union organisation and repression in the transition from segregation to apartheid. He constructs a collective identity, which is political, encompassing ethnic, national and international spheres.

Both Kgasi and Dlamini became mission evangelists, with Paulina Dlamini becoming known as the 'Apostle of Northern Zululand'.[5] Kgasi is conflicted about the mission hierarchy, whereas Dlamini appears to find an independent space in which she sets some distance between her newly invented self and her former life. For both Kgasi and Dlamini, the tropes of 'heathen' and 'Christian' are strong. Such conflicts are largely absent from the life of Mokgatle, who eventually chose a different path. Born into a family in which his mother was a staunch Lutheran and his father agnostic, Mokgatle grew up in the shadow of the mission presence in Phokeng, Kroondal and Rustenburg. Nevertheless, he developed a greater distance from the mission than that achieved by Kgasi and Dlamini. Educated up until Standard 2 at the rival English-medium school of the Pentecostal Holiness Church started by the West-Indian missionary, Kenneth Spooner, he was then confirmed by Ernst Penzhorn of the Hermannsburg Mission. Whereas Kgasi and Dlamini were first-generation converts, Mokgatle's youthful interactions with the mission shaped his everyday understanding of white people and segregation. Whereas Kgasi's relationship has been seen to be one of chafing subordination,[6] Dlamini's is one of apparent gratitude and equality. This chapter traces the respective routes taken by these three people into and through the mission, and examines their contrasting narratives in terms of race, gender and class. Taken together, they cast refracted light on the construction of a collective identity, doing so through the very different experiences and responses of each to the mission's educational project.

Paulina Dlamini

In the case of Dlamini and Mokgatle, white people appear in the text in many guises. Dlamini recounts disrespectful youthful encounters with the Rev. Schmidt, 'who was held in high esteem at the royal *umuzi*' but with whom she and her fellow playmates 'played the fool'.[7] As she explains, however, 'He never became angry but was always of a kind and friendly disposition'.[8] She was impressed when Sir Theophilus Shepstone came to proclaim Cetshwayo King of the Zulus, noting that the festivities accompanying the Feast of the First Fruits were also attended by childless Norwegian missionaries, whom Cetshwayo presented with a girl 'who was to be both servant and daughter' and on whose behalf they should receive *lobola* cattle when she eventually married.[9] Dlamini suggests that Cetshwayo was 'secretly intrigued' by the mission message, but did not make this public lest he should 'lose his crown'.[10] She recounts the visits and influence of John Dunn (1834–1895), legendary Natal settler and confidante of Cetshwayo who took several Zulu wives, and whom Cetshwayo granted a stretch of land from Eshowe to the Ngoye Mountains.

Dlamini's conversion to Christianity, writes Sheila Meintjes, 'can really only be understood in the context of the complete disruption of traditional life after the 1879 war and subsequent civil war'.[11] Following the Anglo-Zulu war and the civil war between Cetshwayo and Zibhebhu in the early 1880s, Dlamini and her family were driven into hiding, seeking refuge 'among the rocks and krantzes and a cave in the mountain called Ngwibi'.[12] There they suffered great hunger, until one day they saw a white man driving a cart, and asked to join him. At Greytown, he registered the family as 'belonging to van Rooyen's establishment'.[13] Paulina 'lived inside his house' while 'he built a hut for her parents just outside his yard'. The family worked for 'Shede Foloyi' (Gert van Rooyen), though she describes the work as being 'very light'.[14] After a period of three years, she has a visitation, a vision of a 'gleaming white person', which Van Rooyen persuades her is a call from God. She is taken to the missionary Johannes Reibeling, who instructs her in the faith and baptises her. She then returns to Melkboom near Babanango, again staying with the Van Rooyen family. She and Van Rooyen start working together as lay preachers. She explains how she was able to change the attitude and practice of a white man who was working African men as if they were animals. This was a turning point for Dlamini, also in her relations with local African people who had hitherto been suspicious of her preaching, and who now saw her relationship with white people as having positive effects.[15]

It was while Dlamini was at Lemgo, her ancestral home near Babanango, that young Heinrich Filter arrived at the Esibongweni mission station. The year was 1925, and she was an elderly woman in her late sixties, while he was a newly married thirty-two-year-old. Sadly, the next year, his wife would die in childbirth. He had behind him a stint at the missionary seminary in Hermannsburg, Germany, an internment at Spandau during the First World War for being a South African, and by implication a British subject, and training as a nurse. According to Bourquin, Filter then started a compilation of Dlamini's memories. In 1939 his second wife moved into his home at the Nazareth mission station, and he brought Dlamini from Lemgo to stay with them.[16] Both Filter and Bourquin describe the process of writing down her memories in long-hand, organising them under specific headings and in chronological sequence, and then turning them into a narrative that was 'not a verbatim record [but] adhered as closely as possible to the original record'.[17] Bourquin points out the 'padding', the 'editorial interference', and the translation issues involved in a text that moved between Zulu, German and English.

The question is whether Dlamini's life, as represented both before and also after her conversion, may be ascribed to Filter's 'editorial interference', or to her knowledge of her interlocutor and his expectations, or to genuine shared understandings. As Meintjes points out, it is clear that Filter's narrative choices shaped the story – spoken in Zulu, the oral narrative was transcribed in key words and sentences in German, and then translated and edited by Bourquin. Filter exercised some licence in the use of direct speech.[18] However, the fascination with the life of a young woman who was part of the royal Zulu household, and who lived with the king himself, is evident in the detail of the accounts that Dlamini shared. While the details are fascinating in their own right, they may also have been of special interest to Filter, for a variety of reasons. The account of her relations with older and younger men, as well as with the king, is presented through the eyes of a person who saw these relationships as natural and normal at the time, but now judged them as wrong. This is a perception that may well have been shared by Filter, the writer, and Dlamini, his subject. And so she describes the process by which a relative requests of her father that she, a girl of about 14 years old, be taken to join Cetshwayo's *isigodlo*, thereby becoming part of the homestead consisting of the huts of the king's wives and children.[19] Her mother having died when she was younger, she was close to her father, so her removal was an unavoidable, 'repugnant' wrench for both of them, as she would henceforth belong to Cetshwayo.[20] She joined his household in 1872, the year that Mpande, who had been king of the Zulus since 1840, passed away.[21] She describes everyday life as involving tasks such as fetching water, attending to planting and harvesting, performing domestic duties in the huts of the royal wives, or being 'at the disposal of the king as concubines'.[22] She and other young women like her also built the royal hut at Ondini, supplying the thatch and plaiting the grass, with the ever-present threat of summary execution if anyone stepped out of line.

Dlamini details the casual brutality and numerous executions which often made 'fear and anxiety' part of everyday life.[23] Ceremonies such as the puberty ceremony, certain beliefs now seen as mere superstitions, and 'the king's nightlife with the *isigodlo* girls' fill her with shame; she confesses that she can 'no longer speak about such things'.[24] Despite all this, however, girls also enjoyed themselves, and after being tutored by older girls had many suitors and fell in love. Her own fiancé died during the civil war, a period of hardship, privation and molestation by men.[25] She never married, and her relationship with men, both white and black, appears to have been one of equal standing. As an independent woman, respected for the work she did with black as well as white people, she enjoyed respect and – within the confines of the times – a degree of dignity.

Naboth Mokgatle

Naboth Mokgatle's *Autobiography of an Unknown South African* is categorised as autoethnography, the genre that Starfield uses to describe the histories produced by Dr S Modiri Molema, who wrote a little earlier than Mokgatle, but on similar themes. During apartheid, such genres were typically employed by African writers so as to provide 'corrective versions of mainstream South African history'.[26] As with Molema, autoethnography enabled Mokgatle to represent his own life alongside that of his community, as well as his growing political awareness and absorption into trade union work.

Kgasi clearly acknowledges his debt to thinkers of his day, and the voice of Paulina Dlamini is explicitly mediated via Filter and Bourquin, but the narrative voice of Mokgatle's autobiography provides no such indication of outside assistance or interference. Having fled South Africa, Mokgatle began to write the book in 1961, not long after he had arrived in London with no documents and no money. Largely self-educated and widely read, it is likely that he did not rely on editorial assistance; there is no introduction to the book, there are no acknowledgements, and no sources are provided. He was welcomed by Mary Benson, a South African writer who worked with the Africa Bureau, founded in 1952 to support Africans by providing advice in their contestations with colonial governments.[27] The London publisher of his book was also the publisher of Jack Simon's 1968 study, *African Women: Their Legal Status in South Africa*, so there was probably a link between Mokgatle and the broader network of anti-apartheid and Communist Party intellectuals in London at the time. The fact that the book does not contain acknowledgements, and that consequently no names are mentioned, may well have been part of the necessary secrecy and anonymity typical of Communist Party traditions of the period.[28]

What is suggestive of Mokgatle's intellectual debt, either to Molema or other writers, is his fine attention to anthropological detail related to 'tribal traditions and customs', such as family tribal relations, circumcision, marriage, and death. Significantly, the language slips in its use of 'my/our' and 'their' – setting up an 'us'/'them' dichotomy. The second chapter, 'Tribal Origins', for example, opens with the following:

> My tribe, known in the Transvaal as the Bafokeng tribe, is Bosotho and its language is Sesotho. Like other tribes all over the Province, they call themselves Bosotho. Our tribal symbol is a crocodile (*kwena*) and we call ourselves and are known as Bakwena. Other tribes too have their tribal symbols. . . . These symbols are so sacred to them that whenever they see them or come into contact with them, they must not kill them but only admire them, and recite poems of praise to them.[29]

A substantial part of the introductory sections of the book is taken up by a history of Mokgatle's family. Just as Kgasi does in *Thutô ke eng?*, Mokgatle 'undertakes the task of humanising the African past by consciously justifying and rationalising traditional beliefs and practices'.[30] In this regard, Mokgatle's narrative voice has been the focus of some investigation. For Thengamehlo Ngwenya, his main purpose was 'to demonstrate to his reader that his ancestors' way of life was based on functional, rational and orderly principles'.[31] Mokgatle's representation of his youth as a time of simple innocence of the 'tribal' boy is puzzling to Ngwenya, who expects that a communist would have inserted an awareness of the economic and political factors responsible for the momentous changes affecting the lives of the Bafokeng during this period.[32] Thomas Thale reads Mokgatle's representation of this history of the Bafokeng as an attempt to legitimate his position within his own ethnic history and, later, in the liberation struggle.[33] Noting the author's significant silences 'about the two occasions when his paternal ancestor, Mokgatle Mokgatle, collaborated with the Boers in the . . . frontier wars', colluding in the suppression first of the Matabele and then the Bapedi, and also offering 'some of his subjects to Piet Potgieter as labourers on farms',[34] Thale suggests that Mokgatle perceives and uses his past as 'a resource for locating [himself] within the discourse of resistance politics' around which his identity is constructed. Accordingly, his youthful experiences are simply a precursor to his later activism. The trade union becomes his family, and his activism a process of learning and alternative education. His self is constructed within the framework of trade union and Communist Party activism.[35]

In Mokgatle's account of his interactions with the Hermannsburgers there is an absence of conflict and rancour. His account of their arrival at Phokeng suggests that the first missionary and his family had come at the invitation of the local African community, the Bafokeng, who fetched them from Durban with ox wagons. But he does show how conflicts arose between missionaries with different approaches, and how members of the community chose to adopt either one or the other, or selectively appropriate aspects of each, or to ignore them altogether. He describes how, in a community such as Phokeng, 'far away from areas inhabited by white people', where the only white people were Rev. Ernst Penzhorn and his family, they were not perceived as such. The children played together, but 'because they spoke our language so well, we never noticed the distinction between us in colour. We never noticed that they were white'.[36] At the age of twelve, working for his uncle, and not yet having attended school, Mokgatle recalls running away on account of his uncle's unjust and cruel treatment. He ran to nearby Kroondal, the German settlement that served the white mission community. He had been told that boys could earn a cow for themselves by working for a German farmer. Attracted by this prospect, he went to seek work at Kroondal. There he was to learn 'two things which I did not know existed. The European way of life as practised in South Africa, and Segregation, Apartheid'.[37] Differences in sleeping arrangements, and not being permitted to sit on the same bench as a white person, were indications of this.

However, like Dlamini, he does not judge his employers harshly. 'During the two years I spent with him [Herman Lange] I did not once hear him swear or beat anyone, although he was very strict . . .. Though [Lange and his wife, Ida] practised segregation like other farmers of Kroondal and the rest of the Europeans in South Africa, they were good and kind people . . .. They cared very much for their workmen and women'.[38] Mokgatle is a sharp observer of how the missionary children learnt to speak fluent Sotho even though they spoke German at home, and attended a separate church with a separate priest: 'Black and white Lutheran congregations did not mix'.[39] Also, the farmers' children and those of the squatters on their farms attended different schools. When, some years later, Mokgatle encounters the Lange daughters, Ida and Elizabeth, in the streets of Pretoria, segregation again rears its head and so he does not greet them, 'to avoid embarrassing them, with great sorrow and regret'.[40] As the women depart, he thinks to himself: 'If anyone asked me where I thought Hell was situated, I would say, "Where I stand now." Hell is where people are denied meeting because they differ in colour'.[41]

In July 1925 he leaves the employ of the Langes to start his schooling, which is constantly interrupted by being called out to help the family in the fields during harvest time and to do odd jobs in Rustenburg. Here again, he is confronted by the conditions under which Africans laboured when he encounters not only the need to register with the office of the native commissioner, but also the subservience expected of Africans when in the presence of whites.[42] After working on an orange farm during the school vacation to earn some money, he is faced with a farmer who tries to dissuade him from going back to school: 'What will you do with your education?' he tells young Mokgatle, 'You are wasting your time'.[43] In the end, though, it is his sister who dissuades him from continuing with his schooling when he reaches the age of 17, encouraging him instead to go for confirmation classes with the missionary, Mr Penzhorn. These classes were a rite of passage from childhood into adulthood, and once they were completed Mokgatle found it difficult to go back to school. Nevertheless, his experiences with whites were hard lessons for him, leaving memories that would not be erased until later on in his life: 'Until I was in politics I thought that Europeans needed us only as long as they could make use of us, to create pleasures for themselves and nothing more. I thought that they looked upon us as a man would look upon his cow or ox. . . . Before these experiences [with whites] I had never known that South Africa was occupied by people who thought of men not as equals, but as superiors and inferiors'.[44]

The first half of the book provides a narrative of family and work, while the latter is a narrative of growing political awareness, struggle and repression. Mokgatle's move to Pretoria brings him into contact with the ANC and the Communist Party of South Africa, which changes its name to the South African Communist Party in 1953. He attends weekend open-air meetings, joins night classes where he is given political education and becomes a frequent visitor of the Left Book Club 'run by the Pretoria Communists and others of Left opinions'.[45] His relations with women are many and varied, in Johannesburg and Pretoria, until he meets Nana Thlogo, whom he eventually marries in 1941. This is a period of rising African trade unionism, also in Pretoria. Once the Communist Party takes an anti-fascist stance on the War, he decides to join it, becoming secretary of the Pretoria district committee in 1942; he is chairman when it is eventually dissolved in 1950 on account of the Suppression of Communism Act (No. 44 of 1950). During the 1940s, living in Marabastad with Nana, he attends the Party National School and becomes secretary of the Pretoria Non-Distributive Workers' Union in 1943. When a branch of the Transvaal Council of Non-European Trade Unions was formed in Pretoria in 1945, Mokgatle was elected secretary, thus holding positions within both the party and the union movement. Three years later, in 1948, he formed the African General Workers' Union. At this time, Mokgatle also became schooled in legal work and represented himself in several cases: 'While the Communist Party was a political school for me,' he writes, 'trade union work became my legal school'.[46]

Once the political narrative picks up, the personal story disappears. As Ngwenya observes, Mokgatle provides no hint of his family life, except for the names of his wife, Nana, and two children, Keitumetsi and Matshediso. It is at this point in his life that he leaves home for good. There is little more than a fleeting reference to his wife's loyalty, and he also refers to their incompatibility. Nana does not share his convictions, instead, he tells us, she is 'always trying to pull me down, urging me to be like everyone else, and saying that I was making trouble for myself'.[47] Ngwenya speculates that this could be the result of an 'unresolved conflict between his roles as husband and a father and his public obligations as a political activist'.[48] Mokgatle was able to write far more freely about his relationships with his mother, aunt and sisters, and it is possible that this silence was as much about the difficulty of writing about the personal when conflict was involved, as it was a strategy for protecting those close to him. It is noteworthy that the book was published in 1971, the height of repressive apartheid. Even though his family remained in South Africa, they were still in danger because of him.

Mokgatle describes the 'poison' being served up by Eiselen's Commission of Inquiry into Education at the same time as a commission comes into being that is intended to stifle African trade unionism. In 1950 the Suppression of Communism Act (No. 44 of 1950) is introduced, and soon afterwards Mokgatle was harassed, arrested, tried, sentenced and served with a banning order. Under the Suppression of Communism Act, banning orders were instituted against people considered a threat to the state; restrictions were placed on their ability to work, their movements, how many people they could see at any one time, and their right to attend gatherings. When an opportunity to escape presents itself in the form of an invitation from the Romanian trade union council, Mokgatle decides to leave. Miraculously, he is permitted to board an aeroplane without documents of any kind, or a return ticket, and soon Saron, Phokeng, Kroondal and Rustenburg are far behind him. The narrative describes his sense of loss as a necessary aspect of his growing awareness of the nature of South African society. He transitions through it, out of it, and beyond it. His journey into exile introduces a new, transnational connection, one with feedback loops and entanglements across Africa and Europe. His book is, therefore, an attempt to claim and also to assert the coexistence of ethnic, nationalist and internationalist identities.

The attempt to assert and reconcile African and European understandings of South African society that we see in Micah Kgasi's *Thutô ke eng?* is also evident in Dlamini's account, though the latter appears to be less conflicted in its attempt. The narrative voice of Paulina Dlamini is clearly a blend of her own and that of the missionary. The lenses trained on her early history are similarly anthropologically oriented, but they also reflect the mission distinctions between Christian and non-Christian life. Mokgatle's narrative voice is sober and measured, positioning the author in relation to fraught issues such as ethnicity, race and gender with a surprising degree of equanimity; in this there are similarities with the voice of Dlamini, for all its more complex, ambiguous character.

Conclusion

Kgasi's reflections, Dlamini's reminiscences and Mokgatle's memoir all provide evidence of the complex networks involving missionaries and Africans that were developed over time, and the social fabric that they jointly wove. These interweavings form part of the mix of identities in terms of which the authors defined themselves – Kgasi in intractable conflict with the European strand, Dlamini identifying with and absorbing it, and Mokgatle rejecting it outright. In each case, the author transcended narrow forms of school education, embracing instead connections that constructed identity in a manner that challenged the narrow racialised and gendered constructions of the society of which they formed a part. In this sense, the mission was a significant step in a complex journey for all three writers. Kgasi's route was one that caused anguish but also held out hope for a more inclusive and equal world than that in which he lived. As represented, Dlamini's route was one that led from hunger and oppression to a measure of security and independence. In the process of claiming the new identity of Christian, a tension appears to emerge between this and her earlier 'tribal' self. Part of this identity includes changing oppressive race relations. Mokgatle's route into the mission was short-lived and a rite of passage, and in the process he learnt of kindness – as well as hypocrisy and inequality. From this he moved out and away towards a secular political kingdom critical of the church. For him at least, there was no conflict between his rural and urban, internationalist and cosmopolitan identities. In each case, Kgasi, Dlamini and Mokgatle appropriated the rather basic education provided by the Hermannsburgers, and actively transformed it for their own purposes.

CONCLUSION

The Hermannsburg Mission Society no longer plays any role in South Africa in running schools, teacher training colleges or seminaries for the training of African pastors. All that remains of previous endeavours are the ruins of settlements founded by the mission, and the private schools for children of German parentage which are rapidly losing their German and Hermannsburger character. All that is left, in effect, are the few remaining people who went through the institutions, their children who are now scattered across the country and the world, books produced in the course of the mission's history, and its various archives. In Germany these archives are carefully catalogued and cared for. In South Africa they are under constant threat of neglect, destruction, and even fire.

In KwaZulu-Natal, the abandoned and dilapidated buildings of the mission headquarters and the old Mission Press at Moorleigh near Estcourt speak of a bygone era. Farm schools have by and large been closed, and the former Bantu community schools are now incorporated into KwaZulu-Natal as public schools. Closed down in 2002, Umpumulo languishes, disused and decaying amid the lush vegetation of the surrounding hills, and in North West province, on the road between Coligny and Ventersdorp, Bethel is now a secondary school for girls, hidden among a grove of trees planted by the mission. Over time, the buildings have expanded considerably, and there is only a dim memory of the school's origin as a mission school, let alone a German one. In the villages around Rustenburg, likewise, the missionaries have left, and Kroondal, the centre of the former German community in that area, is now a shadow of its former self, criss-crossed by highways cutting away whatever charm the village might once have had. All that remains is a church and shady graveyard, and headstones bearing the names of settlers and missionaries. The Hermannsburg book depot no longer exists, and the Mission Press no longer produces school textbooks. The short-lived Primary Education Upgrade Programme, begun just a few decades ago, is a remnant of a past considered best forgotten.

The past that this book deals with is not a comfortable past for South Africans. It does not conform to the narratives of grand, heroic resistance that fires the imaginations of new generations of scholars. It deals with the losers in a long history of struggle. Probing non-English-speaking sources and integrating them into standard narratives of educational history brings into view a history that has been obscured by the focus on the bigger, more prominent missions whose histories are documented in English. Founded in colonial Natal in 1854, in the shadow of British imperialism, Hermannsburger schools struggled into existence up to 1955, when a new dispensation, to which they adapted, began a process of taking control of education. The general poverty of the Hermannsburg schools continued into the apartheid period, as did its series of school readers. Its emphasis on the mother tongue became associated with a shameful history of a system whose purpose was to keep people down, to oppress them and keep them powerless. Moreover, the Lutheran insistence on separation of church and politics sat uneasily alongside broader political currents within mission history in South Africa propagating a secular theology and intervention to address social inequalities. Only very gradually, and then only in the post-war years, in the context of broader pressures and interactions, did some within the Lutheran fold begin to challenge this separation.

Why, then, should one examine this history? For the simple reason, perhaps, that the ideas which animated its theorists and practitioners are still very much alive today. Ideas around education as a Western colonial import, the destructiveness of European intervention, the need for removing its influence, the indigenisation of education and the importance of mother-tongue education – all once held by Lutheran missionaries themselves – are promoted by a new generation of students and scholars seeking to free the university and society from the incubus of colonialism. And, as Cynthia Kros has argued, these ideas were given their most articulate expression by W.W.M. Eiselen in his commission report that became the ideological basis of the Bantu Education Act.[1] Of this there is little knowledge or memory today – indeed, even less so of the troubled history that enabled such ideas, or of the contradictions and tensions these ideas provoked at the time.

Furthermore, homogenising tendencies that oversimplify history and the – often invisible – people who make that history ignore its fluid, ever-changing character. History is neither static nor a single story. This book has tried to show not only that there were differences concerning these ideas among Lutherans and people who came within the ambit of the Hermannsburg Mission, but also that many of the ideas were themselves essentially the product of a transnational movement that included most Protestant missions, whether English- or German-speaking, as well as many Africans associated with them. Thus the emphasis on local languages and their development was as much a product of European endeavour as of African involvement in such matters. The schools themselves were shaped both by missions and the local communities they served. Transnational connections, both within the country and across borders, had many and varied consequences and effects over time within the local context of institutions in which the Hermannsburgers were involved. Once the apartheid state had taken over the mission schools, and the Hermannsburgers became engaged in a broader educational initiative at Umpumulo, their approach – inevitably, perhaps – underwent change.

This is also the case with the role of women. The public history of the mission until the 1970s is largely that of men. This book has examined the gendered nature of its recruitment and employment strategies, its curricula and social practices, and the attempt to regulate and control what it perceived as transgressive sexual behaviour and related mores. Moreover, until the 1970s when Hermannsburg women increasingly began to enter the public sphere, a stultifying mission culture relegated women to secondary roles as wives and mothers. Although this was modified within the compromised sphere of Bantustan politics, limited in its own way by traditional forms of patriarchy, it nevertheless signalled a change from previous decades.

The colonial project of education was deeply contradictory, ultimately undermined as much by achievement of its very purpose as by the changes it wrought within the people who fell under its ambit. Conflict as much as compliance characterised efforts to establish schools among communities. Alliances with one group of people invariably meant conflict with another. These conflicts spilt over into schools in dramatic ways. By the 1940s, with the transition to state control increasingly likely, this would have decisive implications for the schools. Many communities in the Western Transvaal in particular clearly voiced their opposition to mission control, seeking secular, state-controlled schools instead. This is perhaps an under-recognised aspect of the transition to state control – the demand by local educational communities themselves for such control.

At first glance, the mission itself seemed relieved that the state would free it of the financial burden of running schools. Moreover, there was much sympathy for policies such as the promotion of mother-tongue education. But there was also considerable disquiet about the consequences of state takeover for schools, for relationships with communities, and ultimately for the mission's own role in South Africa. Without a role, it would be unable to fulfil its religious purpose, and without this, there would no longer be a place for the mission. And so, in the first instance the Hermannsburgers sought compromises which would enable them to continue in a pastoral or other affiliated role. But in the end what communities themselves demanded – as did the logic of the new system – was secular state-controlled education rather than one in which private religious bodies played any significant role. And yet, as the mission lost all power and influence, the state used religion to bolster its authority. From the perspective of Bantu Education ideologues wielding their bible of Christian National Education, the corrupting European presence was removed from direct control of schools, in accordance with the grand apartheid plan. In this sense, the decolonisation move entailed a re-colonisation: one form of white control was simply replaced by another on the grounds of the putative necessity to maintain the 'purity' of African ethnicities determined by the state itself. It was a spurious argument, but it illustrates the coloniality of the apartheid education project itself: a coloniality which asserted itself at the very moment that, paradoxically, it claimed to expunge colonial control.

The coloniality of the mission endeavour itself is not, of course, in question. The very process of conversion through schooling, through teaching reading and writing, and the hidden messages contained in social practices as much as school and teacher-training curricula, all served to underline a preferred, 'superior' way of bringing up children. The school itself was part of a wider colonising project, which could not be disguised merely by emphasising and prescribing local African content, history and languages in curricula and textbooks, even when many of the latter were written by Africans themselves. And so, throughout the history of this mission, as with others, there were ambiguous responses by Africans. These ranged from wholesale adoption and outright appropriation to secessions and rebellions of various kinds. Umpumulo, a joint German and Scandinavian Lutheran project, which before the advent of Bantu Education provided teacher training of a kind that expanded yet also confined horizons of Africans, re-established itself as a seminary – partially in response to the loss of mission educational institutions to the state. Criticism, including of the role of missionaries themselves, thrived at Umpumulo. However, the critique of their role intensified outside of the mission also, and this had the effect of reinforcing the assault on the missionaries, who gradually withdrew from the space they occupied. Nevertheless, networks established through the mission remained strong, and were represented most clearly in the role played by Hermannsburgers and a broader mission network in Bantustan educational experimentation within the framework of apartheid. A comparison between the theological and primary school education offered by Umpumulo and in Bophuthatswana respectively reveals how differently Hermannsburgers in each sphere responded to the wider context.

The transition from mission to Bantu education was not a neat and clear-cut process, however much the policymakers desired this. It also didn't live up to any expectations that Hermannsburgers, whether white or black, might have had. The nature of the Hermannsburg Mission in education changed after 1955, but its presence continued to be felt for well-nigh forty years. By and large, Hermannsburgers made compromises with the system, although a few of them did break ranks. While the latter story has not been told here, it is one that needs to be told.

When the Hermannsburgers finally decided to close the chapter of missionary work in South Africa, they had been in the country for close to 150 years. The process of transition that began in South Africa in 1990 may not yet have realised the dreams and aspirations held out at its inception, but it has fully embraced the secularity of a system that falls under state control, a system demanded by those communities opposed to the missions, and which took a uniquely harmful form under apartheid. Education for Africans was state-controlled and unequally funded during the apartheid years, and it was neither compulsory nor a right until constitutionally entrenched.[2] Although it may be foolhardy to attempt to draw any definitive conclusions or lessons from the relationship between past and present, it does alert us as much to continuity and change in history, as to its irreducibly unpredictable and contingent character.

NOTE ON SOURCES

This book is based mainly on mission and government archival sources. The main mission archives were the Hermannsburg Mission archive in Hermannsburg, Germany, and the related Lutheran Theological Institute archives of the Cooperating Lutheran Missions in Pietermaritzburg, South Africa. The sources include correspondence, minutes of meetings, reports, examination papers, annual magazines and related documents.

The mission archives proved particularly useful, given the paucity of the Bantu Education archive in the National Archives of South Africa in Pretoria. Although specific files can be tracked down, there does not appear to be a consolidated archive of the state's Bantu Education department during the period covered in this book. In contrast, the mission records include all the circulars missionaries received from, as well as correspondence with, the state, such as prescribed textbook gazettes, negotiations over the transfer of control to the state, and related reports to fellow missionaries. The records also contain comprehensive reports of various kinds concerning conflicts between missionaries and local communities. The meticulousness with which the missionaries kept their records, and the mission its archives, has resulted in considerable information and testimony of missionary educational activities, as well as invaluable evidence of the nature of the interactions between the state, missionaries and local communities.

These mission records, as well as the Christian and Heidi Kohn papers, and the textbook holdings of the German Africana archive held at the University of South Africa (Unisa), appear in several languages: English, Afrikaans, German, Tswana and Zulu. Missionaries used different languages in different contexts and for different purposes – German for minutes of meetings and conferences and correspondence with one another and the head office, English and Afrikaans for certain meetings and correspondence with government officials and bureaucrats, and Tswana and Zulu for correspondence with local communities, school committees, boards, principals and teachers. These were often translated, and therefore appeared in two languages.

With the exception of Heinz Dehnke's chapter, 'The Mission and the School', and unless otherwise stated in the endnotes, all German and Afrikaans translations are my own, though some were checked by colleagues and friends such as Ralf Krüger and Ulrike Kistner. The arduous task of translating Dehnke's chapter, written in Sütterlin script – the historical form of German writing – was done by Margot von Beck. Micah Kgasi's book, *Thutô ke Eng?*, was translated by Enos Makhele. I received translation help with Tswana and Zulu letters and phrases from my colleagues Katlego Tshiloane, Sandile Zwane and Mondli Hlatshwayo.

The sources I used share the strengths and limitations of all mission archives. Male missionaries are the main authors and actors in the dramas enacted. The voices of mostly male African school principals, teachers, students and community participants in schools are patchily present, giving expression to the varied but largely unequal relationships that existed between missionaries and the educational communities with and among whom they worked. And the voices of women – white as well as African – are, as in other archives, largely absent. Read against the grain, the archives nonetheless provide remarkable evidence of unfolding events related to missions and also to schooling.

I was fortunate to be able to use the Lutheran Theological Institute archive in Pietermaritzburg shortly before its tragic closure owing to financial reasons in 2016. This archive held all the reports on institutions as well as activities in which Hermannsburgers were jointly involved through the Cooperating Lutheran Mission. Sources for Umpumulo all originate from that archive. According to Georg Scriba and Martin von Fintel, the institute's archival holdings were taken to Metrofile in Pinetown for storage in April 2017. These records are all in English.

It was possible to use both archival sources and interviews in some of the chapters. It is a commonplace of historical research, however, that interviews with social actors must be treated similarly to archival, documentary sources, and with the same concerns for validity and reliability. Memory and recollection are faulty processes – and similarly constitute processes of 'self-making' and representation. I have tried to deal with interviews not simply as 'statements of fact' about the past, but also as windows into the beliefs and assumptions held by individuals.

Regarding classroom activity, curricula are an important source, as are text-books, examinations and school publications, such as school annual magazines. Formal curricula, however, are not always implemented. How they are implemented, or what is deemed important and valuable in teaching the curriculum at any one time, is best assessed through the examinations students take, and the textbooks that are actually used in schools and classrooms. Like curricula, textbooks are all too frequently produced but not used. I deliberately sought and discussed those textbooks for which I found evidence of use in Hermannsburger classrooms. Teachers themselves are crucial to the educational process, and here a set of exam papers for qualifying teachers in the Lutheran Theological Institute provides insight into what was expected of teachers at the time.

A significant section of this book deals with textbooks produced by missionaries, before and during the apartheid era. The August Hesse German Africana archive at Unisa has a comprehensive collection of everything that the Hermannsburg Mission Press produced, while the National Library of South Africa, as a deposit library, contains extensive holdings of school textbooks produced for all schools, in all subjects, during the apartheid period. In the research for this book I merely scratched the surface of this collection, which merits more extensive research.

This book is, ultimately, a history of Lutheran missionaries in education, and responses to them as represented in and through various secondary and primary sources. My own selection and interpretation were guided by an interest, on the one hand, in the complexities of educational transition, as well as the ongoing continuities and discontinuities between past and present, and local, national and international interactions. On the other hand, I was interested in the social relations and conflicts around education as manifested in relationships between the state and missionaries; educational actors, the state and traditional authorities; and the pedagogical ideas with which, and educational institutions in which, these entities worked, individually and collectively.

NOTES

Introduction

1   Norman Etherington, 'Mission Station Melting Pots as a Factor in the Rise of South African Black Nationalism', *The International Journal of African Historical Studies*, IX (4) (1976): 592–605; Norman Etherington, *Preachers, Peasants and Politics in Southeast Africa 1835–1880: African Christian Communities in Natal, Pondoland and Zululand* (London: London Royal Historical Society, 1978).

2   John Comaroff and Jean Comaroff, *Of Revelation and Revolution, Volume I: Christianity, Colonialism and Consciousness in South Africa* (Chicago: University of Chicago Press, 1991), 36.

3   John L. Comaroff and Jean Comaroff, 'The Colonization of Consciousness', in *A Reader in the Anthropology of Religion*, ed. Michael Lambek (Oxford: Blackwell, 2002).

4   Patrick Harries, 'Missionaries, Marxists and Magic: Power and the Politics of Literacy in South East Africa', *Journal of Southern African Studies* 27 (3) (2001): 409.

5   Isabel Hofmeyr, *The Portable Bunyan: A Transnational History of the Pilgrim's Progress* (Princeton: Princeton University Press, 2004), 117.

6   Stephen Volz, *African Teachers on the Colonial Frontier: Tswana Evangelists and their Communities during the Nineteenth Century* (New York: Peter Lang, 2011).

7   Peter Limb, 'Intermediaries of Class, Nation, and Gender in the African Response to Colonialism in South Africa, 1890s–1920s', also Stephen Volz and Part T. Mgadla, 'Conflict and Negotiation along the Lower Vaal River: Correspondence from the Tswana-language Newspaper, Mokaeri oa Becuana', in *Grappling with the Beast: Indigenous Southern African Responses to Colonialism, 1840–1930*, eds Peter Limb, Norman Etherington and Peter Midgley (Leiden: Brill, 2010).

8   Richard Elphick, *The Equality of Believers: Protestant Missionaries and the Racial Politics of South Africa* (Charlottesville: University of Virginia Press, 2012); Ingie Hovland, *Mission Station Christianity: Norwegian Missionaries in Colonial Natal and Zululand, Southern Africa, 1850–1890* (Leiden: Brill, 2013).

9   Richard Elphick, 'Introduction', *Christianity in South Africa: A Political Social and Cultural History*, eds Richard Elphick and Rodney Davenport (Cape Town: David Philip, 1997), 1–16; Richard Elphick, 'Writing Religion into History: The Case of South African Christianity', in *Missions and Christianity in South African History*, eds Henry Bredenkamp and Robert Ross (Johannesburg: Wits University Press, 1995), 11–27; Richard Elphick, *The Equality of Believers*.

10 Hovland, *Mission Station Christianity*.

11 Hovland, *Mission Station Christianity*, 126.

12 See for example Deborah Gaitskell, 'Devout domesticity? A Century of African Women's Christianity in South Africa', in *Women and Gender in Southern Africa to 1945*, ed. Cheryl Walker (London: James Currey, 1990), 251–272; Deborah Gaitskell, 'Ploughs and Needles: State and Mission Approaches to African Girls' Education in South Africa', in *Christian Missionaries and the State in the Third World*, eds Holger Hansen and Michael

Twaddle (Oxford: James Currey, 2002), 98–120; Deborah Gaitskell, 'Race, Gender and Imperialism: A Century of Black Girls' Education in South Africa'. Paper presented at seminar, Wits University African Studies Institute, August 1998.

13   See for example Kirstin Fjelde Tjelle, *Missionary Masculinities, 1870–1930: The Norwegian Missionaries in South-East Africa* (Basingstoke: Palgrave MacMillan, 2013). Tjelle's discussion, adaptation and development of the dominant approach to masculinity taken in South Africa that distinguishes between 'hegemonic' and 'subordinate' masculinities is especially useful for an exploration of Lutheran mission masculinities. See also Robert Morrell, 'Of Boys and Men: Masculinity and Gender in Southern African Studies', *Journal of Southern African Studies* 24 (4) (1998): 605–630.

14   Kristin Fjelde Tjelle, *Missionary Masculinities*, 63, 98.

15   Cynthia Kros, 'W.W.M. Eiselen: Architect of Apartheid Education', in *The History of Education under Apartheid 1948–1994*, ed. Peter Kallaway (Cape Town: Maskew Miller Longman, 2002); Cynthia Kros, *The Seeds of Separate Development: The Origins of Bantu Education* (Pretoria: Unisa Press, 2010).

16   Andrew Bank, 'The Berlin Mission Society and German Linguistic Roots of *Volkekunde*: The Background, Training and Hamburg Writings of Werner Eiselen, 1899–1924', *Kronos* 41 (1) (Nov. 2015): 166–192.

17   Sue Krige, 'Segregation, Science and Commissions of Enquiry: The Contestation over Native Education Policy in South Africa, 1930–1936', *Journal of Southern African Studies* 23 (3) (Sept. 1997): 491–506; Jonathan Hyslop, 'Food, Authority and Politics: Student Riots in South African Schools 1945–1976', in *Regions and Repertoires: Topics in South African Politics and Culture*, ed. Stephen Clingman (Johannesburg: Ravan, 1991), 84–115; Jonathan Hyslop, "A Destruction Coming In": Bantu Education as Response to Social Crisis', in *Apartheid's Genesis 1935–1972*, ed. Philip Bonner, Peter Delius and Deborah Posel, 393–411 (Johannesburg: Ravan/Wits University Press, 1993); Brahm Fleisch, 'State Formation and the Origins of Bantu Education', in *The History of Education under Apartheid*; Kros, 'W.W.M. Eiselen'.

18   Elphick, *The Equality of Believers*.

19   Hyslop, 'A Destruction Coming In'; Jonathan Hyslop, 'State Education Policy and the Social Reproduction of the Urban African Working Class: The Case of the Southern Transvaal 1955–1976', *Journal of Southern African Studies* 14 (3) (April 1988): 446–476.

20   Meghan Healy-Clancy, *A World of their Own: A History of South African Women's Education* (Charlottesville: University of Virginia, 2014).

21   Saul Dubow, *Apartheid 1948–1994* (Oxford: Oxford University Press, 2014).

22   Leon Tikly, 'Postcolonialism and Comparative Education', *International Review of Education* 45 (5–6) (1999): 603–621.

23   Gary McCulloch, 'Empires and Education: The British Empire', in *International Handbook of Comparative Education*, eds Robert Cowen and Andreas Kazamias (Dordrecht: Springer, 2009), 169–179.

24   Andrew Zimmerman, *Alabama in Africa: Booker T. Washington, the German Empire, and the Globalization of the New South* (Princeton: Princeton University Press, 2010); Rebecca Swartz, '"Ignorant and Idle": Indigenous Education in Natal and Western Australia, 1833–1875' (PhD diss., University of London, 2015).

25   Jonathan Hyslop, 'Comparative Historical Sociology and Transnational History: A
      Response to Julian Go's Patterns of Empire', *Comparative Studies of South Asia, Africa and
      the Middle East* 34 (3) (2014): 610–617; see also Barnita Bagchi, Echkardt Fuchs and
      Kate Rousmaniere, eds., *Connecting Histories of Education: Transnational and Cross-Cultural
      Exchanges in (Post)Colonial Education* (London: Berghahn, 2014).

26   Timothy Gibbs, *Mandela's Kinsmen: Nationalist Elites and Apartheid's First Bantustan*
      (Johannesburg: Jacana, 2014).

27   Robert Cowen, 'Then and Now: Unit Ideas and Comparative Education', in *International
      Handbook of Comparative Education, Vol. 22*, eds Robert Cowen and Andreas Kazamias
      (Dordrecht: Springer, 2009), 339.

28   Tjelle, *Missionary Masculinities*, 55.

29   Tjelle, *Missionary Masculinities*, 114–132.

30   Tjelle, *Missionary Masculinities*, 123–124.

31   Tikly, 'Postcolonialism and Comparative Education'.

32   Peter Kallaway and Rebecca Swartz, eds, *Empire and Education in Africa: The Shaping of a
      Comparative Perspective* (New York: Peter Lang, 2016).

33   Kirsten Rüther, *The Power Beyond: Mission Strategies, African Conversion and the
      Development of a Christian Church in the Transvaal* (Hamburg: LIT Verlag, 2001), 107.

34   Fritz Hasselhorn, *Bauernmission im Südafrika: Die Hermannsburger Mission im
      Spannungsfeld der Kolonialpolitik 1880–1939* (Hermannsburg: Verlag der Ev-Luth. Mission,
      1989), 1.

35   Heinrich Voges, 'Die Arbeit im Südlichen Afrika', in *Vision: Gemeinde Weltweit: 150 Jahre
      Hermannsburger Mission und Ev-luth. Missionswerk in Niedersachsen*, ed. E-A. Lüdemann
      (Hermannsburg: Verlag der Missionshandlung, 2000), 233–357.

36   Georg Scriba with Gunnar Lislerud, 'Lutheran Missions and Churches in South Africa',
      in Elphick and Davenport, *Christianity*, 173–195.

37   Hasselhorn, *Bauernmission*; Rüther, *The Power Beyond*.

38   Hanns Lessing et al., eds, *The German Protestant Church in Colonial South Africa: The
      Impact of Overseas Work from the Beginnings until the 1920s, Vol. I* (Wiesbaden: Cluster,
      2012); Hanns Lessing et al., eds, *Contested Relations: Protestantism between Southern Africa
      and Germany from the 1930s to the Apartheid Era, Vol. II* (Wiesbaden: Harrassowitz Verlag,
      2015).

39   Hasselhorn, *Bauernmission*; Rüther, *The Power Beyond*.

40   Bernard Mbenga, 'Dutch Reformed Church Mission Education and the Emergence of
      Secular Schooling among the Bakgatla-ba-Kgafela Community of Rustenburg District,
      South Africa, 1903–1930s'. Paper presented at the African Studies Association (ASA)
      of America Annual Meeting, Roosevelt Hotel, New Orleans, Louisiana, November
      18–22, 2009.

41   See Andrea Schultze, *In Gottes Namen Huetten Bauen: Kirchlicher Landbesitz in Südafrika:
      die Berliner Mission und die Evangelisch-Lutherische Kirche Suedafrikas zwischen 1834 und
      2005* (München: Fritz Steiner Verlag, 2005), 493–510.

42   See *In Gottes Namen*, where Schultze argues that the distinctions that Hasselhorn makes
      between different forms of land acquisition by the Hermannsburg Mission are not as
      clear-cut as he maintains. Hasselhorn distinguishes between five forms: (i) purchase of

land by missionaries on the market (ii) purchase by individual missionaries (iii) purchase in Trust with means provided by communities (iv) grants by chiefs (v) grants by the British colonial government and (vi) land granted by testament. In particular, Schultze argues firstly that purchase of land in Trust was not a form of protest against discrimination but a practical decision based on chronic scarcity of financial resources. Many missionaries indeed disliked this form of purchase. Secondly, she holds that most missionaries could not afford to buy land and that much land that was claimed to be in their individual ownership was in fact purchased and built up through mixed financing that included African contributions. And thirdly, land granted to missionaries in Zululand by Mpande was given not as permanent private property but for their use only. After the conclusion of the Anglo-Zulu War in 1879, land thus given to missionaries was converted into grants and reduced in size, and the remaining area turned into locations that eventually became the Bantustans.

43   Graeme Simpson, 'Peasants and Politics in the Western Transvaal, 1920–1940' (MA thesis, University of the Witwatersrand, 1986).

44   Simpson, 'Peasants', 358ff.

45   Simpson, 'Peasants', 412.

46   Simpson, 'Peasants', vii.

47   Thomas Thale observes that 'the major contradiction in Penzhorn's philosophy is [that] while he considered himself a custodian of Bafokeng culture, he was at the same time responsible for the destruction of some of the cultural practices observed by Bafokeng and for giving them a new identity as a polity', 'Of Tribal Boys and Communists: Naboth Mokgatle's *The Autobiography of an Unknown South African*', *Current Writing*, 6 (1) (1994): 50.

48   'Rebels' was the term used by contemporaries to refer to breakaway movements at the mission.

49   Belinda Bozzoli with Mmanto Nkotsoe, *Women of Phokeng, Consciousness, Life Strategy and Migrancy in South Africa, 1900–1983* (Johannesburg: Ravan, 1991), 57–81.

50   See Bernard Mbenga and Andrew Manson, *People of the Dew: A History of the Bafokeng of Phokeng-Rustenburg Region, South Africa, from Early Times to 2000* (Johannesburg: Jacana, 2010), 66; also Bernard Mbenga, 'The Rev. Kenneth Mosley Spooner: African-American Missionary to the Fokeng of Rustenburg District, South Africa, 1915–1937' (*Journal of Southern African Studies*, forthcoming).

51   See Simpson, 'Peasants', Chapter 6: 'Christian Peasants and Politics'; also Bozzoli with Nkotsoe, *Women*, Chapter 2: 'Church, School and Tribe, 1910–1925'.

52   Naboth Mokgatle, *Autobiography of an Unknown South African* (London: C. Hurst, 1971).

53   Simpson, 'Peasants', 358ff; Bozzoli with Nkotsoe, *Women*, 57.

54   Rüther, *The Power Beyond*, 222.

55   Rüther, *The Power Beyond*, 236.

56   Lessing et al., eds, *Contested Relations, Vol. II*.

57   Fritz Hasselhorn, '"Why can't we celebrate at the church up there anymore?" The Segregation of the Congregations in Hermannsburg (Natal)', in Lessing et al., *The German Protestant Church, Vol. I*, 471–485.

58   Martin Eberhardt, 'German Settler Communities in Southern Africa and the Third Reich', in Lessing et al., *Contested Relations, Vol. II*, 99.

59   Kevin Ward, 'German Lutherans and English Anglicans in Southern Africa to 1918: A Shared and Divergent History', in Lessing et al., *The German Protestant Church, Vol. 1*, 422.

60   Kevin Ward, 'Afrika! Mayibuye! Equality, Freedom and Humanity', in Lessing et al., *Contested Relations, Vol. II*, 233.

61   Etherington, *Peasants, Preachers and Politics*, 45–46.

62   Gunther Schendel, 'Exploring the Territory between Universalism, *Volkstum* and Race Policies. Discourses on South Africa in the Berlin and the Hermannsburg Mission Societies', 155–177; Rudolf Hinz, 'Conflicts in Dealing with Apartheid: The Churches and Missions of German Origin Working in Southern Africa until the End of the 1960s', 287–312; and Kevin Ward, 'Afrika! Mayibuye! Equality, Freedom and Humanity: The Struggle for South African Christianity in the Twentieth Century', in Lessing et al., *Contested Relations, Vol. II*, 231–243.

63   Peter Kallaway, 'Volkskirche, Volkekunde and Apartheid: Lutheran Missions, German Anthropology and Humanities in African Education,' 140–155; Gunther Schendel, 'Exploring the Territory between Universalism, Volkstum and Race Policies. Discourses on South Africa in the Berlin and the Hermannsburg Mission Societies, 155–177; Hinz, 'Conflicts in Dealing with Apartheid,' 287–312.

64   Gunther Schendel, *Die Missionsanstalt Hermannsburg und der National-sozialismus. Der Weg einer lutherischen Milieuinstitution zwischen Weimarer Republik und Nachkriegszeit.* (Munster: 2009).

65   Scriba with Lislerud, 'Lutheran Missions', 173.

66   Hinz, 'Conflicts in Dealing with Apartheid'.

67   Elphick, *Christianity*, 7.

Chapter 1

1   Fritz Hasselhorn, *Bauernmission in Südafrika: Die Hermannsburger Mission in Spannungsfeld der Kolonialpolitick 1880-1939* (Hermannsburg: Verlag der Ev-Luth. Mission, 1998); Kirsten Rüther, *The Power Beyond: Mission Strategies, African Conversion and the Development of a Christian Culture in the Transvaal* (Hamburg: LIT Verlag, 2001); Heinrich Voges, 'Die Arbeit im Südlichen Afrika', in *Vision: Gemeinde Weltweit: 150 Jahre Hermannsburger Mission und Ev-luth. Missionswerk in Niedersachsen*, ed. Ernst-August Lüdemann (Hermannsburg: Verlag der Missionshandlung, 2001); Hanns Lessing et al., eds, *Umstrittene Beziehungen: Protestantismus zwischen dem südlichen Afrika und Deutschland von den 1930er Jahren bis in die Apartheidzeit – Contested Relations: Protestantism between Southern Africa and Germany from the 1930s to the Apartheid Era* (Wiesbaden: Harrassowitz Verlag, 2015).

2   Gunther Pakendorf, 'A Brief History of the Berlin Mission Society in South Africa', *History Compass* 9 (2) (2011): 107.

3   Interview with Heinrich Voges, 9 October 2015, Pretoria.

4   Pakendorf, 'A Brief History', 108.

5   Hans-Jurgen Oschadleus, 'Lutherans, German: Hermannsburgers', *Natalia*, 22 (1993): 33.

6   Etherington, *Preachers, Peasants and Politics*, 27; Oschadleus, 'Lutherans', 31.

7   Christina Landman, 'The Piety of German Women in South Africa', *Studia Historiae Eccclesiasticae* 40 (2) (Dec. 2014): 125.

8   Tjelle, *Missionary Masculinities*, 123–124.

9   In his historical account of Hermannsburg schooling, Heinz Dehnke wrote: 'All reports concur that more girls than boys attend the school and that they attend school much more regularly than boys. That is so, even today. In the upper grades there are predominantly girls; the reason for the absence of the boys is, today as in those days, that they are herdsmen'. See Heinz Dehnke, 'Die Mission und die Schule: Unsere besonderer Berücksichtigung der Transvaalmission', in *Und die Vögel des Himmels wohnen unter Seinen Zweigen: Hundert Jahre Bauernmission in Südafrika*, ed. Winfried Wickert, trans. Margot von Beck (Hermannsburg: Missionshandlung, 1949), 18.

10   See James Campbell, *Songs of Zion: The African Methodist Episcopal Church in the United States and South Africa* (Oxford: Oxford University Press, 1995), 114; see also Rüther, *The Power Beyond*, passim.

11   Naboth Mokgatle, *Diary of an Unknown South African* (Berkeley: University of California Press, 1971).

12   Bernard Mbenga and Andrew Manson, *'People of the Dew'*. However, see also Schultze's modification of this argument, *In Gottes Namen*, fn. 42.

13   See Rüther, *The Power Beyond*, Introduction.

14   Rüther, *The Power Beyond*, 94; see also Hasselhorn, *Bauernmission*, passim.

15   Rüther, *The Power Beyond*, 117.

16   While these schools are not the subject of this book, the topic is deserving of a fuller treatment.

17   Unisa, August Hesse Collection of German Africana, ADA 266.416 82 SCHU: CAR Schulenberg, 'Die Hermannsburgse Sending in Transvaal', Voordrag gelewer vir die Eugène Nielen Marais-tak van die Suid-Afrikaanse Akademie vir Wetenskap en Kuns (paper presented at the University of South Africa, Pretoria, August 27, 1981), 8.

18   Voges, 'Die Arbeit im Südlichen Afrika', 259.

19   Compiled from the Evangelisch-Luthersiches Missionswerk Hermannsburg, ELM H SA. Acc. 76.1157 Statistische Uebersicht über die Betschuanenmissionen im Jahre 1949, 1 Magaliesberg-Kreis, 2 Mariko-Kreis; Statistische Uebersicht über die Zulumission im Jahre 1949; Gesamt-Uebersicht.

20   Dehnke, 'The Mission and the School', 8.

21   Tjelle, *Missionary Masculinities*, 71.

22   Herman Schluyter, *The History of the Co-operating Lutheran Missions in Natal 1912–1951* (Durban: Moorleigh Press, 1951).

23   For a history of the emergence of a 'patchwork' of Lutheran Missions in South Africa, see Georg Scriba with Gunnar Lislerud, 'Lutheran Missions and Churches in South Africa', in *Christianity in South Africa: A Political, Social and Cultural History*, eds R. Elphick and R. Davenport (Berkeley: University of California Press, 1997), 173–95.

24   See Hovland, *Mission Station Christianity*.

25   Schluyter, *The History of the Co-operating Lutheran Missions*, 9–11.

26 Ingolf Hodne, *Missionary Enterprise in African Education: The Cooperating Lutheran Missions in Natal, South Africa, 1912–1955: A Documentation* (Stavanger: Misjonshogskolens forlag, 1997).

27 Hodne, *Missionary Enterprise*, 29; Schluyter, *The History of the Cooperating Lutheran Missions*, 13.

28 Hodne, *Missionary Enterprise*, 24.

29 ELM H SA Acc. 76.572, A Scheme of Cooperation between Lutheran Missions drawn up in Natal at a meeting held at Umpumulo Mission Station, 19–24 April 1911.

30 Schluyter, *The History of the Co-operating Lutheran Missions*, 18.

31 Schluyter, *The History of the Co-operating Lutheran Missions*, 36.

32 Hodne, *Missionary Enterprise*, 38.

33 Joseph Reilly, *Teaching the 'Native': Beyond the Architecture of an Unequal Education System* (Pretoria: Human Sciences Research Council Press, 2016).

34 Hodne, *Missionary Enterprise*, 69, 75.

35 Schluyter, *The History of the Co-operating Lutheran Missions*, 59.

36 Schendel, 'Exploring the Territory', 177; Pakendorf, 'A Brief History', 114.

37 Union Education Department (UED), Report of the Interdepartmental Committee on Native Education, 1935–36, Government Printer, Pretoria, Union Government 29/1936.

38 Sue Krige, 'Segregation, Science and Commissions of Enquiry: The Contestation over Native Education Policy in South Africa, 1930–1936', *Journal of Southern African Studies*, 23 (3) (Sept. 1997): 491–506.

39 Hodne, *Missionary Enterprise*, 132.

40 ELM H SA Acc. 76.1329, 'Our Reaction to the Attempts of the Education Department to take control of Native Teachers out of the Hands of Grantees'.

41 ELM H SA Acc. 76.1329, 'Our Reaction', 2.

42 ELM H SA Acc. 76.1329, 'Our Reaction', 2.

43 ELM H SA Acc. 76.1329, 'Our Reaction', 56.

44 ELM H SA Acc. 76.1329, 'Our Reaction', 56.

45 ELM H SA Acc. 76.1357, W.O. Rindahl, B. Schiele, O. Sarndal, 'Memorandum of Committee appointed to formulate the Views of the Co-operating Lutheran Missions in Natal in Connection with the Report of the Commission on Native Education, 1949–1951', Dundee, Natal, 10 June 1952, 1–6.

46 ELM H SA Acc. 76.1357, 'Memorandum', Section II: General Principles, 1.

47 ELM H SA Acc. 76.1357, 'Memorandum', 1, Section III: Tribal Culture, 1, and Section IV: The Missions and Bantu Education, 2.

48 ELM H SA Acc. 76.1357, 'Memorandum', Section V: Control of Schools, 3.

49 ELM H SA Acc. 76.1357, 'Memorandum', Section VI: Financial Matters, 4.

50 ELM H SA Acc. 76.1357, 'Memorandum', Section VII: Type of Schools, 4.

51 ELM H SA Acc. 76.1357, 'Memorandum', Section VIII: Medium of Instruction, 5.

52 ELM H SA Acc. 76.1357, 'Memorandum', Section IX: Official Languages, 5.

53 ELM H SA Acc. 76.1357, 'Memorandum', Section X: Religious Instruction, 5.

54 See Scriba with Lislerud, 'Lutheran Missions', 173.

55 Pakendorf, 'A Brief History', 109.

56   Elphick, *Christianity in South Africa*, 4.

57   Interview with Voges, 9 October 2015, Pretoria.

58   'The General Missionary Conference was formed in 1904 to bring together various missionary groups to discuss and act upon common issues. This was replaced in 1936 by the Christian Council of South Africa (CCSA). This body changed its name to the South African Council of Churches (SACC), as well as its structure, at its 17th biennial meeting on 28 May 1968'. Last modified 9 May 2017, http://www.archivalplatform.org/registry/entry/south_african_council_of_churches/

59   Voges, 'Die Arbeit im Südlichen Afrika', 321–322.

60   See Rudolf Schmidt, *Die Wertung des Volkstums bei Louis Harms, Vortrag gehalten anlässlich einer Freundesratstagung der Hermannsburger Mission* (Hanover: Verlag der Missionshandlung Hermannsburg, n.d.), 1–20. For a discussion of interpretations of *Volkstum*, see G. Schendel, *Die Missionsanstalt Hermannsburg und der Nationalsozialismus. Der Weg einer Lutherischen Milieuinstitution zwischen Weimarer Republik und Nachkriegszeit* (Münster: Lit Verlag, 2009), 331–356.

61   For example, Rev. K Meister's claim: 'bastardisation has so many dangers that there has to be geographical separation'. ELM H SA Acc. 76.572, 'Attitude of the Lutheran Church to the Racial Question' (paper presented at the General Lutheran Conference, Durban, September 12–13, 1950).

62   See Voges, 'Die Arbeit im Südlichen Afrika', and contributions by Peter Kallaway, Gunther Schendel and Kevin Ward, in Lessing et al., *Contested Relations*, Vol. II.

63   ELM H SA Acc. 76.382, R. Tönsing and O. Brümmerhoff, 'Memorandum by the Hermannsburg Mission on Questionnaire of Native Education Commission signed by R. Tönsing and O. Brümmerhoff on behalf of the Select Committee of the Hermannsburg Mission, Krugersdorp, 30 June 1949.

64   Heinz Dehnke, 'The Mission and the School'; Micah Kgasi, *Thutô ke eng?*, trans. Enos Makhele (Lovedale: Lovedale Press, 1949 [1939]).

65   Ronald Herr, *'Heinz Dehnke. Ein Missionar in der Auseinandersetzung um die Kirchwerdung und den Schwarzen Politischen Aufbruch in Südafrika'* (MTheol thesis, University of South Africa, 1992); for a brief history, see also Heinrich Pape, *Hermannsburger Missionare in Südafrika*, Vol. 1 (Wonderboom: Barrodel, 1986), 35– 36.

66   Herr, 'Heinz Dehnke', 122.

67   Herr, 'Heinz Dehnke', 122.

68   Schendel, *Die Missionsanstalt Hermannsburg*, 346–477, 352, 401–402, 409. Schendel depicts a man whose closeness to national socialist thought is best represented in his work, 'Volkstum und Schule auf dem Hermannsburger Missionsfeld', in W. Gerber, *Vom Missionsdienst der Lutherische Kirche* Band 2 (Leipzig: Verlag Wallman, 1938), 68–72.

69   Herr, 'Heinz Dehnke', Abstract, 3.

70   Dehnke, 'The Mission and the School', 11.

71   Dehnke, 'The Mission and the School', 14.

72   Dehnke, 'The Mission and the School', 32.

73   Herr, 'Heinz Dehnke', 49.

74   http://www.sahistory.org.za/people/king-mzilikazi, last modified May 9, 2017.

75   Kgasi, *Thutô ke eng?* (*What is Education?*), 30. (Translated by Enos Makhele).

76   Kgasi, *Thutô ke eng?*, 32.

77   Kgasi, *Thutô ke eng?*, 34.

78   Kgasi, *Thutô ke eng?*, 34.

79   Kgasi, *Thutô ke eng?*, 43.

Chapter 2

1   Central Archives Depot (CAD), Native Affairs Files (NTS) South African Police
      (SAP) 509, 15.8.53. Report from Office of the Deputy Commissioner, Transvaal, to
      Commissioner of the South African Police re Riot: Bethel Native Training Institution,
      22 May 1953.

2   Kerry Chance, '"Where there is Fire, there is Politics": Ungovernability and Material Life
      in Urban South Africa' in *Cultural Anthropology*, 30 (3) (2015): 401.

3   Tjelle, *Mission Masculinities*, 111.

4   See Jonathan Hyslop, 'Food, Authority and Politics: Student Riots in South African
      Schools 1945–1976', in *Regions and Repertoires: Topics in South African Politics and Culture*,
      ed. Stephen Clingman (Johannesburg: Ravan, 1991), 84–115; Colin Bundy, 'Schooled for
      Life? The Childhood and Education of Govan Mbeki' (seminar paper presented at Yale
      University, New Haven, December 2, 1992).

5   For a discussion of the limitations and possibilities of using mission sources, see Rüther,
      The Power Beyond.

6   Teacher training qualifications offered by the Bethel Training Institution in 1951:
      (a) Native Teachers' Higher Certificate, for which the qualification was the Junior
      Certificate (J.C.); (b) the Native Teachers' Lower Certificate, which required as entrance
      qualification Form 1 or Std VI and a special entrance examination administered by the
      Department of Native Education in the Transvaal; (c) Matriculation, which also required
      J.C. The Institution awarded a limited number of loan bursaries for teachers. There
      were also a few free bursaries awarded by the department. Boarding fees were £14 p.a.,
      sports fees amounted to 5 shillings p.a., and 'book accounts amounted to approximately
      £3 per annum'. See Wits Historical Papers Research Archive, Collection Number
      AD1715, South African Institute of Race Relations (SAIRR), 1892–1974, 'A Survey
      Conducted by the South African Institute of Race Relations: Careers for Africans, Part II
      Training Colleges and Industrial Schools', Johannesburg, 1951, 18–19.

7   Paul-Lenert Breutz, *Die Stamme van die Distrik Lichtenburg en Delareyville*, Union
      of South Africa, Native Affairs Department, Ethnological Series no 37, Pretoria,
      Government Printer, 1957, par. 112, pp 50–51.

8   Trust farms were bought on behalf of, and held in trust for, Africans by missionaries,
      usually with both mission and African resources.

9   Breutz, *Die Stamme*, par. 54–57, pp.24–28. For further information on trust farms, see
      Introduction above, endnote 42.

10   Heinrich Voges, '*Die Arbeit im Südlichen Afrika*', 269; see also Horst Meyberg, *Gedanken
      & Worte Band 4: Bethel, Südafrika, eine Schule von Menschen geplant, von Gott geführt*
      (Pretoria: H. Meyberg, 2002), 13–14.

11   Evangelisch-lutherisches Missionswerk (ELM) in Niedersachsen, Hermannsburg, ELM H
      SA Acc. 76.518, Bethel Diamond Diggings 1924; Dept of Mines and Industries
      Certificate of Owner's Claims no. 43, signed 16 May 1924, Klerksdorp; see also ELM H
      SA Acc. 76.1456.

12   The original German reads 'sozusagen eine "Palastrevolution"'. See Meyberg, *Gedanken &
      Worte*, 19–20. (Author's translation.)

13   Meyberg, *Gedanken & Worte*, 20.

14   Herr, 'Heinz Dehnke', 26.

15   Meyberg, *Gedanken & Worte*, 24.

16   ELM H SA Acc. 76.395.2, Hermann Greve, 'Jahresbericht des Lehrerseminars, Bethel in
      Transvaal, 1945' (Annual Report of the Teacher Training College, Bethel, Transvaal [for]
      1945), Bethel, Jan. 1946.

17   ELM H SA Acc. 76.395.2, Greve, 'Jahresbericht des Lehrerseminars, Bethel in Transvaal,
      1945' (Annual Report of the Teacher Training College, Bethel, Transvaal [for] 1945),
      Bethel, Jan 1946.

18   ELM H SA Acc. 76.386, Minutes of the Sitting of both Mission Councils on 10 May
      1945, Krugersdorp; Application by Brümmerhoff, acting Superintendent of the HMB to
      Additional Native Commissioner Mr van Heerden at Hammanskraal, 17 May 1945; the
      permit was granted on 6 June 1945.

19   ELM H SA Acc. 76.395.2, Sondersitzung zur Einführung von Br. Greve am 31. Juli-1.
      Aug., 1945 (Special Meeting at the Introduction of Brother Greve from 31 July – 1
      August 1945). The minutes indicate that the response to the student petition was guided
      by the wishes of the parents for the students to continue working. Therefore the require-
      ment for an additional £3 would fall away and things would continue as before. While
      the student petition is not in the file, the response indicates that the students wanted
      answers to the decisions of the institution following the circular to, and response of, the
      parents.

20   ELM H SA Acc. 76.395.2, Greve, 'Jahresbericht des Lehrerseminars, Bethel in Transvaal,
      1945' (Annual Report for the Teacher Training College, Bethel, Transvaal [for] 1945),
      Bethel, Jan. 1946.

21   ELM H SA Acc. 76.395.2, Greve, 'Jahresbericht des Lehrerseminars, Bethel in Transvaal,
      1945' (Annual Report for the Teacher Training College, Bethel, Transvaal [for] 1945),
      Bethel, Jan. 1946).

22   CAD, Bantoe-Onderwys (BO) vol. 84, ref. NEI/38268, G.H. Franz, 'Bethel-
      Opleidingskool: Verhoudings tussen Superintendent en Onderwysende Staf' (Relationships
      between the Superintendent and Teaching Staff). And G.H. Franz, Addendum to
      Memorandum on Bethel, 11.6.1953.

23   See Mbenga and Manson, *People of the Dew*, 116–122.

24   Schultze, *In Gottes Namen*, 508.

25   ELM H SA Acc. 76.388, Letter from H. Greve to Otto [Brümmerhoff], 20.1.1953.

26   See Tjelle, *Missionary Masculinities*, ch. 5: 'Norwegian Mission Masculinity and "Other"
      Zulu Masculinity,' 85–113.

27   ELM H SA Acc. 76.388, 'Ein Bericht über das Betragen der Schüler am Sonntagabend,
      den 12 April, und die darauffolgenden Untersuchungen' (A Report on the Behaviour of

the Students on Sunday evening 12 April and the Subsequent Investigations), 18 April 1953; see Letter from H. Greve to Otto [Brümmerhoff], 2.05.1953.

28 ELM H SA Acc. 76.388, Letter from [Otto Brümmerhoff] to Hermann [Greve], 9.5.1953.

29 ELM H SA Acc. 76.388, 'Bethel Opleidingskool: Memorandum van Onderhoud tussen H.I.N.O. [Hoof Inspekteur Naturelle Onderwys] en Beherende Liggaam van die Inrigting oor die Jongste Onluste' (Memorandum of the Interview between the H.I.N.O. [Chief Inspector of Native Education] and the Governing Body of the Institution about the recent Disturbances. (Undated, author's translation). The likely author of the memorandum is G.H. Franz.

30 Meyberg, *Gedanken & Worte*, 32–33. (Author's translation).

31 Meyberg, *Gedanken & Worte*, 34; ELM H SA Acc. 76.543, Letter from Winfried Wickert to the Brothers of the Hermannsburg Mission (undated); The *Deutsche Presse Agentur*, Hamburg, raised 500 DM for Bethel and transferred the amount through Mr H.J. Krueger. The value in Sterling was £42 12s 7d. Minutes of the Council Meeting, 1.07.1953. ELM H SA Acc. 76.388.

32 Gottfried Heinrich Franz was born on 30 Sept 1896 on Berlin Lutheran Mission station near Houtbosdorp in the Pietersburg district, where his father was a missionary. After a period in Pietersburg, he matriculated at Pretoria Boys' High School in 1914. He then attended the Transvaal University College [now the University of Pretoria], where he obtained a BA degree and a Higher Teachers' Diploma. He started teaching in Pietersburg in August 1919, and from 1921 to 1926 he assisted J.C. Johns, Inspector of Native Schools in Pietersburg, with refresher courses for teachers. In May 1926 he was appointed Inspector of Native Education in Bloemfontein, with the Orange Free State as his circuit. In 1930 he was transferred to Pretoria where he remained for the remainder of his career, except for the period 1942 to 1945, when he was Inspector in Pietersburg. In August 1947 he succeeded Dr W.W.M. Eiselen as Chief Inspector of Native Education in the Transvaal. After the creation of the new Division of Bantu Education Mr Franz was transferred to Head Office, where he took charge of language issues and the preparation of teacher lesson guides. He died shortly after his retirement in Sept 1956. Summarised from 'G.H. Franz: An Appreciation', *African Studies* 16 (1) (1957): 83.

33 ELM H SA Acc. 76.389.2, Letter from Saron, Phokeng to W. Wickert, 28.5.1953.

34 See reports in ELM H SA Acc. 76.388: P.A. Hoffman (Voorsitter), H.J. van Zyl, H. Dehnke, C.T. Muller, 'Verslag van die Kommissie van Ondersoek Bethel Opleidingsinrigting (Vertroulik)' (Report of the Commission of Enquiry Bethel Training Centre – Confidential). (Undated, author's translation); [Author probably G.H. Franz], 'Bethel Opleidingskool: Memorandum van Onderhoud tussen H.I.N.O. [Hoof Inspekteur Naturelle Onderwys] en Beherende Liggaam van die Inrigting oor die Jongste Onluste' (Memorandum of the Interview between the H.I.N.O. [Chief Inspector of Native Education] and the Governing Body of the Institution about the recent Riots. (Undated, author's translation). The likely author of the report is G.H. Franz. Although it is undated, it is evident that this interview was held and the memorandum prepared after the Commission of Inquiry had done its work; National Archives of South Africa, Pretoria, Bantoe Onderwys, 1/38268, Hoof Inspekteur, 'Verslag oor Bethel Onluste,

ASOD'), (Chief Inspector, 'Report on the Bethel Riots'). (Undated, author's translation); Pretoria National Archives, BO vol. 84, ref. NEI/38268, Signed Statements by Rev. H. Greve, Bethel, 3 June 1953; Georg Heinrich Theodore Meyer, Bethel, 4 June 1953, K.T.M. Kgomongwe, Bethel, 4 June 1953; K.K. Sephoti, Mr B. Volker and Johannes Poo, Bethel, 4 June 1953.

35   Winfried Wickert, 'Südafrika: Das Unglück von Bethel' (South Africa: The Disaster at Bethel), *Hermannsburger Missionsblatt* 93 (7) (1953): 74. (Author's translation.)

36   CAD, BO, vol. 84, ref. 1/38268. Submission from Chief Inspector of Native Education, 25.5.1953 (marked ASOD) CAD, BO, vol. 84, ref. 1/38268; Notice from the Secretary of the Transvaal Education Department, G. Jones: Bethel Training Institution: Commission of Inquiry, undated.

37   The name is spelt either Poo or Pooe in the documents.

38   See ELM H SA Acc. 76.388, 'Bethel Opleidingskool: Memorandum van Onderhoud tussen H.I.N.O. [Hoof Inspekteur Naturelle Onderwys] en Beherende Liggaam van die Inrigting oor die Jongste Onluste' (Memorandum of the Interview between the H.I.N.O. [Chief Inspector of Native Education] and the Governing Body of the Institution about the recent Unrest). (Undated, author's translation). The likely author of the memorandum is G.H. Franz.

39   CAD BO vol. 84, 1/38268, Hoof Inspekteur, 'Verslag oor Bethel Onluste, ASOD'), (Chief Inspector, 'Report on the Bethel Disturbances'). (Undated, author's translation).

40   CAD, BO, vol. 84, 1/38268, Hoof Inspekteur, 'Verslag oor Bethel Onluste, ASOD'), (Chief Inspector, 'Report on the Bethel Disturbances'). (Undated, author's translation).

41   CAD, BO, vol. 84, NEI/38268, GH Franz, 'Bethel-Opleidingskool: Verhoudings tussen Superintendent en Onderwysende Staf', 11.6.1953.

42   CAD, BO vol. 84, ref. NEI/38268 [Author probably G.H. Franz], 'Bethel-Opleidingskool: Memorandum van Onderhoud tussen H.I.N.O. [Hoof Inspekteur Naturelle Onderwys] en Beherende Liggaam van die Inrigting oor die Jongste Onluste' (Memorandum of the Interview between the H.I.N.O. [Chief Inspector of Native Education] and the Governing Body of the Institution about the recent Disturbances. (Undated, author's translation). See also ELM H SA Acc. 76.142.7. A letter from W. Eiselen to Meyer (undated) suggests that Eiselen supported Franz's position and considered Meyer's approach to the entire incident to be unsatisfactory. In this letter, written in Afrikaans, he comments on the incident where the principal dismissed six students, remarking that the student protest could not be considered entirely unreasonable, that 'the reasons for the dismissal . . . were certainly not satisfactory', that 'the punishment that was applied was disproportionately heavy – here are paying students who doubted the legality of an instruction who were punished more heavily than the teachers who draw a salary and who make themselves guilty of gross immorality', and that the information with which he was provided was 'incomplete and misleading'. In these circumstances, the department had decided that all candidates would be admitted for the exam and that instructions to other training schools to refuse admission to the students would be cancelled. (Author's translation of the original Afrikaans: '(c) dat die protes van die leerlinge nie as heeltemal onredelik kan beskou word nie . . . (e) dat die redes vir die ontslag van ses bepaalde leerlinge uit die hele groep geensins voldoende is nie (f) dat die straf wat toegepas is

buite verhouding swaar is (Hier is betalende studente omdat hulle getwyfel het aan die
wettigheid van 'n bevel swaarder gestraf as wat gebeur het in die geval van salaristrek-
kende onderwysers wat hulle b.v. aan growwe onsedelikheid skuldig maak) (g) dat die
plaaslike outoriteite by die melding van die geval aan die Dept baie onvolledig en derh-
alwe misleidende informasie verskaf het. Onder hierdie omstandighede is besluit dat al die
kandidate tot die Departmentele eksamen sal toegelaat word, end dat die instruksies aan
ander opleidingskole om die betrokke leerlinge nie op te neem nie gekanselleer salword
om hulle weer in Bethel op te neem'.).

43   CAD BO vol. 84, ref. 1/38268, Signed statement by K.K. Sephoti (teacher).

44   CAD, NTS, SAP, vol. 509, Ref. No 15/8/1953, Transvaal Office of the Deputy
     Commissioner of Police to the Commissioner of South African Police, 'Report on the
     Riot: Bethel Native Training Institution', 24 June 1953; see also Meyberg, *Gedanken &*
     Worte, 35.

45   ELM H SA Acc. 76.388, ('Abschrift des Protokolls der Seminarratssitzung in Bethel am
     30 Juni und 1 Juli 1953') (Transcript of the Minutes of the College Council meeting in
     Bethel on 30 June and 1 July 1953). (Author's translation.)

46   ELM H SA Acc. 76.388, ('Abschrift des Protokolls der Seminarratssitzung in Bethel am
     30 Juni und 1 Juli 1953') (Transcript of the Minutes of the College Council meeting in
     Bethel on 30 June and 1 July 1953). (Author's translation.)

47   ELM H SA Acc. 76.388, 'Dikgang tsa Kopanô tsa di 20 tsa January 1954 mo Bethel'
     (News of the meeting held on 20 January 1954 at Bethel.) (Translation by Kgatlego
     Tshiloane.)

48   Meyberg, *Gedanken & Worte*, 41.

49   ELM H SA Acc. 76.395.2, 'Abschrift des Protokolls der Seminarratssitzung in Kroondal'
     (Transcript of the Minutes of the College Council meeting at Kroondal), 6.8.1953.
     (Author's translation.)

50   CAD BO vol. 84, ref. 1/38268, Secretary of the Transvaal Education Department
     to H. Greve, 14.7.1953; ELM H SA Acc. 76.389.2, ('Abschrift des Protokolls der
     Seminarratssitzung in Langlaagte am 11.8.1953' (Transcript of the Minutes of the College
     Council meeting in Langlaagte, 11.8.1953). (Author's translation.)

51   ELM H SA Acc. 76.388, 'Dikgang tsa Kopanô tsa di 20 tsa January 1954 mo Bethel'
     (Minutes of the Council of Friends meeting held on 20 January 1954 at Bethel).
     (Translation by Kgatlego Tshiloane.)

52   ELM H SA Acc. 76.388, Letter to Otto Brümmerhoff from Heinz [Dehnke], 9.4.1954.

53   ELM H SA Acc. 76.389.2, Letter from H. Greve to Otto [Brümmerhoff], z. Zt [zur
     Zeit: currently based at] Ramoutsa, 11.8.1954. (Author's translation.)

54   ELM H SA Acc. 76.388, Letter from Bethel Training College to Secretary of Native
     Affairs, Pretoria (undated, but probably October 1954, as the last meeting mentioned in
     the letter was held on 29 September 1954).

55   See H. Voges, *'Arbeit im Südlichen Afrika'*, 298.

56   ELM H SA Acc. 76.388. See letter from Lucas Mangope, Chairman of Bethel Training
     College, Bodenstein, to Regional Director of Bantu Education, Pretoria, 20.12.1955.

57   'Kgosi Lucas Manyane Mangope, Doctor of Laws, LLD 28/04/1984' last modified June 8,
     2016, http://www.nwu.ac.za/sites/www.nwu.ac.za/files/files/Lucas%20Mangope.pdf

58   'Governmentality' is a Foucauldian concept that refers to the 'art of government'. See
      Michel Foucault, *The Birth of Biopolitics: Lectures at the College de France 1978–1979*,
      ed. Michael Senellart, trans. Graham Burchell (New York: Palgrave MacMillan, 2010).
      Governmentality is also associated with 'disciplinary power', a concept that Foucault
      developed in *Discipline and Punish: The Birth of the Prison* (Middlesex: Penguin, 1975).
59   ELM H SA Acc. 76.694, Letter from Department of Bantu Education, Pretoria, to
      Principal of Bethel Training College, P.K. Bodenstein (undated).
60   Meyberg, *Gedanken & Worte*, 102–3.

Chapter 3

1   Muriel Horrell, *Bantu Education to 1968* (Johannesburg: South African Institute of Race
      Relations, 1968), 24.
2   See for example Frank Molteno, 'The Historical Foundations of the Schooling of Black
      South Africans' in *Apartheid and Education: The Education of Black South Africans*, ed. Peter
      Kallaway (Johannesburg: Ravan, 1984), 93.
3   Jonathan Hyslop, 'State Education Policy and the Social Reproduction of the Urban
      African Working Class: The Case of the Southern Transvaal 1955–1976', *Journal of
      Southern African Studies*, 14 (3) (April 1988): 446–476.
4   See Bernard Mbenga, 'Dutch Reformed Church Mission Education and the Emergence
      of Secular Schooling among the Bakgatla-ba-Kgafela Community of Rustenburg District,
      South Africa, 1903–1930s' (paper presented at the African Studies Association of America
      Annual Meeting, The Roosevelt Hotel, New Orleans, USA, 18–22 November 2009), 1–13.
5   Simpson, 'Peasants', Chapter 5.
6   Simpson, 'Peasants', 333.
7   Simpson, 'Peasants', 334.
8   Simpson, 'Peasants', 335.
9   ELM H SA Acc. 76.395.2, Karl Bühr, 'Jahresbericht über die Missionsstation Bethanie
      Tvl über das Jahr 1939' (Annual Report for the Mission Station Bethanie Transvaal over
      the Year 1939), Bethanie, 10 February 1940. (Author's translation.)
10   See Pape, *Hermannsburger Missionare*, vol. I, 26-7.
11   Simpson, 'Peasants', 335.
12   ELM H SA Acc. 76.395.2, Moruti Joseph Mogotsi, 'Jahresbericht über Bethanie im
      Rustenburg-distrikt' für 1944' (Annual Report for Bethanie in the district of Rustenburg
      for 1944), 31 January 1945.
13   ELM H SA. Acc. 76.395.2, Karl Bühr, 'Jahresbericht über die Missionsstation Bethanie
      Tvl. über das Jahr 1944' (Annual Report prepared for the Mission Station Bethanie
      Transvaal for the year 1944), Bethanie, 30 January 1945.
14   ELM H SA. Acc. 76.395.2, Karl Bühr, 'Jahresbericht über die Missionsstation Bethanie
      Tvl. über das Jahr 1944' (Annual Report prepared for the Mission Station Bethanie
      Transvaal for the year 1944), Bethanie, 30 January 1945.
15   ELM H SA. Acc. 76. 395.2, Karl Bühr, 'Jahresbericht über die Missionsstation Bethanie
      Tvl. über das Jahr 1945', (Annual Report for Mission station Bethanie Transvaal for the
      year 1945), Bethanie, 25 January 1946.

16   ELM H SA Acc. 76.388. Otto Brümmerhoff apparently wrote and distributed a
     Rundbrief (circular) regarding the role of missionaries as school superintendents, and
     though there seems to be no record of the circular, this file contains three additional
     documents, from H. Lange, 'Vorschläge für Veränderung der Schulsuperintendenteur',
     (Proposals for Changing the School Superintendency) (n.d., author's translation), K.
     Bühr, 'Entwurf: Bedingungen, unter denen wir bereit wären, unsere Schulen an die
     Regierung abzutreten', (Draft: Conditions under which we would be prepared to hand
     over our schools to the government) (3 March 1945, author's translation) and H. Dehnke,
     'Superintendeur der Schule' (School Superintendency) (n.d. Author's translation). In
     these documents, reference is made to the tense relationship between state and mission
     concerning the control of mission schools, and also to tense relationships between
     missionaries and communities on mission stations, which were linked to these issues. Both
     Lange and Bühr refer to hints that the Education Department intended to take over
     schools, and they propose communication with the department to secure the influence of
     missionaries in specific fields, such as Religious Instruction. For Dehnke, the priority is to
     use his influence to ensure a closer relationship between the school and community or the
     parents. A debate follows in which the proposals are considered by some and dismissed
     by others. Significantly, they refer as early as 1945 to problems in mission schools
     between church and state, and also between missions and mission communities.

17   August Friedrich Otto Brümmerhof was born on 5 Dec 1906. He was the son of a peas-
     ant from the Lüneberger Heide in Germany. After training as a missionary he went to the
     Transvaal Mission in 1931. He learnt Tswana and his first postings were at the stations
     Krugersdorp and Salem. A best man at his wedding was Heinz Dehnke, who was in mis-
     sion service at Krugersdorp, Salem-Jericho-Saron-Krugersdorp. In January 1944 he became
     Superintendent of the Magaliesburg district, and retired on 1 January 1973. In 1974 he
     suffered a heart attack and in 1984 a stroke, from which he never recovered. He died in
     the H.F. Verwoerd Hospital, Pretoria, on 17 October 1984. See H. Pape's *Hermannsburger
     Missionare in Südafrika Band 1* (Wonderboom: Barrodel Drukkers, 1986), 25–6.

18   Simpson argues that the conflict at Bethanie at this time had little to do with the earlier
     Jericho/Hebron opposition to Mamogale, and more with successionist issues resulting
     from the appointment of unwanted chiefs by the Native Affairs department. The role of
     the mission in supporting unpopular chiefs was integral to these battles.

19   ELM H SA Acc. 76.388, Letter to Pastor O. Brümmerhoff, senior Pastor of
     Hermannsburg church in Phokeng, 26.3.1946.

20   Simpson, 'Peasants', 336.

21   ELM H SA Acc. 76.386.2, Letter from Chief B. Ramakoka, P.O. Ramakokstad, via Brits,
     to Assistant Native Commissioner, Pilanesberg, 26 March 1946.

22   P-L Breutz, *The Tribes of Rustenburg and Pilanesberg Districts*, Union of South Africa,
     Department of Native Affairs, Ethnological Publications No 28, Pretoria, Government
     Printer, 1953, 321–341.

23   ELM H SA Acc. 76.386.2, Assistant Native Commissioner to Native Commissioner,
     Rustenburg 8.4.1946; Native Commissioner, Rustenburg, to Inspector of Education,
     Rustenburg, 9.5.1946 re Bethel Tribal School Ramakokstad.

24   ELM H. SA Acc. 76.386.2, Inspector of Schools C.A. Jansen to Rev. Brümmerhoff of
     Saron P.O. Phokeng, re Ramakokstad Native School.

25   ELM H SA Acc. 76.385.

26   ELM H SA Acc. 76.385, C.A. Jansen, Inspector of Transvaal Education Department to
     O. Brümmerhoff, 17 January 1947.

27   See 'Peter Gerdes Meyerhoff', in Pape, *Hermannsbürger Missionare*, vol. I, 123.

28   Mbenga and Manson, '*People of the Dew*', 78.

29   Mbenga and Manson, '*People of the Dew*', 93, citing Saul Dubow's 'Holding a "Just
     Balance between White and Black": The Native Affairs Department in South Africa, c.
     1920–1933', *Journal of Southern African Studies* 12 (2) (April 1986): 22–23.

30   Mbenga and Mason, '*People of the Dew*', 121.

31   He was co-director from 1932 to 1934 and again from 1937 to 1957. See Voges, 'Die
     Arbeit im Südlichen Afrika', 353.

32   Winfried Wickert, 'Der Fall Saron' (The Case of Saron), *Hermannsburger Missionsblatt*, 94
     (December 1954): 135–137. (Author's translation.)

33   ELM H SA Acc. 76.1457.1, First Defendant's reply to Plaintiff's Declaration in the
     matter between James Tomogale Molotlegi and Reverend O. Brümmerhoff and Mission
     Society of Hermannsburg, Hanover, Germany.

34   ELM H SA Acc. 76.1457, Letter from Gratus, Sacks & Bernard Melman to Reverend
     O. Brümmerhoff, 28.2.1952, cc. W. Wickert at Moorleigh, Natal, 9.4.1952. According
     to Mokgatle, 'Paramount Chief Manotshe James Molotlegi changed his name from
     Mokgatle to Molotlegi after his father when he became the Paramount Chief'. Mokgatle,
     Autobiography, 83.

35   ELM H SA Acc. 76.388, Letter from Otto B[rümmerhoff], Saron, Phokeng, to
     Chief Inspector of the Transvaal Education Department, Mr G.H. Franz, 4.8.1951.

36   Jonathan Hyslop, 'School Boards, School Committees and Educational Politics: Aspects
     of the Failure of Bantu Education as a Hegemonic Strategy, 1955–1976', in *Holding Their
     Ground: Class, Locality and Culture in 19th and 20th Century South Africa*, ed. P. Bonner
     et al. (Johannesburg: Ravan/Wits University Press, 1989), 211–212.

37   Horrell, *Bantu Education*, 24.

38   ELM H SA Acc. 76.388, Letter from Otto B[rümmerhoff], Saron, Phokeng, to Chief
     Inspector of the Transvaal Education Department, Mr G.H. Franz, 4.8.1951.

39   ELM H SA Acc. 76.1457.1, Extract from the standard work of the Hermannsburg
     Mission Society, G. Haccius, *Hannoversche Missionsgeschichte*, vol. 3, 1, 237ff.

40   Haccius, *Hannoversche Missionsgeschichte*, vol. 3, 2 and 173ff.

41   ELM H SA Acc. 76.1457.1, Memorandum re Native Affairs Department. In the
     Supreme Court of South Africa, Transvaal Provincial Division. J.T. Molotlegi and Rev.
     O. Brümmerhoff and Mission Society of Hermannsburg, 3.

42   ELM H SA Acc. 76.1457.1, Memorandum re Native Affairs Department. In the
     Supreme Court of South Africa, Transvaal Provincial Division. J.T. Molotlegi and Rev.
     O. Brümmerhoff and Mission Society of Hermannsburg, 3.

43   ELM H SA Acc. 76.1457.1, Stegmann, Oosthuizen & Jackson [solicitors for
     Brümmerhoff] to Rev. O. Brümmerhoff, 5 June 1952.

44 ELM H SA Acc. 76.1457.1, Letter from Brümmerhoff to Stegmann, Oosthuizen &
    Jackson, 2 May 1953 and Letter to Solicitor in Estcourt, 12.5.1953.
45 ELM H SA Acc. 76.1457.1, Letter from Congregation of Saron to Rev. Wickert,
    12 June 1954. The signatories were the churchwardens of Saron: Th. Montsho, Joh. Nke,
    E. Mokgatle, A. Phokela, Noa Diale, David Rapoo, A. Ramutla, Fredrik Mokgatle, M.
    Mokoe and E. Radinka.
46 ELM H SA Acc. 76.1457.1, Stegmann, Oosthuizen & Jackson to Solicitors, Estcourt,
    20 July 1954.
47 ELM H SA Acc. 76.1457.1, In the Supreme Court of South Africa, Transvaal Provincial
    Division, James Tomagale Molotlegi vs Rev. O. Brümmerhoff and Mission Society of
    Hermannsburg, 3 September 1954, 6.
48 Cited in the Supreme Court of South Africa, Transvaal Provincial Division, 3 September
    1954.
49 Mbenga and Manson, 'People of the Dew', 122.
50 Simpson, 'Peasants', 358.

Chapter 4

1 ELM H SA Acc. 76.1139, File No. 252/302, Union of South Africa, Department of
   Native Affairs, Division of Bantu Education, Circular to all Grantees, Superintendents
   or Managers of State-Aided schools from W.W.M. Eiselen, 'Regarding the Transfer of
   control of state-aided schools to Bantu community organisations, except in the case of
   teacher training schools,' 2.08.1954.
2 Deborah Posel, 'The Apartheid Project 1948–1970' in The Cambridge History of South
   Africa, Volume 2: 1885-1994, eds Robert Ross et al. (Cambridge: Cambridge University
   Press, 2012), 323.
3 Posel, 'The Apartheid Project', 345–348, 355–359.
4 Schultze, In Gottes Namen, 508.
5 Johann Kistner's son was of a more liberal persuasion and questioning disposition than
   his father. The son was principal and superintendent of the Hermannsburg School from
   1955–1965, when he became mission superintendent at Moorleigh. He was a pastor in
   Germany from 1969–1972, when he joined the staff of the newly-formed Theological
   College in Pietermaritzburg. In 1977 he was appointed director of the Division of Justice
   and Reconciliation of the South African Council of Churches (SACC), a post he held
   until 1988. See 'Wolfram Kistner 1923–2006 United Evangelical Lutheran Church South
   Africa', Dictionary of African Christian Biography, accessed March 3, 2017 http://www.dacb.
   org/stories/southafrica/kistner_wolfram.html.
6 Fritz Scriba, The Ehlanzeni Mission Station 1856–1973, ed. and trans. J.H. Scriba, April
   2014. Information about the life of Fritz Scriba was compiled from an interview by the
   author with Georg Scriba, December 2015, and from H. Pape, Hermannsburger Missionare
   in Südafrika Band 1 Lebens-und Arbeitsberichte mit Bildern. Ein Beitrag zur Südafrikanische
   Geschichte (Wonderboom: Barrodel Printers, 1986), 183–84.
7 Interview with Heidi and Christian Kohn, 7 November 2016, Hanover, Germany.

8   ELM H SA Acc. 76.1139, Letter from Superintendent of the Hermannsburg Mission in Natal and Zululand, Fritz Scriba, P.O. Moorleigh to W.W.M. Eiselen, 24.8.1954. ELM H SA Acc. 76.1139.
9   ELM H SA Acc.76.610, Letter from Superintendent of the Hermannsburg Mission in Natal and Zululand, Fritz Scriba, to Secretary of Native Affairs, Pretoria, regarding Transfer of State-Aided Schools to Bantu Education, 13.12.1954.
10 ELM H SA Acc. 76.1139, H.F. Verwoerd to all Grantees, etc.: Regulations for the Registration of Bantu Schools. ELM H SA Acc. 76.1139.
11 ELM H SA Acc. 76.1139, Circular N 24/10300 C.M. 3/1955.
12 ELM H SA Acc. 76.1139, Circular from Department of Native Affairs Bantu Education section, Heyfries Building, Schoeman Street, Pretoria, to Managers and Grantees of Schools owned by Churches and Religious Societies which will become Bantu Community Schools and Regional Directors and Inspectors of Bantu Education. 1.04.1955.
13 ELM H SA Acc. 76.1329, Rev. W. Wickert to Regional Director of Bantu Education re Government-Aided Native Schools and Mission Schools of the Hermannsburg Mission in Natal and Zululand, 2.1.1955.
14 ELM H SA Acc. 76.1329, Department of Native Affairs, Department of Bantu Education, Pietermaritzburg, to Heads of Churches and Mission Societies, Grantees and Managers and Circuit Inspectors and Administrative Organisers re New Classification of Aided Bantu Schools. C M 18/1955; N 26/10300. ELM H SA Acc. 76.1329.
15 ELM H SA Acc. 76.12.35, Regional Director of Bantu Education, S.R. Dent, to Rev. J. von Fintel, 10.9.1956. ELM H SA Acc. 76.12.35.
16 ELM H SA Acc. 76.1330, 'DRC Native Schools will have to close too. From our Correspondent in Pretoria', *The Natal Mercury*, 25.7.1958.
17 ELM H SA Acc. 76.1329, Fritz Scriba, Empangweni, 'Schullage' (School analysis), 28.4.1956.
18 ELM H SA Acc. 76.1329, Fritz Scriba, Empangweni, 'Schullage', 28.4.1956.
19 ELM H SA Acc. 76.1329.
20 ELM H SA Acc. 76.1330, Department of Bantu Education, Building Section 3.11.1960 to Treasurer of Hermannsburg Mission Society re Hiring of Buildings from Churches and other Parties for use as Bantu Community schools.
21 ELM H SA Acc. 76.1330, Fritz Scriba 18.1.1960.
22 ELM H SA Acc. 76.1330, Fritz Scriba 18.1.1960.
23 ELM H SA Acc. 76.1330, Fritz Scriba 18.1.1960. Potgieter's comment was made on 3 February 1961 in response to a letter from Scriba dated 18 January 1961. The latter was responding to the Department of Bantu Education, Building Section, Pretoria, that had sent a circular to the Treasurer of the Hermannsburg Mission Society re 'Hiring of Buildings from Churches and other Parties for use as Bantu Community schools' on 3 November 1960.
24 ELM H SA Acc. 76.1330, Heini Fedderke, 'Bericht über die Lage der Bantu Community Schools unserem Missionsgebiet in Natal und Zululand', Georgenau, 5 April 1961.
25 ELM H SA Acc. 76.1330, Heini Fedderke, 'Bericht über die Lage der Bantu Community Schools unserem Missionsgebiet in Natal und Zululand'.

26   ELM H SA Acc. 76.1330, Circular dated June 1961, Reference A5/1/256.

27   ELM H SA Acc. 76.1330, Letter from S.R. Dlangalala, 17.11.1961; Letter to Fritz
      Scriba from Umvoti and Kranskop School Boards 14.6.1961, and from Msinga Bantu
      School Board 20.6.1961.

28   ELM H SA Acc. 76.1330, Stillfried von Fintel, Hermannsburg 16 May 1962, to
      Missionary Fedderke, P.O. Wartburg Regarding the Emthombeni Lease. Report on
      meeting, 9.05.1962.

29   ELM H SA Acc. 76.1328, Letter from Inspector of Bantu Education, Pietermaritzburg,
      to Rev. Fritz Scriba, Moorleigh, Estcourt, 1.8.1957.

30   ELM H SA Acc. 76.1328, Report by Fritz Scriba on Hermannsburg Schools sent to
      H. Schubert, General Manager of Schools and Hostels, South Eastern Region, Natal,
      10.7.1969.

31   ELM H SA Acc. 76.1329, Fritz Scriba, Empangweni, 'Schullage', 28.4.1956.

32   ELM H SA Acc. 76.1139, Fritz Scriba to Bantu Education Regional Director, 9.03.1957.

33   ELM H SA Acc. 76.1328, Letter from Hellett & De Waal Solicitors, Notaries and
      Conveyancers to Rev. Scriba, 18.05.1957.

34   ELM H SA Acc. 76.1328, Letter from Gunter Krause to Fritz Scriba and Ingolf Hodne,
      28.8.1958.

35   ELM H SA Acc. 76.1328, Fritz Scriba, Superintendent of Hermannsburg Mission Natal
      and Zululand to Secretary of Native Affairs, Pretoria, regarding classification of Müden
      Farm School, 27.8.1957.

36   ELM H SA Acc. 76.1328, Department of Native Affairs, Bantu Education Division,
      Circular to all Managers/Owners of farm schools, 28.06.1958.

37   ELM H SA Acc. 76. 397 1–3, Annual Report for 1958 by W. Kaiser 3.2.1959.

38   Anti-Slavery Society, *Child Labour in South Africa* (London: Anti-Slavery Society, 1980).

39   ELM H SA Acc. 76.1140, see correspondence between Missionary Henneke and
      Fritz Scriba, 1966; ELM H SA Acc. 76.1328; see also correspondence in ELM H SA
      Acc. 76.1140.

40   ELM H SA Acc. 76.1140, see for example circular received by Rev. Henneke of Piet
      Retief on 13 Feb. 1968 requesting information and his response.

41   ELM H SA Acc. 76.1297 1-3, see correspondence between the Inspector of Bantu
      Education and Scriba about Müden near Greytown and Ophathe near Weenen,
      27.6.1963, 13.8.1963, 14.8.1963, 5.10.1963.

42   ELM H SA Acc. 76. 1297, see correspondence between Bodenstein and Scriba,
      28.7.1959, 3.8.1959, 20.8.1959, 3.9.1959.

43   See ELM H SA Acc. 76.1140.

44   ELM H SA Acc. 76.1296, Letter from Acting Superintendent-General Scriba to Bantu
      Affairs Commissioner, Piet Retief, 25 June 1964.

45   ELM H SA Acc. 76.1296, Letter to Mr Lammerding, Sendelingspos (also known as
      Zendelingspost) via Paulpietersburg from Fritz Scriba, 22.10.1964.

46   ELM H SA Acc. 76.1296, Letter to Mr Lammerding, Sendelingspos (also known as
      Zendelingspost) via Paulpietersburg from Fritz Scriba, 22.10.1964.

47   ELM H SA Acc. 76.399, Annual Report for the year 1964, Esibongweni Mission
      Station, Shiyane Circuit, Natal.

48   Voges, 'Die Arbeit im Südlichen Afrika', 321.

49   Wendy Leeb and John Aitchison, 'Report to the ELC Property Management Company: ELCSA (SED) Farm Schools – A Development Study', Pietermaritzburg, 1990, 38. Pietermartizburg: Centre for Adult Education, University of KwaZulu-Natal.

50   Leeb and Aitchison, 'Report', 26.

51   Leeb and Aitchison, 'Report', 26.

52   ELM H SA Acc. 76.1329, Fritz Scriba, 'Schullage'.

53   ELM H SA Acc. 76.1297, Fritz Scriba to Right Rev. Bishop Helge Fossues, ELC P.O. Mapumulo, Natal (Mapumulo also spelt as Umpumulo or Umphumulo).

54   ELM H SA Acc. 76.1328, Report by Fritz Scriba on Hermannsburg Schools sent to H. Schubert, General Manager of Schools and Hostels, South Eastern Region, Natal, 10.7.1969.

55   ELM H SA Acc. 76.1328.

56   'Introduction' to *Africa's Hidden Histories: Everyday Literacy and the Making of the Self*, ed. Karin Barber (Bloomington: Indiana, 2006), 9.

57   ELM H SA Acc. 76.640, see Principal of Keatesdrift School to Rev. Seinwill, 22.1.1957.

58   ELM H SA Acc. 76.640, see Principal of Keatesdrift School to Rev. Seinwill, 22.1.1957.

59   ELM H SA Acc. 76.640, Letter from Principal Robert Kuzwayo, Keates Drift school to Superintendent of the Lutheran Church, Rev. F Scriba, Natal, 28.10.1957.

60   ELM H SA Acc. 76.640, Letter from teacher E.E. Ndwawonde to priest in charge of Keatesdrift, 5.1.1962.

61   ELM H SA Acc. 76.640, H.M.D. Mbhele to Fritz Scriba, 28.4.1958.

62   ELM H SA Acc. 76.640, H.M.D. Mbhele to Scriba, 28.4.1958.

63   ELM H SA Acc. 76.640, Letter from Rev. Fritz Scriba, Moorleigh, to Mbhele, 9.5.1958.

64   ELM H SA Acc. 76.640, Letter from Rev. Fritz Scriba, Moorleigh, to Mbhele, 9.5.1958.

65   ELM H SA Acc. 76.640, Rev. Seinwill to Principal Robert Kuzwayo of Keatesdrift School, 27.9.1957.

66   ELM H SA Acc. 76.1235, Correspondence between Education Department and Rev. Welke of Obersfelde (also spelt Oebisfelde), P.O. Dalton, 26.7.1949, 1.8.1939, 4.8.1939.

67   ELM H SA Acc. 76.1119, Letter from Rev. Filter of Sendelingspos (also known as Zendelingspost: LC) Native School, Entombe, to Mr J. de Jager, Inspector of Native Education, Standerton, 28.11.1949; Handwritten notes of the School Committee meeting, 25.11.1949, regarding an allegation by Joseph Mdlalose that he found E. Dladla in his sister's room; Letter from Transvaal Education Department to Mr J. de Jager, 8.12.1949.

68   ELM H SA Acc. 76.1137, Letter from Mr J. de Jager, Inspector of Native Education in Standerton, to Rev. Filter, 4.8.1947; Rev. Filter to Inspector J. de Jager, 16.3.1948; Dick Nkambule to Rev. Filter, 28.8.1948.

69   ELM H SA Acc. 76.1297, Letter from F.W. Schmidt 25.6.1959, giving particulars of a teacher employed at the Bangisizuzu Native Bantu School since 1951; see also N. Erlank, 'Sexual misconduct and church power on Scottish mission stations in Xhosaland in South Africa in the 1840s', *Gender and History* 15 (1) (2003): 69–84.

70   ELM H SA Acc. 76.1296, Proposed Conditions of Service for Teachers Employed by the Owner of a State-Aided Farm School, Departmental Circular.

71   ELM H SA Acc. 76.640, Rev. Seinwill to R. Khuzwayo, 8.9.1959.

72   ELM H SA Acc. 76.640, Principal to Rev. Seinwill, 11.9.1959.

73   ELM H SA Acc. 76.640, Rev. Seinwill to J.J.P. de Wet Nel, November 1961.

74   ELM H SA Acc. 76.640, J.J.P. de Wet Nel to Rev. Seinwill, 11.11.1961.

75   ELM H SA Acc. 76.640, Rev. Seinwill to J.J.P. de Wet Nel 11.1.1962. This was an
      ongoing issue: see also letter from C.V. Roettcher, manager of Müden Mission Farms, to
      Lukas Gcaba, 3.8.1964, complaining about meetings held in the church that went on into
      the early hours of the morning, and forbidding these under threat of 'further steps being
      taken'. Scriba observed to W.T. Kruse: 'Now this evening music must stop; it in no way
      has the approval of the church'. 22.8.1964.

Chapter 5

1   See for example Naboth Mokgatle's account of mission schooling in Phokeng. He makes
      it clear that the purpose of schooling provided by the Hermannsburger, Ernst Penzhorn,
      was confirmation and religious education. Referring to his experience in Penzhorn's
      mission school in 1929, he wrote: 'We were all prepared to become good Lutherans and
      devout Christians'. See Mokgatle, *Autobiography*, 162. However, as the Comaroffs have
      revealed with reference to an earlier period, this does not negate the role of the mission
      and school in working to reconfigure 'space and time, separating the sacred from the
      secular, work from leisure, the public from the private, the inner from the outer'. See
      J. and J. Comaroff, *Of Revelation and Revolution*, 234.

2   See Unisa August Hesse Collection of German Africana, Acc. 74.

3   Union of South Africa, *Debates of the House of Assembly* (Hansard), First Session –
      Eleventh Parliament, 3 July to 2 October, 1953, Vols, 82, 83, col. 3635–3636.

4   Horrell, *Bantu Education to 1968*, 90.

5   Horrell, *Bantu Education to 1968*, 140.

6   Michael Apple, *Ideology and Curriculum*, (New York: Routledge, 1990); Michael Apple
      and Linda Christian-Smith, eds, *The Politics of the Textbook* (New York: Routledge, 1991);
      Michael Apple, *Education and Power* (New York: Routledge, 1995); Michael Apple, *Power,
      Meaning and Identity: Essays in Critical Educational Studies* (New York: Peter Lang, 1999);
      Michael Apple, *Official Knowledge: Democratic Education in a Conservative Age* (New York:
      Routledge, 2000); Michael Apple, 'The Political Economy of Text Publishing', *Educational
      Theory* 34 (4) (1984): 307–319.

7   Eckhardt Fuchs, 'Current Trends in History and Social Studies Textbook Research',
      Journal of International Cooperation in Education 14(2) (2011): 17–34; Jason Nicholls,
      'Introduction: School History Textbooks across Cultures from the Perspective of
      Comparative Education', in *School History Textbooks across Cultures: International Debates
      and Perspectives*, ed. Jason Nicholls (Oxford: Oxford University Press, 2006).

8   See for example Franz Auerbach, 'An Enquiry into History Textbooks and Syllabuses
      in Transvaal High Schools' (MEd thesis, University of the Witwatersrand, 1963); Franz
      Auerbach, *The Power of Prejudice in South African Education* (Cape Town: A.A. Balkema,
      1965); Elizabeth Dean, Paul Hartmann and May Katzen, *History in Black and White: An
      Analysis of South African School History Textbooks* (Paris: UNESCO, 1983); Cynthia Kros,
      'Telling Lies about History and Hoping to Forget All about History', *South African*

Historical Journal 42 (2000): 69–88;. Ryôta Nishino, *Changing Histories: Japanese and South African Textbooks in Comparison 1945–1995* (Göttingen: V&R Unipress, 2011); Sasha Polakow-Suransky, 'Historical Amnesia? The Politics of Textbooks in Post-Apartheid South Africa' (paper presented at the Annual Meeting of the American Educational Research Association, New Orleans, Louisiana, April 1–5, 2002).

9   See for example: Archie Dick, *The Hidden History of South Africa's Book and Reading Cultures* (Toronto: University of Toronto Press, 2012); *Print, Text and Book Cultures in South Africa*, ed. Andrew van der Vlies (Johannesburg: Wits University Press, 2012); Isabel Hofmeyr, Preben Kaarsholm and Bodil Frederiksen, 'Introduction: Print Cultures, Nationalisms and Publics of the Indian Ocean', *Africa* 81 (1) (2011): 1–22.

10   Comaroff and Comaroff, *Of Revelation and Revolution*, 218–19.

11   Comaroff and Comaroff, *Of Revelation and Revolution*, 223.

12   See Peter Vail, 'Introduction', *The Creation of Tribalism in Southern Africa*, ed. Leroy Vail (Berkeley: University of California Press, 1989); Patrick Harries, *Butterflies and Barbarians: Swiss Missionaries and Knowledge in South-East Africa* (Oxford: James Currey, 2007).

13   Vail, 'Introduction', 11–12.

14   Vail, 'Introduction', 12.

15   Sarah Pugach, 'Carl Meinhof and the German Influence on Nicholas van Warmelo's Ethnological and Linguistic Writing, 1927–1935', *Journal of Southern African Studies* 30 (4) (2004), 830.

16   Pugach, 'Carl Meinhof', 831.

17   Bank, 'The Berlin Mission Society', 178–181.

18   J. and J. Comaroff, *Of Revelation and Revolution*, 223.

19   Scriba and Lislerud, 'Lutheran Missions and Churches', 186.

20   Voges, 'Die Arbeit', 257.

21   Herman Schluyter, *The History of the Co-operating Lutheran Missions in Natal 1912–1951* (Durban: Moorleigh Press, 1951), 36.

22   Schluyter, *The History of the Co-operating Lutheran Missions*, 73.

23   For a set of such publications, see August Hesse Collection, Unisa, Acc. 74.

24   Union of South Africa, Union Education Department (UED), Report of the Interdepartmental Committee on Native Education, 1935–36, Pretoria, Government Printer, UG 29–1930, 135. This Report was known as the Welsh Report.

25   Welsh Report, 135–137.

26   Welsh Report, 83.

27   Welsh Report.

28   Welsh Report.

29   Welsh Report.

30   Welsh Report, 80.

31   Isabel Hofmeyr, *The Portable Bunyan: A Transnational History of the Pilgrim's Progress* (Princeton: New Jersey, 2004), 114–130.

32   South African Institute of Race Relations (SAIRR), Historical Papers Research Archive, University of the Witwatersrand, Johannesburg, Collection number AD1715 D 111623; African Authors Conference, Johannesburg 1936, in 'Conferences on Literature for the South African Bantu' (Lovedale: Lovedale Press, n.d.); See also Union Education

Department (UED), Report of the Interdepartmental Committee on Native Education, 1935–36, Pretoria, Government Printer, UG 29–1930, 135–37.

33   South African Institute of Race Relations (SAIRR), Historical Papers Research Archive, University of the Witwatersrand, Johannesburg, Collection number AD1715 D 111623, 'Conferences on Literature for the South African Bantu', Bloemfontein, June 1936, and Johannesburg, October 1936. (Lovedale Press, n.d.), accessed May 18, 2017.

34   ELM H SA Acc. 76.300, Missionsfest und Konferenz in Kana, Report, 24–26 April 1938, 5. See statements by School Inspector Kriel and Brother Brümmerhof.

35   ELM H SA Acc. 76.300, Transvaal Education Department forms for Education of Native and Coloured children for Zendelingspost, 1947 and 1948.

36   ELM H SA Acc. 76.1137. Note by principal of Zendelingspost school, D. D. Nkambule, on the back of the Transvaal Education Department form requiring enrolment and related information, 25 June 1948.

37   ELM H SA Acc. 76.617. School expenditure for Endhlovini, Obanjani, Enyezane, Hebron and Bangisizungu, 1 April 1947 to 31 March 1954.

38   Brian Rose and Raymond Tunmer, eds, *Documents in South African Education* (Johannesburg: Ad Donker, 1975), 250.

39   Horrell, *Bantu Education to 1968*, 58.

40   Horrell, *Bantu Education to 1968*.

41   Horrell, *Bantu Education to 1968*, 60.

42   Natal Archives Depot, A 1381 Zulu Society File IV/2/3-IV/2/5 in File IV/1-1/3 8, Edendale Joint Schools Committee (JSC), 'Memorandum on Native Education' (undated). Evidence suggests that the memorandum was in response to separationist proposals, circa 1944.

43   Edendale JSC, 'Memorandum on Native Education', 2.

44   Edendale JSC, 'Memorandum on Native Education'.

45   Edendale JSC, 'Memorandum on Native Education', 9.

46   Horrell, *Bantu Education to 1968*, 58.

47   Horrell, *Bantu Education to 1968*, 59.

48   ELM H SA Acc. 76.609, 'Preliminary List of Books for use in Primary Schools', *Bantu Education Journal* 1 (6) (May 1955): 170; 'Books for Primary Schools: Preliminary List of Books', *Bantu Education Journal* 1 (August 1955): 321–322.

49   ELM H SA Acc. 76.609, *Bantu Education Journal* 1 (6) (May 1955): 170–178; *Bantu Education Journal* 1 (6) (August 1955): 320–326.

50   Department of Basic Education Library P13/0069, Pretoria, Department of Native Affairs, Bantu Education, 'Library Books for Government, Community, Farm, Mine and Factory Schools', in *Handbook of Regulations and Instructions* (Pretoria: Government Printer, 1957), 190.

51   *Bantu Education Journal* 1 (6) (August 1955): 320–321.

52   ELM H SA Acc. 76.1235. See case of Seven Oaks Bantu School, February and March 1957, 1.8.1959 and 24.8.1959.

53   These authors included G.H. Franz, H.J. van Zyl, Jack Dugard and J.R. Dent.

54   Interview with Heinrich Voges, Pretoria, 9 October 2015. Voges was in charge of the Hermannsburg Mission Book Depot in Rustenburg in the 1970s.

55 Nishino, *Changing Histories*, 47–48.

56 National Library of South Africa (NLSA, 54/5413 and 54/5414), *Sadie Merber Readers for African Schools*, Book 1 (Johannesburg: Afrikaanse Pers Boekhandel, 1947); *Sadie Merber Readers for African Schools*, Book 2 (Johannesburg: Afrikaanse Pers Boekhandel, 1947); *Sadie Merber Readers for African Schools*, Book 3 (Johannesburg: Afrikaanse Pers Boekhandel, 1947).

57 *Sadie Merber Readers*, Book 3, Chapter 2, 'Lazy Jim'.

58 *Sadie Merber Readers*, Book 2.

59 National Library of South Africa, (CR) 372.412. J.J. Ross, 'Preface', A.S.V. Barnes, ed. G.H. Franz, *English Readers for Southern Africa, First Steps in Reading*, Book I (Bloemfontein: Via Afrika, 1951), 5–6; see also A.S.V. Barnes, ed. G.H. Franz, *English Readers for Southern Africa, Cabbages and Kings*, Book III (Bloemfontein: Via Afrika, 1951); A.S.V. Barnes, ed. G.H. Franz, *English Readers for Southern Africa, Here and There*, Book IV (Bloemfontein: Via Afrika, 1951); A.S.V. Barnes and J.H. Dugard, ed. G.H. Franz, *English Readers for Southern Africa*, Book I and Book II (Bloemfontein: Via Afrika, 1992). G.H. Franz was Chief Inspector of Native Schools in the Transvaal.

60 Unisa August Hesse Collection, Acc. 74, *Morutapuo* series (Rustenburg: Hermannsburg Mission Depot and Mission Press, 1939, 1942, 1945, 1956) *Mogorosi I and II* (Rustenburg: Hermannsburg Mission Depot and Mission Press, 1956, 1957, 1959, 1964).

61 C.M. Doke, ed., *Imvulamlomo, First Primer*, Longmans' Zulu Readers (London: Longmans, 1946); C.M. Doke, ed., *Ingqaqamazinyo, Second Primer*, Longmans' Zulu Readers (London: Longmans, 1946); C.M. Doke, ed., *Ufundukhuphuke, Standard I*, Longmans' Zulu Readers (London: Longmans, 1946); C.M. Doke, ed., *Unokuhlekisa Standard II*, Longmans' Zulu Readers (London: Longmans, 1947); C.M. Doke, ed., *Unozizwe, Standard III*, Longmans' Zulu Readers (London: Longmans, 1947); C.M. Doke, *Usokuzula, Standard IV*, Longmans' Zulu Readers (London: Longmans, 1947).

62 Unisa August Hesse Collection, Acc. 74, *Morutapuo I*, (Rustenburg: Hermannsburg Mission Depot and Press, 1956); *Mogorosi I* (Rustenburg: Hermannsburg Mission Depot and Press, 1957); *Mogorosi II* (Rustenburg: Hermannsburg Mission Depot and Press, 1956); *Morutapuo I* (Rustenburg: Hermannsburg Mission Depot and Press, 1956); Doke, Longmans' Zulu readers.

63 Mamokgethi Setati et al., 'Incomplete Journeys: Code-switching and Other Language Practices in Mathematics, Science and English Language Classrooms in South Africa', *Language and Education* 16 (2) (2002): 128–149.

Chapter 6

1   Daniel Magaziner, *The Law and the Prophets: Black Consciousness in South Africa 1968–1977* (Ohio: Ohio University Press, 2010), 55; Philippe Denis, 'Seminary networks and black consciousness in South Africa in the early 1970s', *Journal of Southern African Studies*, 62 (1) (2010): 162–182.

2   Magaziner, *The Law and the Prophets*, 158.

3   Philippe Denis and Graham Duncan, *The Native School that Caused all the Trouble: A History of the Federal Theological Seminary of Southern Africa* (Pietermaritzburg: Cluster Publications, 2011), 283.

4   Denis and Graham, *The Native School*, 49.

5   Denis and Graham, *The Native School*, 142.

6   Denis and Graham, *The Native School*, 83, 85.

7   Hodne, *Missionary Enterprise*, 110.

8   Hodne, *Missionary Enterprise*, 115.

9   Eshowe Zulu Lutheran High School was founded in 1893 by Norwegian missionaries as a government-aided teacher training seminary; it became a high school in 1948.

10   Lutheran Theological Institute (LTI), Inkanyezi (INK) 1, Box 40, *Inkanyezi* Umpumulo Institution Magazine for 1936–1948, and INK 2, Box 40, *Inkanyezi* Umpumulo Institution Magazine for 1950–1962.

11   LTI, INK 1 and INK 2.

12   Union of South Africa, Debates in the House of Assembly (Hansard), vol. 82–83, column 3586, 17 September 1953, Minister of Native Affairs.

13   University of the Witwatersrand, Johannesburg, South African Institute of Race Relations (SAIRR) Collection, 1892–1974, collection number AD 1715, 'A Survey conducted by the South African Institute of Race Relations: Careers for Africans', (Johannesburg, SAIRR, n.d.), 8.

14   See Chapter 1 above, where reference is made to C.T. Loram's promotion of an 'adapted' and 'practical' education for Africans. See Reilly, '*Teaching the 'Native'*.

15   ELM H SA Acc. 76.572, Annual Report of the Executive Committee of the Cooperating Lutheran Missions in Natal for 1943.

16   LTI, Government Correspondence (GOV) 1–3, Umpumulo Training College, Government Correspondence, Box 32.

17   LTI, GOV 1–3, Umpumulo Training College, Government Correspondence, Box 32. The Table provides a sample of exam papers. Records were not kept systematically, and so the Table is merely an indication of exam papers that were written.

18   Jane Starfield, 'Dr S. Modiri Malema (1891–1965): The Making of an Historian' (PhD diss., University of the Witwatersrand, 2008), 113–117; Jeanne Prinsloo, 'Possibilities of Critical Literacy: An exploration of schooled literacies in the province of KwaZulu-Natal' (PhD diss., University of the Witwatersrand, 2002); see also Jeanne Prinsloo, 'Examining the Examination: The "Worlding" of the Matriculation Language Papers in KwaZulu-Natal', *Perspectives in Education* 22 (1) (March 2004): 81–97; Jeanne Prinsloo, 'Making visible constructions of dis/advantage through genealogical investigation – South African schooled literacies', *Critical Arts* 21 (1) (2007): 190–211.

19   I analysed papers for: Reading; Language; Composition; Composition and Reproduction; and Reproduction and Literature papers for English (1949 and 1954); Organisation and Management of Schools (1945, 1949 and 1954); Principles of Psychology papers (1945 and 1949); and Methods of Teaching (1945 and 1949).

20   Prinsloo's PhD dissertation focuses on the literacy practices that the 1990 Matric English Language papers of the white, Indian and African departments (now integrated into the KwaZulu-Natal Department of Education) revealed. She argues that 'there is a startling continuity of particular literacy practices that continue (from 1920) up to the year 2000, despite changing demands on students' literacy skills. Most striking is the resilience of a form of assessment designed in colonial times. The examination is omposed of three

elements that continue to provide the dominant form and structure of current literacy examinations: literature, language and writing. Prinsloo analyses the 1990 Language papers of the racially categorised departments of education (one each for whites, Indians, coloureds, Africans in urban areas, and Africans in the Bantustans) in order to discover which tradition and what competencies each promoted. The study also looks at the way in which the papers position the students – as global or local citizens, for example. Here Prinsloo uses a Foucauldian genealogical approach to determine how exams constitute subjects. She identifies the following influences on the development of South African literacy practices from 1920 to 2000: the Grammar/Skills approach, the Cultural Heritage approach, the Personal Growth approach, and the Critical approach.

21   Pietermaritzburg LTI, GOV 1–3 Umpumulo Training College, Government Correspondence, Box 32: English Composition and Reproduction Paper 1949.

22   LTI, GOV 1, Umpumulo Training College, Government Correspondence, Box 32: Department of Native Affairs, Bantu Education, Natal Region, 'Bantu Teachers' Junior Third Class (T3) Second Year Certificate Examination, 1954: English Composition', Question 2.

23   LTI, GOV 1, Umpumulo Training College, Government Correspondence, Box 32: Department of Native Affairs, Bantu Education, Natal Region, 'Bantu Teachers' Junior Third Class (T3) Second Year Certificate Examination, 1954: English Literature', Question 5.

24   The Direct Method focuses on using the target language in the classroom, and does not permit the home language or mixing or switching of languages.

25   Saul Dubow, *Scientific Racism in Modern South Africa* (Cambridge: Cambridge University Press, 1995).

26   Saul Dubow, *A Commonwealth of Knowledge: Science, Sensibility and White South Africa 1820–2000* (Oxford: Oxford University Press, 2006); Brahm Fleisch, 'The Teachers' College Club' (DPhil diss., Columbia University, 1995); Linda Chisholm, 'Reformatories and Industrial Schools in South Africa: A Study in Class, Colour and Gender 1882–1939' (PhD diss., University of the Witwatersrand, 1989); see also Ellen Condliffe Lagemann, *An Elusive Science: The Troubling History of Education Research* (Chicago: University of Chicago Press, 2000).

27   LTI, INK 2, Box 40, *Inkanyezi*, Umpumulo Institute Magazine, 1950, 39, and 1951, 6.

28   ELM H SA Acc. 76.572, Cooperating Lutheran Mission in Natal and Zululand, Reports 1953: Umpumulo Institution Principal's General Report for the Year 1953.

29   ELM H *Ausland: Südliches Afrika* (ASA) 432b), Minutes of the 67th and Extra-ordinary meeting of the Exco of the CLM in Natal and Zululand held in Durban, November 4–5, 1954.

30   ELM H ASA 432b), CLM in Zululand and Natal Reports 1956; Chairman's Annual Report for the Year 1956, 24 April 1957.

31   ELM H ASA 432c), Minutes of the 75th and Annual Meeting of the Exco of the CLM in Natal and Zululand held in Durban on April 22–24 1958, Report of the College Board for 1958, and Umpumulo Institution General Report for the Year 1958.

32   ELM H ASA 432c), Minutes of the 79th and Extraordinary Meeting of the Exco of the CLM in Natal and Zululand held in Durban on 3–5 November, 1959, at Umpumulo.

33   ELM H ASA 432c), CLM in Natal and Zululand Reports 1959, CLM Chairman's
     Report for the Year 1959, C. Otte, Entumeni, 8.4.1960.

34   ELM H ASA 432c), CLM in Natal and Zululand Reports 1957, CLM Chairman's
     Report for the Year 1957, C. Otte, Entumeni, 16.4.1958, Eshowe Training College
     Superintendent's Report for the Year 1957.

35   ELM H ASA 432c), Minutes of the 80th and Extraordinary Meeting of the Exco of the
     CLM in Natal and Zululand held in Durban, 26–28 April 1960.

36   ELM H SA Acc. 76.234, H. Greve, 'Marang' Lutheran Theological Seminary, *Newsletter*,
     5 May 1965.

37   ELM H SA Acc. 76.234, '*Kurzer Bericht ueber die Sitzung der "Commission on Seminary"
     Oscarsberg/Umpumulo*', 31 August bis (until) 2 September 1960.

38   ELM H SA Acc. 76.234, *Aktennotiz* (File note).

Chapter 7

1   Bengt Sundkler, *The Christian Ministry in Africa* (Uppsala: Swedish Institute of
     Missionary Research, 1960).

2   Lutheran Theological Institute (LTI), Fritz Scriba Papers, Unsorted files, CLM in Natal and
     Zululand Reports for 1960. Chairman's Annual Report for 1960, signed May 1961, Eshowe.

3   Eric Sharpe, 'The Legacy of Bengt Sundkler', *International Bulletin of Missionary Research*
     (April 2001): 60.

4   Sundkler, *The Christian Ministry*, 188–281.

5   Sundkler attributes this notion to anthropologist Monica Wilson, who was his doctoral super-
     visor. *The Christian Ministry*, 198. See also Sean Morrow, *The Fires Beneath: The Life of Monica
     Wilson, South African Anthropologist* (Cape Town: Penguin Books, 2016), 253–254.

6   Sundkler, *The Christian Ministry*, 198, 220.

7   Sundkler, *The Christian Ministry*, 219.

8   Sundkler, *The Christian Ministry*, 223.

9   Sundkler, *The Christian Ministry*, 262.

10   Tjelle, *Missionary Masculinities*, 91.

11   See LTI, Lutheran Theological Seminary (LTS): Umpumulo, 1971 Annual Report by
     H-J. Becken. In his report, Becken thanks member churches, supporting missions and
     churches, the United Evangelical Lutheran Church in Germany, the Lutheran World
     Federation, *Evangelische Arbeitsgemeinschaft für Weltmission*, the Theological Education
     Fund, the Bantu Welfare Trust, as well as congregations, agencies and individuals who
     assisted through grants and donations.

12   The Hermannsburgers closed down their own seminary at Hermannsburg and joined up
     with Umpumulo once doctrinal issues and the conflict with the Berlin Mission Society
     over the continued existence of Marang were resolved. Interview with Heinrich Voges,
     23 August 2016, Pretoria.

13   The churches included the Evangelical Lutheran Church in Southern Africa (Cape
     Orange region, Transvaal Region, Tswana region and South-Eastern region), the Eastern
     Cape Moravian Church, the Bantu Synod, and the African Evangelical Lutheran Church
     of Southern Rhodesia.

14   A block grant was a general grant made by a Mission Society to an institution, to be
     used as it saw fit.

15   ELM H SA Acc. 76.1420. Letter from the Principal, Gunnar Lislerud, to Fritz Scriba,
     28.10.1960, documenting resolution 39 of the CLM Minutes of April 1960 in this
     regard.

16   ELM H SA Acc. 76.1420. Letter from Hermannsburg Mission to Dr A. Sovik, c/o
     Johannesstift, Berlin, Germany, 26 July 1961, with reference to: 'Participating of our
     Hermannsburg Mission in the Work of the Joint Lutheran Theological Seminary at
     Oscarsberg, in future Umpumulo'. The author of the letter was probably the general
     superintendent of the Hermannsburg Mission, Wolfram von Krause, who arrived in South
     Africa in 1957.

17   LTI, Fritz Scriba Papers, LTS, Umpumulo, Rector's Report on the Lutheran Theological
     College (LTC) for 1966.

18   LTI, Fritz Scriba Papers, LTS, Umpumulo, Annual Report for Umpumulo, 1969.

19   LTI, Fritz Scriba Papers, LTS, Umpumulo File, Exhibit: Memorandum on the Future
     Structure of LTC.

20   LTI, Fritz Scriba Papers, LTS, Umpumulo File, LTC Rector's Report for 1971.

21   Axel-Ivar Berglund, *Zulu Thought Patterns and Symbolism* (Cape Town: David Phillip,
     1976).

22   Axel-Ivar Berglund, 'Concepts of Water and Baptism amongst some Africanist Zionist
     Movements', *Credo: Lutheran Journal of Southern Africa* 16 (1) (1965): 4–11; 'Pack-oxen
     and cattle-riding among the Zulu', *African Studies* 27 (1) (1968): 29–30.

23   Hans-Jürgen Becken, 'I Love to Tell the Story: Oral History in the Nazaretha Church',
     in *Empirical Studies in African Independent/Indigenous Churches*, eds I. Hexham and
     G. C. Oosthuizen (New York: Edward Mellen, 1992), 29–44.

24   LTI, Fritz Scriba Papers, LTS, Umpumulo File, Chairman of the Governing Body,
     W. O. Rindahl, in a letter to the members of the Governing Board, 15.6.1966.

25   ELM H SA Acc. 76.403, Annual Reports 1964–1973.

26   ELM H SA Acc. 76.403, H-J. Becken, Hermannsburger Mission, Lutheran Theological
     College. Mapumulo Süd-Ost-Region, 'Jahresbericht für das Jahr 1964' (Annual Report for
     the Year 1964).

27   ELM H SA Acc. 76.403, H-J. Becken, Hermannsburger Mission, Lutheran Theological
     College, Mapumulo Süd-Ost-Region, 'Jahresbericht für das Jahr 1965' (Annual Report for
     the Year 1965), 2, 11.

28   ELM H SA Acc. 76.403, H-J. Becken, 'Jahresbericht für das Jahr 1965', 4.

29   ELM H SA Acc. 76.403, H-J. Becken, 'Jahresbericht für das Jahr 1965', 14.

30   ELM H SA Acc. 76.403, H-J. Becken, Hermannsburger Mission, Lutheran Theological
     College, überregionaler Dienst (Supraregional Service), 'Jahresbericht für das Jahr 1966'
     (Annual Report for the Year 1966), 2. (Author's translation.)

31   ELM H SA Acc. 76.403, H-J. Becken, 'Jahresbericht für das Jahr 1966', 12.

32   ELM H SA Acc. 76.403, H-J. Becken, Hermannsburger Mission, Lutheran Theological
     College, Mapumulo, Oberregionaler Dienst: Südafrika (Supraregional Service:
     South Africa), 'Jahresbericht für das Jahr 1971', 1.

33   ELM H SA Acc. 76.403, Karl Bunjer, Hermannsburger Mission, Lutheran Theological
     College, Mapumulo, Natal, 'Jahresbericht für das Jahr 1969', 1–2.

34   ELM H SA Acc. 76.403, Bunjer, 'Jahresbericht für das Jahr 1969', 2.

35   Heinrich Voges, teacher and principal at Marang from 1961 until its closure in 1992,
     interview, 23 August 2016, Pretoria.

36   LTI, Fritz Scriba Papers, LTS, Umpumulo, LTC Annual Report for 1965.

37   ELM H SA Acc. 76.1419, Peter Beyerhaus, Annual Report for 1964, 5.

38   For discussion of the women's associations (known as 'manyanos') in several South African
     churches, see Gaitskell, 'Power in Prayer and Service', 253–268.

39   ELM H SA Acc. 76.1419.1, Constitution of the Lutheran Theological College, Final
     version as adopted by the Governing Board, 25 November 1965, 7.

40   LTI, Fritz Scriba Papers, CLM in Natal and Zululand Reports for 1962, Gunnar
     Lislerud, LTC Annual Report.

41   LTI, GOV 3, Box 32, Government Correspondence, Letter from LTS, Rorke's Drift, to
     Rev. B. Schiele, Berlin-Lichterfelde West, Augustastr., 3.05.1961.

42   Extension of University Education Act (No. 45 of 1959), accessed May 19, 2017, https://
     www.nelsonmandela.org/omalley/index.php/site/q/03lv01538/04lv01828/05lv01829/0
     6lv01898.htm

43   LTI, GOV 3, Box 32, Government Correspondence, Letter from LTS, Rorke's Drift, to
     Rev. B. Schiele, Berlin-Lichterfelde West, Augustastr., 3.05.1961.

44   Bill Nasson's use of the term 'pigment permits' signals the contempt in which such
     permits were generally held. See *History Matters: Selected Writings 1970–2016* (Cape Town:
     Penguin Random House, 2016), 25.

45   LTI, Box 32, GOV 3, Government Correspondence, Letter from Hjlamar Astrup,
     Andreas Løken and Gunnar Lislerud to Minister of Bantu Education, J. H. van Eck,
     4.01.1963.

46   LTI, Box 32, GOV 3, Government Correspondence, Department of Bantu Education to
     Chairman of the CLM, 7.3.1963.

47   LTI, Box 32, GOV 3, Government Correspondence, W.W.M. Eiselen to Minister of
     Bantu Education and Minister of Indian Affairs, 21.7.1964; response from W.A. Maree,
     Minister of Bantu Education, 30.10.1964.

48   LTI, Box 32, GOV 3, Government Correspondence.

49   LTI, Fritz Scriba Papers, LTS, Umpumulo, Report on Interview with the Secretary for
     Department of Bantu Education, Pretoria, undated.

50   LTI, Fritz Scriba Papers, LTS, Umpumulo, LTC, Axel-Ivar Berglund, Annual Report for
     1968; letter from Berglund to ASATU, 22.4.1968.

51   LTI, Fritz Scriba Papers, LTS, Umpumulo, LTC, H-J. Becken, Annual Report for 1965.

52   LTI, Fritz Scriba Papers, LTS, Umpumulo, LTC, Gunnar Lislerud, Annual Report for
     1966.

53   ELM H SA Acc. 76.1420, Gunnar Lislerud, Annual Report 1960, Lutheran Theological
     Seminary.

54   ELM H SA Acc. 76.234, Letter from H-J. Becken to Wolfram Kistner at Moorleigh,
     Natal, undated, and SA Acc. 76.1419, Rules for the Missiological Institute (MI).

55   LTI, LTS, Umpumulo, and LTI, Missiological Institute. 1978.

56   LTI, LTS, Umpumulo, Findings of the Missiological Institute Consultation on Church
      and Nationalism, Umpumulo, September 1974.

57   The English translations do not adequately convey the meaning of these terms. For a full
      discussion of the origins and deployment of these concepts within the rise of Afrikaner
      nationalism in South Africa, see Dan O'Meara, *Volkskapitalisme: Class, Capital and Ideology
      in the Development of Afrikaner Nationalism 1934–1948* (Cambridge: Cambridge University
      Press, 1983).

58   LTI, LTS, Umpumulo, Findings of the Missiological Institute Consultation on Church
      and Nationalism, Umpumulo, September 1974.

59   LTI, MI 1978, Box 47, 'Ideologies of Change'. See also Karl Nürnberger, *Ideologies of
      Change in South Africa and the Power of the Gospel (Capitalism – Socialism – Marxism): An
      Inter-disciplinary Study-Program of the Missiological Institute, Mapumulo* (Durban: Lutheran
      Publishing House, 1979) and *Socio-Economic Ideologies in a Christian Perspective* (Durban:
      Lutheran Publishing House, 1979).

60   Klaus Nürnberger, *Ideologies of Change.*

61   See Denis and Duncan, *The Native School*; Magaziner, *The Law and the Prophets.*

62   Magaziner, *The Law and the Prophets*, 65.

63   Magaziner, *The Law and the Prophets*, 119.

64   LTI, LTS, Umpumulo, Annual Report of the Governing Board of the LTC at
      Umpumulo, signed S. Nielsen, 1971.

65   LTI, Students (STUDS) 1, Box 28.

66   LTI, STUDS 1, Box 28, Letter from Barney Pityana, Secretary-General of SASO, to
      Rector, LTC, regarding Resolution 55/72, 8.11.1972.

67   John Evenson, 'Introduction', Tshenuwani Farisani, *Diary from a South African Prison*
      (Philadelphia: Fortress Press, 1987). Farisani, according to Evenson, was born in 1947 near
      Louis Trichardt. He grew up with the ever-present threat of removal, with destitution
      staring his family in the face. After two forced removals, the family was again uprooted in
      1951 when Farisani was four years old, and again in 1959 when he was twelve. They were
      forced to sell cattle amassed since 1951 and move to the barren area of Mbabada, where
      Farisani entered a community school. There, a German missionary, Hanna Lechler, had an
      enormous impact on him. He became politicised at secondary school, and was a member
      of the Venda Students' Association while also vice-chairman of the Student Christian
      Movement. He was a theology student at Umpumulo from 1970 to 1972.

68   See for example Jane Hofmeyr, 'An examination of the influence of Christian National
      Education on the principles underlying white and black education in South Africa
      1948–1982' (MEd thesis, University of the Witwatersrand, 1983).

69   According to the Lutheran catechism, the Sixth Commandment is 'Thou Shalt Not
      Commit Adultery'.

70   See LTI, STUDS 1 Box 28, 'Disciplinary Suspensions, etc'..

71   LTI, Pietermaritzburg, STUDS 1, Box 28, 'Disciplinary/Suspensions, etc'., Case File
      Mthiyane, August 1962–March 1964.

72   LTI, Pietermaritzburg, STUDS 1, Box 28, 'Disciplinary/Suspensions, etc'., Case File
      Mabaso, March 1964.

73 LTI, Pietermaritzburg, STUDS 1, Box 28, 'Disciplinary/Suspensions, etc'., Case File Busiswe Buthelezi and Sipho Nyandeni, December 1962.

74 LTI, Pietermaritzburg, STUDS 1, Box 28, 'Disciplinary/Suspensions, etc'., Case File Christopher Hlongwane and Nurse Aid Mirriam Nzimande, April 1965.

75 LTI, Pietermaritzburg, STUDS 1, Box 28, 'Disciplinary/Suspensions, etc'., Case File A. Farao and Mrs Matthews, 1965–1966.

Chapter 8

1   Nick Taylor, 'Falling at the First Hurdle: Initial Encounters with the Formal System of African Education in South Africa', Research Report No 1, Education Policy Unit, University of the Witwatersrand, 1989, 38.

2   Maren Bodenstein (daughter of Christel and Hans Bodenstein), email messages to author, 10 March, 2012.

3   Interviews with Christel Bodenstein, 6 and 16 August, 2009, Johannesburg.

4   Interviews with Christel Bodenstein, 6 and 16 August 2009, Johannesburg.

5   Interview with Heinrich Voges, 23 August 2016, Pretoria.

6   Popagano is the Tswana term for 'unity'.

7   Maren Bodenstein, email message to author, March 10, 2013.

8   Hans Bodenstein, 'Fröhlich singend über die Brücken', in *Geschichten, die das Leben schreibt: Rückblick unserer Freunde der Alten Garde*, ed. Helmut Stäcker (Kroondal: Stups, 1998).

9   Bodenstein, 'Fröhlich singend', 132.

10 Bodenstein, 'Fröhlich singend', 135.

11 Bodenstein, 'Fröhlich singend', 136.

12 For a history of this community, see Marcus Melck, 'The Afrikadeutschen of Kroondal, 1849–1949' (MA diss., University of Pretoria, 2012).

13 Republic of Bophuthatswana, Report of the National Education Commission, Education for Popagano, Mafikeng, Government Printer, 1978.

14 See Linda Chisholm, 'Education Policy Borrowing across African Borders: Histories of Learner-Centred Education', in: *Policy Borrowing and Lending: World Yearbook of Education 2012*, eds Gita Steiner-Khamsi and Florian Waldow (London: Routledge, 2012), 206–226.

15 Richard Tabulawa, 'Pedagogical Classroom Practice and Social Context: The Case of Botswana', *International Journal of Educational Development* 17 (2) (1997): 189–204; Richard Tabulawa, 'Education Reform in Botswana: Reflections on Policy Contradictions and Paradoxes', *Comparative Education* 45 (1) (2009): 87–107.

16 Shireen Ally and Arianna Lissoni, 'Let's Talk about the Bantustans', *South African Historical Journal* 64 (1) (2012): 1; William Beinart, 'Beyond Homelands: Some Ideas about the History of African Rural Areas in South Africa', *South African Historical Journal* 64 (1) (2012): 6.

17 Anne Mager and Maanda Mulaudzi, 'Popular Responses to Apartheid: 1948–c.1975', in *The Cambridge History of South Africa, Vol. 2, 1885–1994*, eds Robert Ross, Anne Mager and Bill Nasson (Cambridge: Cambridge University Press, 2102), 390.

18 Michael Lawrence and Andrew Manson, '"Dog of the Boers": The Rise and Fall of Mangope in Bophuthatswana', *Journal of Southern African Studies* 20 (3) (1994): 451. In Special Issue, 'Ethnicity and Identity in Southern Africa', September 1994.

19   Lawrence and Manson, 'Dog of the Boers'.

20   Bernard Magubane, 'Resistance and Repression in the Bantustans', in *The Road to Democracy in South Africa. Volume 2 (1970–1980)*, eds South African Democracy Education Trust (Pretoria: Unisa Press, 2004), 754.

21   E.P. Lekhela, W.M. Kgware, T. Vorster, and J.E. Rossouw, *A Survey of the Development of Education among the Batswana of Bophuthatswana* (Mafikeng: n.p., 1972), 16, 37.

22   Peter Buckland, 'Education Policy and Rural Development in Southern Africa: A Review of Four Regional Commissioned Reports on Education Policy. A Report submitted to the Committee on Rural Education', Human Sciences Research Council, Pretoria, 1983.

23   Ken Hartshorne, 'Curriculum and the Reality of Context: The Bophuthatswana Beginnings', in *Education Curriculum and Development: Papers presented at Conferences at the University of Cape Town and the University of the Witwatersrand, 1979–1981*, eds A. Hunter, M. Ashley and C. Millar (Centre for Continuing Education, University of the Witwatersrand, 1983), 392; Ken Hartshorne, *Crisis and Challenge: Black Education 1910–1990* (Oxford: Oxford University Press, 1992), 127.

24   Hartshorne, 'Curriculum and the Reality of Context', 391.

25   The term 'home language' continues to be used today: curriculum policy refers to Home Language, rather than Mother Tongue, and First Additional and Second Additional Language for the second and third languages. The rationale for this is that the mother tongue is not always and not necessarily the language spoken at home. The home language could be the language of the father, or of neither parent(s)/carer(s). See for example Republic of South Africa, Department of Basic Education, Curriculum and Assessment Policy Statement. Grades R–3. Home Language, accessed June 1, 2017, http://www.education.gov.za/Portals/0/CD/National%20Curriculum%20Statements%20 and%20Vocational/CAPS%20English%20HL%20GRADES%20R-3%20FS.pdf? ver=2015-01-27-154201-167

26   Curtis Nkondo, 'Comparison of the Syllabus of the Bantu Education Department with that of the Transvaal Education Department and Other Related Matters', *Reality* 11 (4) (July 1979): 17–19.

27   Nkondo, 'Comparison of the Syllabus', 18.

28   Andrew Paterson, 'Agricultural and Industrial Curricula for South African Rural Schools: Colonial Origins and Contemporary Continuities', in *Shifting Understandings of Skills in South Africa: Overcoming the Impact of a Low Skills Regime*, eds Simon McGrath et al. (Cape Town: Human Sciences Research Council Press, 2004), 89.

29   Peter Kallaway, 'Conference Litmus: The Development of a Conference and Policy Culture in the Interwar Period with Special Reference to the New Education Fellowship and British Colonial Education in South Africa', in *Transformations in Schooling: Historical and Comparative Perspectives*, ed. Kim Tolley (New York: Palgrave/Routledge, 2007), 123–149.

30   David F. Labaree, 'Progressivism, Schools and Schools of Education: An American Romance', *Paedogogica Historica* 41 (1&2) (2005): 275–288, 277.

31   Labaree, 'Progressivism', 279.

32   'Progressive education – philosophical foundations, pedagogical progressivism, administrative progressivism, life-adjustment progressivism', accessed May 22, 2017, http://education. stateuniversity.com/pages/2336/Progressive-Education.html#ixzz2MmorW02g

33   Labaree, 'Progressivism', 280.

34   Education for Popagano, 18.

35   Bodenstein, 'Fröhlich singend', 137.

36   Education for Popagano, 35.

37   Education for Popagano, 36.

38   Education for Popagano, 36.

39   Education for Popagano, 36.

40   Hartshorne, 'Curriculum and the Reality of Context', 401.

41   Education for Popagano.

42   Hartshorne, 'Curriculum and the Reality of Context', 396.

43   For further discussion, see Chisholm, 'Education Policy Borrowing', 206–225; also Martin Carnoy, Linda Chisholm and Bagele Chilisa, eds, *The Low Achievement Trap: Comparing Schooling in Botswana and South Africa* (Cape Town, Human Sciences Research Council Press, 2012).

44   Brenda Evans, 'JCI's Social Responsibility Funding: The Bophuthatswana Education Upgrading Programme. Revolution on a shoestring', *Mining Survey* 2/4 (1986): 51–55.

45   Ken Hartshorne, *Crisis and Challenge: Black Education 1910–1990* (Oxford: Oxford University Press, 1992), 133.

46   Francine de Clercq, 'High-skilled Manpower, Education and Work in Bophuthatswana', in *Vintage Kenton: A Kenton Education Association Commemoration*, eds Wendy Flanagan et al. (Cape Town: Maskew Miller Longman, 1994), 115.

47   Johan Graaff, 'Is Bop Better? A Case Study in Educational Innovation in Bophuthatswana', in Heather Jacklin and Johan Graaff, Rural Education in South Africa. A Report on Schooling Systems in the Bantustans (unpublished report, 1994), 31.

48   Telephonic interview with PEUP organiser, Bill Holderness, 5 August 2009.

49   Carol Macdonald, *Towards a New Primary Curriculum for South Africa: The Main Report of the Threshold 2 Project* (Pretoria: Human Sciences Research Council Press, 1993), 21.

50   Interview with Christel Bodenstein, 6 August, 2009, Johannesburg.

51   Interview with Christel Bodenstein, 6 August, 2009, Johannesburg.

52   Bill Holderness, 'Upgrading Primary Education in the Seventeen Circuits, 1980–1985: A Celebration of Achievement', Occasional publication 2, Mafikeng, University of Bophuthatswana, Institute of Education, 1986, 2.

53   Holderness, 'Upgrading Primary Education', 3.

54   Jacob Malao, 'Planning an Educational System for Bophuthatswana' (MEd thesis, Potchefstroom University for Christian Higher Education, 1983), 158; Lawrence Schlemmer, 'A Venture in Educational Development: An External Evaluation Report on the Bophuthatswana Teacher Upgrading Project, mounted by the SACHED Trust', University of Natal, Durban Centre for Applied Social Science, 1982, accessed May 22, 2017, http://citeseerx.ist.psu.edu/viewdoc/download? doi=10.1.1.837.5351&rep=rep1&type=pdf

55   See Lawrence Schlemmer, 'A Venture in Educational Development'; Lefentse Malope, 'Planning Educational Reforms in Bophuthatswana: An Evaluation' (MEd thesis, Potchefstroom University for Christian Higher Education, 1992), 70, accessed May 22, 2017, http://nrfnexus.nrf.ac.za/handle/20.500.11892/9875.

56   Holderness, 'Upgrading Primary Education', 5.

57   Interview with Francine de Clercq and Mittah Motstatsi, 2 July 2009, Kempton Park.

58   Telephonic interview with Ken Holderness, 5 August 2009.

59   Maren Bodenstein, email message to author, March 10 2013.

60   Hartshorne, *Crisis and Challenge*, 127.

61   Interview with Christel Bodenstein, 6 August 2009, Johannesburg.

62   Carol Macdonald, *Swimming up the Waterfall: A Study of School-based Learning Experiences*
     (Pretoria: Human Sciences Research Council Press, 1990), 43.

63   Evans, 'JCI's Social Responsibility Funding', 52.

64   Hartshorne, *Crisis and challenge*, 134; Johann Graaff, 'Rural Parents and School Enrolment
     Rates in Two Regions of Bophuthatswana: Subjects for Reconsideration', *Perspectives in
     Education* 9 (2) (1987): 25–43; J. Graaff, 'Is Bop Better? A Case Study in Educational
     Innovation in Bophuthatswana', in Heather Jacklin and Johann Graaff, Rural Education
     in South Africa, A Report on Schooling Systems in the Bantustans (unpublished report,
     1994), 31.

65   National Education Coordinating Committee, *National Education Policy Investigation:
     Report on Systems, Planning and Management* (Cape Town: Oxford University Press,
     1993), 21.

66   Hartshorne, *Crisis and challenge*, 132.

67   Graaff, 'Is Bop Better?', 35–36.

68   Graaff, 'Is Bop Better?'.

69   Graaff, 'Is Bop Better?', 10.

70   Samuel Lehobye, 'An Evaluation of the Primary Education Upgrading Programme in the
     Two Circuits of the Odi Region,' Institute of Education, University of Bophuthatswana,
     1992, 48.

71   Lehobye, 'An Evaluation', 48.

72   Macdonald, *Swimming*; Carol Macdonald, *Crossing the Threshold into Standard
     Three in Black Education: The Consolidated Main Report of the Threshold Project*
     (Pretoria: Human Sciences Research Council Press, 1990), 1–196; Macdonald,
     Primary Curriculum.

73   Lehobye, 'An evaluation', 35.

74   Lehobye, 'An evaluation', 36.

75   Macdonald, *Swimming*.

76   Macdonald, *Swimming*, 25.

77   Macdonald, *Swimming*, 27.

78   Macdonald, *Swimming*, 19–21.

79   Macdonald, *Swimming*, 90.

80   Macdonald, *Crossing the Threshold*.

81   Macdonald, *Crossing the Threshold*, 57.

82   Interview with eight PEUP teachers who were assured of anonymity, 2009, Mafikeng.

83   A phenomenon observed by Angeline Barrett in Tanzanian classrooms. See 'Beyond the
     Polarization of Pedagogy: Models of Classroom Practice in Tanzanian Primary Schools',
     Comparative Education 43 (2) (2007): 273–294.

Chapter 9

1   Inkatha (a Zulu word describing the plaited coil placed on top of the head to help bear the weight of a heavy load) grew out of a cultural movement founded by the Zulu King, Solomon Dinuzulu, in the 1920s. It started out as the Inkatha National Cultural Liberation Movement (INCLM), and became the Inkatha Freedom Party in 1975. It presented itself as being in opposition both to apartheid and to the African National Congress (ANC) and Pan African Congress (PAC). It styled itself as a party committed to individual rights including belonging to cultural groups, free enterprise, and negotiated solutions to the achievement of liberation. Despite Buthelezi's claims to membership of the ANC Youth League, he and his party were closely associated during the 1970s and 1980s with Bantustan politics, the formation of a rival trade union, and violence in Zululand, Natal, and the greater Johannesburg region. See Gerhard Maré and Geraldine Hamilton, *An Appetite for Power: Buthelezi's Inkatha and the Politics of 'Loyal Resistance'* (Johannesburg: Ravan Press, 1987).

2   Praisley Mdluli (pseudonym of Blade Nzimande, current Minister of Higher Education and Training), 'Ubuntu-botho: Inkatha's "People's Education"', *Transformation* 5 (1987): 61–79; Gerhard Maré, 'Education in a Liberated Zone: Inkatha and Education in KwaZulu', *Critical Arts* 4 (4/5) 1 (1988/89): 126–139; Johan Graaff, 'Education as an Instrument of War: The Case of Kwazulu/Natal', in Jacklin and Graaff, 'Rural Education in South Africa', 1994.

3   By this stage, the legislative apparatus for making black people citizens of Bantustans had been set in place: the 1959 Promotion of Bantu Self-Government Act and the 1970 Bantu Homelands Citizenship Act.

4   Maré and Hamilton, *An Appetite for Power*.

5   Mdluli, 'Ubuntu-botho', 61 and Maré, 'Education in a Liberated Zone', 131.

6   PC Luthuli was a professor of philosophy of education at the University of Zululand. His MEd., 'The Metablectic Nature of the Aim in Education' (University of Zululand, 1977) and his PhD on 'The philosophical foundations of Black education in South Africa', (Unisa, c1981) promoted the idea of an African philosophy for a new Zulu system of education. E.P. Ndaba also wrote within the framework of his Afrikaner mentors, Fundamental Paedagogics: E.P. Ndaba, A Psycho-Paedagogical Study of Differentiated Education and its significance for Education in KwaZulu (Unpublished DEd thesis, University of Zululand, 1975).

7   Paul Beard and Wally Morrow, eds, *Problems of Paedagogics* (Durban: Butterworth, 1981).

8   Mangosuthu Buthelezi, Weekly Newsletter to the Nation, Dr Oscar Dumisani Dhlomo, 9 September 2008, accessed May 25, 2017, http://www.ifp.org.za/newsroom/dr-oscar-dumisani-dhomo/, 2; Obituaries: Oscar Dumisani Dhlomo (1943–2008), *Natalia*, 38 (2008): 77; The *Ubuntu-botho* textbooks also contained biographies of Inkatha leaders, including Dhlomo. See for example *Ubuntu-Botho (Good Citizenship) A Textbook in Zulu in a series in Good Citizenship*, Ibanga 7 (Pietermaritzburg: KwaZulu Booksellers, 1989), 11.

9   See for example, Babs Fafunwa, *New Perspectives on African Education* (Lagos: Macmillan, 1967).

10 See for example Loram, *Education of the South African Native*; Reilly, *Teaching the 'Native'*.

11 Oscar Dhlomo, 'An Evaluation of some Problems in Teacher Training with Special Reference to Teacher Training Colleges in KwaZulu' (DEd diss., University of South Africa, 1980).

12 Dhlomo, 'An Evaluation', 2.

13 Daphna Golan, 'Inkatha and its Use of the Zulu Past', *History in Africa* 18 (1991): 113–126.

14 Maré and Hamilton, *An Appetite for Power*, 48–49.

15 The Buthelezi Commission: The Requirements for Stability and Development in KwaZulu Natal Vols I and II (Durban: H+H Publications, 1982). Of German-Jewish extraction, Schlemmer was born into an Afrikaans-speaking family in Pretoria, where he attended Pretoria Boys' High School. He was not a Hermannsburger.

16 Maré and Hamilton, *An Appetite for Power*, 49.

17 Patrick O'Malley digital archives, accessed March 1, 2017, https://www.nelsonmandela.org/omalley/index.php/site/q/03lv02424/04lv02426/05lv02539.htm

18 Maré, 'Education in a Liberated Zone', 135.

19 See Chapter 5 above; see also Golan, 'Inkatha and its Use of the Zulu Past', 122.

20 Inkatha Syllabus as cited in Golan, 'Inkatha and its Use of the Zulu Past', 120.

21 Praisley Mdluli, *Ubuntu-botho (Good Citizenship) A Textbook in Zulu in a series in Good Citizenship*, Ibanga 7 (Pietermaritzburg: KwaZulu Booksellers, 1989), 14–15.

22 Mdluli, *Ubuntu-botho*, 77.

23 Golan, 'Inkatha and its Use of the Zulu Past', 122.

24 Golan, 'Inkatha and its Use of the Zulu Past', 123.

25 During an interview in November 2016, they shared with me not only documents and photographs but also memories of their time in South Africa from 1963 to 1975. A wall hung with hand-welded Zulu spears graced the room in which we spoke, testimony of a significant period in the lives of the Kohns.

26 See Pape, *Hermannsburger Missionare in Südafrika Band 2*; see also interview with Christian and Heidelore Kohn, 11 November 2016, Hanover, Germany.

27 Interview with Christian and Heidelore Kohn, 11 November 2016, Hanover.

28 Kohn's contribution is acknowledged on page 1 of Hans-Jürgen Becken's 'A Healing Church in Zululand: "The New Church Step to Jesus Christ Zion in South Africa"', *Journal of Religion in Africa* 4 (3) (1972): 213–222.

29 This friendship had begun when the Kohns were hostel parents, and Christian was a probationer at Hermannsburg, South Africa. Dr Wolfram Kistner, who was in charge of the Hermannsburg school, was also the leader of the white congregation, and in that position also Christian's tutor (*Vikariatsvater*). Later, when Kistner was in charge of the Hermannsburg Mission in South Africa, their friendship deepened, and continued into the period when he was the director of the Department of Justice and Reconciliation of the SACC.

30 Christian and Heidi Kohn papers, Hanover. Christian Kohn, 'Die Stellung des Hermannsburger Missionars in Südafrika heute' (The Position of Hermannsburg Missionaries in South Africa Today), October 1967. (Author's translation.)

31 Christian and Heidi Kohn papers, Hanover. Christian Kohn, 'The History of the Maqhamusela Lutheran Mission Bible School', 1974.

32   Christian and Heidi Kohn papers, Hanover. Christian Kohn, 'The Present Discussion on Christian Laymen' (undated).

33   Interview, Christian and Heidelore Kohn, 11 November 2016, Hanover, Germany.

34   Christian Kohn, 'Kirche setzt Beispiel für Einheit über Rassengrenzen hinweg', *Missionsblatt* 111 (10) (October 1971): 150–151.

35   Vicky Kolbe, 'Kohns Return to Germany', *Zululand Times*, 19 June 1975.

36   Vicky Kolbe, 'Kohns Return to Germany', *Zululand Times*, 19 June 1975.

37   Christian and Heidi Kohn Papers, Hanover. (n.d.) The South African Liberation Movement Inkatha (Amsterdam: Information Centre on South Africa, Inkatha Institute and Inkatha Office, n.d.)

38   Anon., 'Man as a Whole Must become Free – Dr Sibusiso Bhengu', *Zululand Times*, 20 March 1975.

39   See for example Tjelle's account of Christian Oftenbro's experiences in the Norwegian Mission Society, *Missionary Masculinities*, 45–55.

40   Christian and Heidi Kohn Papers, Hanover. Christian Kohn, 'Impressions after twelve years of service in South Africa' (paper presented at Eshowe to a gathering of the 'Ministers Fraternal', April 28, 1975).

41   Christian and Heidi Kohn Papers, Hanover. Christian Kohn, 'Impressions after twelve years of service in South Africa' (paper presented at Eshowe to a gathering of 'Ministers Fraternal', April 28, 1975).

42   Wesenick occupied the position of mission director from 1959–1974.

43   Ulrike Kistner relaying her sister's recollection, Interview, 14 January 2017, Johannesburg. At the time, Kistner was probably lecturing in Theology at the University of Natal, Pietermaritzburg, a position he left in 1976 to become head of the justice and reconciliation division of the SACC. By 1992, the number of Hermannsburg missionaries in South Africa had declined from 17 in 1970 to 10. Only 2 of the original 33 Swedish missionaries remained, with 1 from the original 13 of the American Lutheran Mission, and none from the Berlin Mission. See Gunther Hermann, *Die Rückseite der Apartheid: Kirche und Mission in den "Homelands" von Südafrika* (Berlin: LIT Verlag, 2011), 42.

44   See for example *Bericht Matshana Projekt* der Kirchenkreise Hannover Mitte und Eshowe/Empangeni, Südafrika 08. Bis 29 Juli 2009. Christian and Heidi Kohn Papers, Hanover.

45   Hermann, *Die Rückseite der Apartheid*, 8–9.

46   Hermann, *Die Rückseite der Apartheid*, 42.

Chapter 10

1   Judith Coullie et al., eds, *Selves in Question: Interviews on Southern African auto/biography* (Honolulu: University of Hawai'i, 2006), 44.

2   Coullie et al., *Selves in Question*, 46–47.

3   Heinrich Filter, comp., *Paulina Dlamini: Servant of Two Kings* (Durban and Pietermaritzburg: Killie Campbell Africana Library and University of Natal, 1986); Naboth Mokgatle, *Autobiography of an Unknown South African* (London: C. Hurst and Company, 1971).

4   Coullie et al., *Selves in Question*, 40.

5   'Introduction', Heinrich Filter, comp., S. Bourquin, ed., *Paulina Dlamini: Servant of Two Kings* (Durban and Pietermaritzburg: Killie Campbell Africana Library and University of Natal Press, 1986), 3.

6   As discussed in Chapter 2 above.

7   Filter, *Paulina*, 24.

8   Filter, *Paulina*, 25.

9   Filter, *Paulina*, 42.

10   Filter, *Paulina*, 42.

11   Sheila Meintjes, 'Book Reviews and Notices: Paulina Dlamini, Servant of Two Kings and Shula Marks, Not either an Experimental Doll: The Separate Worlds of Three South African Women', *Natalia* 7 (1987): 101–105.

12   Filter, *Paulina*, 77.

13   Filter, *Paulina*, 81.

14   Filter, *Paulina*, 81.

15   Filter, *Paulina*, 87.

16   Filter, *Paulina*, 3.

17   Filter, *Paulina*, 4.

18   Meintjes, 'Book Reviews', 101.

19   Filter, *Paulina*, 110

20   Filter, *Paulina*, 20.

21   See South African History Online, Mpande, kaSenzangakhona (1798-1872) http://v1. sahistory.org.za/pages/people/bios/mpande_kasenzangakhona.htm, last modified May 29, 2017.

22   Filter, *Paulina*, 26 & 32.

23   Filter, *Paulina*, 66.

24   Filter, *Paulina*, 82.

25   Filter, *Paulina*, 75.

26   Jane Starfield, 'Dr S. Modiri Molema (1891–1965): The Making of an Historian' (PhD diss., University of the Witwatersrand, 1987). Abstract.

27   South African History Online Biographies: 'Mary Benson': Mary Benson was secretary of the Africa Bureau in London when she met Mokgatle. The Bureau's work initially focused on advice, support and representation on international bodies, but eventually also included a research wing. Its main focus was support of African struggles for independence. Born in Pretoria, she was active in raising funds for the defence in the Treason Trial in 1957, going on to write several books on the liberation struggle in South Africa. http://www. sahistory.org.za/people/mary-benson, last modified May 29, 2017.

28   For some reason, the book seems not to have been reviewed in the *African Communist*, the journal of the South African Communist Party.

29   Mokgatle, *Autobiography*, 4.

30   Thengamehlo Ngwenya, 'Ideology and Form in South African Autobiographical Writing: A Study of the Autobiographies of Five South African Authors' (PhD diss., University of South Africa, 1996), 116.

31   Ngwenya, 'Ideology', 117.

32   Ngwenya, 'Ideology', 124.

33   Thomas Thale, 'Of Tribal Boys and Communists: Naboth Mokgatle's "The Autobiography of an Unknown South African"', *Current Writing* 6 (1) (1994): 47.

34   Thale, 'Of Tribal Boys and Communists', 47.

35   Thomas Thale, 'Paradigms Lost? Paradigms Regained: Working Class Autobiography in South Africa', in *Journal of Southern African Studies* 21 (4) (1995); see also Thomas Thale, 'Of Tribal Boys and Communists'.

36   Mokgatle, *Autobiography*, 95.

37   Mokgatle, *Autobiography*, 113.

38   Mokgatle, *Autobiography*, 114.

39   Mokgatle, *Autobiography*, 116.

40   Mokgatle, *Autobiography*, 115.

41   Mokgatle, *Autobiography*, 116.

42   Mokgatle, *Autobiography*, 138.

43   Mokgatle, *Autobiography*, 143.

44   Mokgatle, *Autobiography*, 161.

45   Mokgatle, *Autobiography*, 198.

46   Mokgatle, *Autobiography*, 266.

47   Mokgatle, *Autobiography*, 329.

48   Ngwenya, Ideology, 137.

48   Thale, 'Of Tribal Boys and Communists', 54.

Conclusion

1   C. Kros, *The Seeds of Separate Development: The Origins of Bantu Education* (Pretoria, Unisa Press, 2010).

2   In terms of Section 29 of the South African Constitution approved by the Constitutional Court in December 1996 and taking effect in February 1997: (1) Everyone has the right (a) to a basic education, including adult basic education; and (b) to further education, which the state, through reasonable measures, must make progressively available and accessible. (2) Everyone has the right to receive education in the official language or languages of their choice in public educational institutions where that education is reasonably practicable. In order to ensure the effective access to, and implementation of, this right, the state must consider all reasonable educational alternatives, including single medium institutions, taking into account (a) equity; (b) practicability; and (c) the need to redress the results of past racially discriminatory laws and practices. (3) Everyone has the right to establish and maintain, at their own expense, independent educational institutions that (a) do not discriminate on the basis of race; (b) are registered with the state; and (c) maintain standards that are not inferior to standards at comparable public educational institutions. (4) Subsection (3) does not preclude state subsidies for independent educational institutions. Constitution of the Republic of South Africa No. 108 of 1996.

REFERENCES

Unpublished Primary Sources

Central Archives Depot (CAD), Pretoria

Christian and Heidi Kohn papers, Hanover, Germany

Evangelisch-Lutherisches Missionswerk in Niedersachsen (ELM), Hermannsburg, Germany

Killie Campbell Library, Durban

Lutheran Theological Institute (LTI), Pietermaritzburg

Natal Archives Depot (NAD), Pietermaritzburg

University of Johannesburg, Archives and Special Collections

University of the Witwatersrand, Johannesburg, Historical Papers, South African Institute of Race Relations (SAIRR) Collection

Printed Primary Sources

Government Reports

Breutz, P.-L. (1953). *The Tribes of Rustenburg and Pilansberg Districts*, Union of South Africa, Department of Native Affairs, Ethnological Publications No. 28, Pretoria: Government Printer.

Breutz, P.-L. (1957). *Die Stamme van die Distrik Lichtenburg en Delareyville*, Union of South Africa, Department of Native Affairs, Ethnological Series No. 37, Pretoria: Government Printer.

KwaZulu (South Africa) Legislative Assembly. (1982). *The Buthelezi Commission: The requirements for stability and development in KwaZulu Natal, volumes I and II*. Durban: H+H Publications.

Republic of Bophuthatswana. (1978). Report of the National Education Commission: Education for Popagano. Mafikeng: Government Printer.

Republic of South Africa. 1996. Constitution of the Republic of South Africa No. 108 of 1996.

Republic of South Africa, Department of Basic Education. South Africa. (2011), Curriculum and Assessment Policy Statement. Grades R–3. Home Language Pretoria.

Union Education Department (UED). (1936). Report of the Interdepartmental Committee on Native Education, 1935–36 UG No. 29/1936. Pretoria. Government Printer, UG 29–1930.

Union of South Africa. (17 September 1955). *Debates of the House of Assembly* (Hansard). (17 September) Cape Town: Government Printer.

Union of South Africa, Department of Native Affairs. (1954). *Bantu education: Policy for the immediate future*. Statement by H.F. Verwoerd, Minister of Native Affairs, in the Senate of the Parliament of the Union of South Africa, 7th June 1954.

Union of South Africa, Department of Native Affairs, Bantu Education. (1957). Library books for government, community, farm, mine and factory schools. In: *Handbook of regulations and instructions*. Pretoria: Government Printer.

Union of South Africa, *Report of the commission on native education, 1949–51*. UG No. 53/1951 (Chair: Eiselen).

Government and Missionary Journals

Bantu Education Journal, May and August 1955.

Hermannsburger Missionsblatt.

Zululand Times.

Unisa August Hesse Collection, Hermannsburg Readers and School Textbooks

Mogorosi I and *II* (1956, 1957, 1959, 1964). Rustenburg and Moorleigh: Hermannsburg Mission Depot and Mission Press.

Morutapuo series (1939, 1942, 1945, 1956). Rustenburg and Moorleigh: Hermannsburg Mission Depot and Mission Press.

National Library of South Africa, School Textbooks

Barnes, A. (1951a). *English readers for southern Africa. Book I, First steps in reading*, edited by G.H. Franz. Bloemfontein: Via Afrika.

Barnes, A. (1951b). *English readers for southern Africa. Book III, Cabbages and kings*, edited by G.H. Franz. Bloemfontein: Via Afrika.

Barnes, A. (1951c). *English readers for southern Africa. Book IV, Here and there*, edited by G.H. Franz. Bloemfontein: Via Afrika.

Barnes, A. and Dugard, J. (1992). *English readers for southern Africa. Book I and 2, Further afield*, edited by G.H. Franz. Bloemfontein: Via Afrika.

Doke, C., ed. (1946a). *Imvulamlomo, first primer. Longmans Zulu readers*. London: Longmans, Green and Co.

Doke, C., ed. (1946b). *Ingqaqamazinyo, second primer. Longmans Zulu readers*. London: Longmans, Green and Co.

Doke, C., ed. (1946c). *Ufundukhuphuke, standard I. Longmans Zulu readers*. London: Longmans, Green and Co.

Doke, C., ed. (1946d). *Unokuhlekisa, standard II. Longmans Zulu readers*. London: Longmans, Green and Co.

Doke, C., ed. (1946e). *Unozizwe, standard III. Longmans Zulu readers*. London: Longmans, Green and Co.

Doke, C., ed. (1946e). *Usokuzula, standard IV. Longmans Zulu readers*. London: Longmans, Green and Co.

Merber, S., (1947a). *Readers for African schools book 1*. Johannesburg: Afrikaanse Pers Boekhandel.

Merber, S., (1947b). *Readers for African schools book 2*. Johannesburg: Afrikaanse Pers Boekhandel.

Merber, S., (1947c). *Readers for African schools book 3*. Johannesburg: Afrikaanse Pers Boekhandel.

Ubuntu-Botho (Good citizenship): A textbook in Zulu in a series in good citizenship. Ibanga [Grade] 7. Pietermaritzburg: KwaZulu Booksellers, 1989.

Autobiographies, Memoirs, Reminiscences

Bodenstein, H. (1998). Fröhlich singend über die Brücken. In: H. Stäcker, ed., *Geschichten, die das Leben schreibt: Rückblick unserer Freunde der Alten Garde*. Kroondal: Stups Printing.

Dehnke, H. (1949). Die Mission und die Schule: Unsere besonderer Berücksichtigung der Transvaalmission (The mission and the school) In: *Und die Vögel des Himmels wohnen unter Seinen Zweigen: Hundert Jahre Bauernmission in Südafrika* (Margot von Beck, Trans.). W. Wickert, 264–301. Hermannsburg: Missionshandlung.

Filter, H., comp., edited by S. Bourquin. (1986). *Paulina Dlamini: Servant of two kings*. Durban and Pietermaritzburg: Killie Campbell Africana Library and University of Natal, Pietermaritzburg Press.

Kgasi, M. (1949 [1939]). *Thutô ke eng? (What is education?)* (Enos Makhele, Trans.). Lovedale: Lovedale Press.

Meyberg, H. (2002). *Gedanken & Worte Band 4: Bethel, Südafrika, eine Schule von Menschen geplant, von Gott geführt*. Pretoria: H. Meyberg.

Mokgatle, N. (1971). *Autobiography of an unknown South African*. London: C. Hurst and Co.

Published Secondary Sources

Ally, M. and Lissoni, A. (2012). Let's talk about the Bantustans. *South African Historical Journal*, 64(1), pp. 1–4.

Anon. (2008). Obituaries: Oscar Dumisani Dhlomo (1943–2008), *Natalia*, 38, p. 77.

Anon. Anti-Slavery Society (1980). *Child labour in South Africa*. London: Anti-Slavery Society.

Apple, M. (1984). The Political Economy of Text Publishing. *Educational Theory*, 34(4), pp. 307–319.

Apple, M. (1990). *Ideology and curriculum*. 2nd ed. New York: Routledge.

Apple, M. (1995). *Education and power*. 2nd ed. New York: Routledge.

Apple, M. (1999). *Power, meaning and identity: Essays in critical educational studies*. New York: Peter Lang.

Apple, M. (2000). *Official knowledge: Democratic education in a conservative age*. 2nd ed. New York: Routledge.

Apple, M. and Christian-Smith, L. eds, (1991). *The politics of the textbook*. New York: Routledge.

Auerbach, F. (1963). *An enquiry into history textbooks and syllabuses in Transvaal high schools* (MEd thesis). Johannesburg: University of the Witwatersrand.

Auerbach, F. (1965). *The power of prejudice in South African education*. Cape Town: A.A. Balkema.

Bagchi, B., Fuchs, E., and Rousmaniere, K., eds, (2014). *Connecting Histories of Education: Transnational and Cross-Cultural Exchanges in (Post)Colonial Education*. London: Berghahn.

Bank, A. (2015). The Berlin Mission Society and German linguistic roots of *Volkekunde*: The background, training and Hamburg writings of Werner Eiselen, 1899–1924. *Kronos*, 41(1), pp. 166–192.

Barber, K., ed., (2006). *Africa's hidden histories: Everyday literacy and the making of the self*. Bloomington: Indiana University Press.

Barrett, A. (2007). Beyond the polarization of pedagogy: Models of classroom practice in Tanzanian primary schools. *Comparative Education*, 43(2), pp. 273–294.

Beard, P. and Morrow, W., eds, (1981). *Problems of paedagogics*. Durban: Butterworth.

Becken, H-J. (1972). A Healing Church in Zululand: 'The New Church Step to Jesus Christ Zion in South Africa'. *Journal of Religion in Africa*, 4(3), pp. 213–222.

Becken, H.-J. (1992). I love to tell the story: Oral history in the Nazaretha church. In: G.C. Oosthuizen and I. Hexham, eds, *Empirical studies of African independent/indigenous churches*, pp. 29–48. Lewiston: Edwin Mellen Press.

Beinart, W. (2012). Beyond 'homelands': Some ideas about the history of African rural areas in South Africa. *South African Historical Journal*, 64(1), pp. 5–21.

Berglund, A.-I. (1965). Concepts of water and baptism amongst some Africanist Zionist movements. *Credo: Lutheran Journal of Southern Africa*, 16(1), pp. 5–6.

Berglund, A.-I. (1968). Pack-oxen and cattle-riding among the Zulu. *African Studies*, 27(1), pp. 29–30.

Berglund, A-I. (1976). *Zulu Thought Patterns and Symbolism*. Cape Town: David Philip.

Bozzoli, B. and Nkotsoe, M. (1991). *Women of Phokeng, consciousness, life strategy and migrancy in South Africa 1900–1983*. Johannesburg: Ravan.

Campbell, J. (1995). *Songs of Zion: The African Methodist Episcopal Church in the United States and South Africa.* Oxford: Oxford University Press.

Carnoy, M., Chisholm, L. and Chilisa, B., eds, (2012). *The low achievement trap: Comparing schooling in Botswana and South Africa.* Cape Town: Human Sciences Research Council.

Chance, K. (2015). 'Where there is fire, there is politics': Ungovernability and material life in urban South Africa. *Cultural Anthropology*, 30(3), pp. 394–423.

Chisholm, L. (2012). Education policy borrowing across African borders: Histories of learner-centred education. In: G. Steiner-Khamsi and F. Waldow, eds, *Policy borrowing and lending: World yearbook of education 2012*, pp. 206–225. New York: Routledge.

Comaroff, J. and Comaroff. J. (1991). *Of revelation and revolution. Christianity, colonialism and consciousness in South Africa.* Volume I. Chicago: University of Chicago Press.

Comaroff, J. and Comaroff, J. (2002). The colonization of consciousness. In: M. Lambek, ed., *A reader in the anthropology of religion*, pp. 464–479. Oxford: Blackwell.

Coullie, J., Meyer, S., Ngwenya, T. and Oliver, T., eds, (2006). *Selves in question: Interviews on Southern African biography.* Honolulu: University of Hawai'i Press.

Cowen, R. (2009). Then and now: Unit ideas and comparative education. In: R. Cowen and A. Kazamias, eds, *International handbook of comparative education*, Volume 22, pp. 1277–1294. Dordrecht: Springer.

Dean, E., Hartmann, P. and Katzen, M. (1983). *History in black and white: An analysis of South African school history textbooks.* Paris: UNESCO.

De Clercq, F. (1994). High-skilled manpower, education and work in Bophuthatswana. In: W. Flanagan, C. Hemson, J. Muller and N. Taylor, eds, *Vintage Kenton: A Kenton Education Association commemoration*, pp. 110–132. Cape Town: Maskew Miller Longman.

Denis, P. (2010). Seminary networks and black consciousness in South Africa in the early 1970s. *South African Historical Journal*, 62(1), pp. 162–182.

Denis, P. and Duncan, G. (2011). *The native school which caused all the trouble: A history of the federal theological seminary of Southern Africa (1963–1993).* Pietermaritzburg: Cluster Publications.

Dick, A. (2012). *The hidden history of South Africa's book and reading cultures.* Toronto: University of Toronto Press.

Dubow, S. (1986). Holding a 'Just balance between white and black': The native affairs department in South Africa, c. 1920–1933. *Journal of Southern African Studies*, 12(2), pp. 217–239.

Dubow, S. (1995). *Scientific racism in modern South Africa*. Cambridge: Cambridge University Press.

Dubow, S. (2006). *A commonwealth of knowledge: Science, sensibility and white South Africa 1820–2000*. Oxford: Oxford University Press.

Dubow, S. (2014). *Apartheid 1948–1994*. Oxford: Oxford University Press.

Eberhardt, M. (2015). German settler communities in Southern Africa and the Third Reich: Hopes - expectations - challenges. In H. Lessing, T. Dedering, J. Kampmann, and D. Smit, eds, *Contested relations: Protestantism between Southern Africa and Germany from the 1930s to the apartheid era*, pp. 64–90. Wiesbaden: Harrassowitz Verlag.

Elphick, R. (1995). Writing religion into history: The case of South African Christianity. In: H. Bredenkamp and R. Ross, eds, *Missions and Christianity in South African history*, pp. 11–26. Johannesburg: Wits University Press.

Elphick, R. (1997). Introduction. In: R. Elphick and R. Davenport, eds, *Christianity in South Africa: A Political and Cultural History*, pp. 1–16. Cape Town: David Philip.

Elphick, R. (2012). *The equality of believers: Protestant missionaries and the racial politics of South Africa*. Charlottesville: University of Virginia Press.

Erlank, N. (2003). Sexual misconduct and church power on Scottish mission stations in Xhosaland in South Africa in the 1840s. *Gender and History*, 15(1), pp. 69–84.

Etherington, N. (1976). Mission station melting pots as a factor in the rise of South African Black nationalism. *The International Journal of African Historical Studies*, IX(4), pp. 592–605.

Etherington, N. (1978). *Preachers, peasants and politics in Southeast Africa 1835–1880: African Christian Communities in Natal, Pondoland and Zululand*. London: London Royal Historical Society.

Evans, E. (1986). JCI's Social Responsibility Funding: The Bophuthatswana Education Upgrading Programme. Revolution on a shoestring. *Mining Survey*, 2(4), pp. 51–55.

Fafunwa, B. (1967). *New perspectives on African education*. Lagos: Macmillan.

Farisani, T. (1987). *Diary from a South African prison*. Philadelphia: Fortress Press.

Fleisch, B. (2002). State formation and the origins of Bantu education. In: P. Kallaway, ed., *The history of education under apartheid 1948–1994*, pp. 39–52. Cape Town: Maskew Miller Longman.

Foucault, M. (2010). *The Birth of biopolitics: Lectures at the College de France 1978–1979*, edited by M. Senellart and translated by G. Burchell. New York: Palgrave Macmillan.

Fuchs, E. (2011). Current trends in history and social studies textbook research. *Journal of International Cooperation in Education*, 14(2), pp. 17–34.

Gaitskell, D. (1990). Devout domesticity? A Century of African Women's Christianity in South Africa. In: Cheryl Walker, ed, *Women and Gender in Southern Africa to 1945*, pp. 251–272. London: James Currey.

Gaitskell, D. (1997). Power in prayer and service: Women's Christian organisations. In: Elphick and Davenport, eds, *Christianity in South Africa: A political, social, and cultural history*, pp. 253–268. Berkeley: University of California Press.

Gaitskell, D. (1998). Race, Gender and Imperialism: A Century of Black Girls' Education in South Africa. Paper presented at seminar, Wits University African Studies Institute.

Gaitskell, D. (2002). Ploughs and Needles: State and Mission Approaches to African Girls' Education in South Africa. In: Holger Hansen and Michael Twaddle, eds, *Christian Missionaries and the State in the Third World*, pp. 98–120. Oxford: James Currey.

Gibbs, T. (2014). *Mandela's Kinsmen: Nationalist elites and apartheid's first Bantustan*. Johannesburg: Jacana.

Golan, D. (1991). Inkatha and its use of the Zulu past. *History in Africa*, 18, pp. 113–126.

Graaff, J. (1987). Rural parents and school enrolment rates in two regions of Bophuthatswana: Subjects for reconsideration. *Perspectives in Education*, 9(2), pp. 25–43.

Haccius, G. (1909). *Hannoversche Missionsgeschichte*. Hermannsburg: Druck und Verlag der Missionshandlung.

Harries, P. (2001). Missionaries, Marxists and magic: Power and the politics of literacy in South-East Africa. *Journal of Southern African Studies*, 27(3), pp. 405–427.

Harries, P. (2007). *Butterflies and Barbarians: Swiss missionaries and knowledge in South-East Africa*. Oxford: James Currey.

Hartshorne, K. (1983). Curriculum and the reality of context: The Bophuthatswana beginnings. In: A. Hunter, M. Ashley, and C. Millar, eds, *Education curriculum and development: Papers presented at conferences at the University of Cape Town and the University of the Witwatersrand, 1979–1981*, pp. 390–414. Johannesburg: Centre for Continuing Education, University of the Witwatersrand.

Hartshorne, K. (1992). *Crisis and challenge: Black education 1910–1990*. Oxford: Oxford University Press.

Hasselhorn, F. (1989). *Bauernmission in Südafrika: Die Hermannsburger Mission im Spannungsfeld der Kolonialpolitick 1880–1939*. Hermannsburg: Verlag der Ev-Luth. Mission.

Hasselhorn, F. (2012). 'Why can't we celebrate at the church up there anymore?' The segregation of the congregations in Hermannsburg (Natal). In: H. Lessing, J. Besten, T. Dedering, C. Hohman, and L. Kriel, eds, *The German Protestant*

Church in colonial South Africa: The impact of overseas work from the beginnings until the 1920s, pp. 471–485. Wiesbaden: Harrassowitz Verlag.

Healy-Clancy, M. (2014). *A world of their own: A history of South African women's education*. Charlottesville: University of Virginia Press.

Hermann, G. (2011). *Die Rückseite der Apartheid: Kirche und Mission in den 'Homelands' von Südafrika*. Berlin: LIT Verlag.

Hinz, R. (2015). Conflicts in dealing with apartheid: The churches and missions of German origin working in Southern Africa until the end of the 1960s. In: H. Lessing, T. Dedering, J. Kampmann, and D. Smit, eds, *Contested relations: Protestantism between Southern Africa and Germany from the 1930s to the apartheid era*, Volume II, pp. 287–312. Wiesbaden: Harrassowitz Verlag.

Hodne, I. (1997). *Missionary enterprise in African education: The co-operating Lutheran missions in Natal, South Africa, 1912–1955: A documentation*. Stavanger: Misjonshogskolens Forlag.

Hofmeyr, I. (2004). *The portable Bunyan: A transnational history of 'The pilgrim's progress'*. Princeton, NJ: Princeton University Press.

Hofmeyr, I., Kaarsholm, P. and Frederiksen, B. (2011). Introduction: Print cultures, nationalisms and publics of the Indian Ocean. *Africa*, 81(1), pp. 1–22.

Horrell, M. (1968). *Bantu education to 1968*. Johannesburg: South African Institute of Race Relations.

Hovland, I. (2013). *Mission station Christianity: Norwegian missionaries in colonial Natal and Zululand, Southern Africa, 1850–1890*. Leiden: Brill.

Hyslop, J. (1988). State education policy and the social reproduction of the urban African working class: The case of the Southern Transvaal, 1955–1976. *Journal of Southern African Studies*, 14(3), pp. 446–476.

Hyslop, J. (1989). School boards, school committees and educational politics: Aspects of the failure of Bantu education as a hegemonic strategy, 1955–1976. In: P. Bonner, I. Hofmeyr, D. James and T. Lodge, eds, *Holding their ground: Class, locality and culture in 19th and 20th century South Africa*, pp. 201–225. Johannesburg: Ravan/Wits University Press.

Hyslop, J. (1991). Food, authority and politics: Student riots in South African schools 1945–1976. In: S. Clingman, ed., *Regions and repertoires: Topics in South African politics and culture*, pp. 84–115. Johannesburg: Ravan.

Hyslop, J. (1993). 'A destruction coming in': Bantu education as response to social crisis. In: P. Bonner, P. Delius and D. Posel, eds, *Apartheid's genesis 1935–1972*, pp. 393–411. Johannesburg: Ravan/Wits University Press.

Hyslop, J. (2014). Comparative historical sociology and transnational history: A response to Julian Go's patterns of empire. *Comparative Studies of South Asia, Africa and the Middle East*, 34(3), pp. 610–617.

Kallaway, P. (2007). Conference litmus: The development of a conference and policy culture in the interwar period with special reference to the new education fellowship and British colonial education in South Africa. In: K. Tolley, ed., *Transformations in schooling: Historical and comparative perspectives*, pp. 123–149. New York, NY: Palgrave/Routledge.

Kallaway, P. (2015). Volkskirche, Volkekunde and apartheid: Lutheran missions, German anthropology and humanities in African education. In: H. Lessing, T. Dedering, J. Kampmann, and D. Smit, eds, *Contested relations: Protestantism between Southern Africa and Germany from the 1930s to the apartheid era*, pp. 140–155. Wiesbaden: Harrassowitz Verlag.

Kallaway, P. and Swartz, R. eds, (2016). *Empire and Education in Africa: The Shaping of a Comparative Perspective*. New York: Peter Lang.

Krige, S. (1997). Segregation, science and commissions of enquiry: The contestation over Native Education Policy in South Africa, 1930–1936. *Journal of Southern African Studies*, 23(3), pp. 491–506.

Kros, C. (2000). Telling lies and then hoping to forget all about history. *South African Historical Journal*, 42(1), pp. 69–88.

Kros, C. (2000). W.W.M. Eiselen: Architect of apartheid education. In: P. Kallaway, ed., *The history of education under apartheid 1948–1994*, pp. 53–73. Cape Town: Maskew Miller Longman.

Kros, C. (2010). *The seeds of separate development: The origins of Bantu education.* Pretoria: Unisa Press.

Labaree, D. (2005). Progressivism, schools and schools of education: An American romance. *Paedogogica Historica*, 41(1&2), pp. 275–288.

Lagemann, E.C. (2000). *An elusive science: The troubling history of education research.* Chicago: University of Chicago Press.

Landman, C. (2014). The Piety of German Women in South Africa. *Studia Historiae Ecclesiasticae*, 40 (2), pp. 119–129.

Lawrence, M. and Manson, A. (1994). 'Dog of the Boers': The rise and fall of Mangope in Bophuthatswana. *Journal of Southern African Studies*, 20(3), pp. 447–461. Special Issue: Ethnicity and Identity in Southern Africa, September.

Lekhela, E., Kgware, W., Vorster, T., and Rossouw, J. (1972). *A Survey of the Development of Education among the Batswana of Bophuthatswana.* Mafikeng: n.p.

Lessing, H., Besten, J., Dedering, T., Hohman, C. and Kriel, L. eds, (2012). *The German protestant church in colonial South Africa: The impact of overseas work from the beginnings until the 1920s.* Wiesbaden: Harrassowitz Verlag.

Lessing, H., Dedering, T., Kampmann, J. and Smit, D. eds, (2015). *Contested relations: Protestantism between Southern Africa and Germany from the 1930s to the apartheid era.* Wiesbaden: Harrassowitz Verlag.

Limb, P. (2010). Intermediaries of class, nation, and gender in the African response to colonialism in South Africa, 1890s–1920s. In: P. Limb, N. Etherington, and P. Midgley, eds, *Grappling with the beast: Indigenous Southern African responses to colonialism, 1840–1930*, pp. 47–86. Leiden: Brill.

Loram, C. (1917). *The education of the South African native*. London: Longmans.

Macdonald, C. (1990). *Crossing the threshold into standard three in black education: The consolidated main report of the threshold project*. Pretoria: Human Sciences Research Council.

Macdonald, C. (1990). *Swimming up the waterfall: A study of school-based learning experiences*. Pretoria: Human Sciences Research Council.

Macdonald, C. (1993). *Towards a new primary curriculum for South Africa: The main report of the threshold 2 project*. Pretoria: Human Sciences Research Council.

Magaziner, D. (2010). *The law and the prophets: Black consciousness in South Africa 1968–1977*. Athens: Ohio University Press.

Mager, A. and Mulaudzi, M. (2011). Popular responses to apartheid: 1948–c.1975. In: R. Ross, A. Mager, and B. Nasson, eds, *The Cambridge history of South Africa, volume 2: 1885–1994*, pp. 369–408. Cambridge: Cambridge University Press.

Magubane, B. (2004). Resistance and repression in the Bantustans. In: South African Democracy Education Trust, ed., *The road to democracy in South Africa, volume 2: 1970–1980*, pp. 749–755. Pretoria: Unisa Press.

Maré, G. and Hamilton, G. (1987). *An appetite for power: Buthelezi's Inkatha and the politics of 'Loyal resistance'*. Johannesburg: Ravan.

Maré, G. (1988/89). Education in a liberated zone: Inkatha and education in KwaZulu. *Critical Arts*, 4(4/5), pp. 126–139.

Mbenga, B. and Manson, A. (2010). *'People of the dew': A history of the Bafokeng of Phokeng-Rustenburg region, South Africa, from early times to 2000*. Johannesburg: Jacana.

Mbenga, B. (forthcoming). The Rev Kenneth Mosley Spooner: African-American Missionary to the Fokeng of Rustenburg District, South Africa, 1915–1937. *Journal of Southern African Studies*.

McCulloch, G. (2009). Empires and education: The British Empire. In: R. Cowen and A.M. Kazamias, eds, *International handbook of comparative education*, pp. 169–179. New York: Springer.

Mdluli, P. (pseudonym of B.E. 'Blade' Nzimande) (1987). Ubuntu-botho: Inkatha's 'People's education'. *Transformation*, 5, pp. 61–79.

Meintjes, S. (1987). Book reviews and notices. Paulina Dlamini: Servant of two kings and Shula Marks (ed): 'Not either an experimental doll': The separate worlds of three South African women. *Natalia*, 7, pp. 101–105.

Molteno, F. (1984). The historical foundations of the schooling of black South Africans. In: P. Kallaway, ed., *Apartheid and education: The education of black South Africans*, pp. 45–107. Johannesburg: Ravan.

Morrell, R. (1998). Of boys and men: Masculinity and gender in Southern African studies. *Journal of Southern African Studies*, 24(4), pp. 605–630.

Morrow, S. (2016). *The Fires Beneath: The Life of Monica Wilson, South African Anthropologist*. Cape Town: Penguin Books.

Nasson, B. (2016). *History matters. Selected writing, 1970–2016*. Cape Town: Penguin Random House.

National Education Coordinating Committee. (1993). *National education policy investigation: Report on systems, planning and management*. Cape Town: Oxford University Press.

Nicholls, J. (2006). Introduction: School history textbooks across cultures from the perspective of comparative education. In: J. Nicholls, ed., *School history textbooks across cultures: International debates and perspectives*, pp. 7–15. Oxford: Oxford University Press.

Nishino, R. (2011). *Changing histories: Japanese and South African textbooks in comparison (1945–1995)*. Göttingen: V&R Unipress.

Nkondo, C. (July 1979). Comparison of the syllabus of the Bantu education department with that of the Transvaal education department and other related matters. *Reality*, 11(4), pp. 17–19.

Nürnberger, K. (1979a). *Ideologies of change in South Africa and the power of the gospel (capitalism-socialism-Marxism): An interdisciplinary study-program of the Missiological Institute, Mapumulo*. Durban: Lutheran Publishing House.

Nürnberger, K. (1979b). *Socio-economic ideologies in a Christian perspective*. Durban: Lutheran Publishing House.

Oschadleus, H.-J. (1993). Lutherans, German: Hermannsburgers. *Natalia*, 22, p. 33.

Pakendorf, G. (2011). A brief history of the Berlin Mission Society in South Africa. *History Compass*, 9(2), pp. 106–118.

Pape, H. (1986). *Hermannsburger Missionare in Südafrika Band 1&2 Lebens-und Arbeitsberichte mit Bildern. Ein Beitrag zur Südafrikanischen Geschichte*. Wonderboom: Barrodel.

Paterson, A. (2004). Agricultural and industrial curricula for South African rural schools: Colonial origins and contemporary continuities. In: S. McGrath, A. Badroodien, A. Kraak, and L. Unwin, eds, *Shifting understandings of skills in South Africa: Overcoming the impact of a low skills regime*, pp. 71–97. Cape Town: Human Sciences Research Council.

Posel, D. (2012). The apartheid project 1948–1970. In: R. Ross, A. Mager, and
  B. Nasson, eds, *The Cambridge history of South Africa, volume 2: 1885–1994*,
  pp. 319–368. Cambridge: Cambridge University Press.

Prinsloo, J. (2004). Examining the examination: The 'Worlding' of the matriculation
  language papers in KwaZulu-Natal. *Perspectives in Education*, 22(1),
  pp. 81–97.

Prinsloo, J. (2007). Making visible constructions of dis/advantage through genealogical
  investigation: South African schooled literacies. *Critical Arts*, 21(1), pp. 190–211.

Pugach, S. (2004). Carl Meinhof and the German influence on Nicholas van
  Warmelo's ethnological and linguistic writing, 1927–1935. *Journal of Southern
  African Studies*, 30(4), pp. 824–845.

Reilly, J. (2016). *Teaching the 'Native': Beyond the architecture of an unequal education
  system*. Cape Town: Human Sciences Research Council.

Rose, B. and Tunmer, R. (1975). *Documents in South African education*. Johannesburg:
  Ad Donker.

Rüther, K. (2001). *The power beyond: Mission strategies, African conversion and the development of a Christian culture in the Transvaal*. Hamburg: LIT Verlag.

Schendel, G. (2009). *Die Missionsanstalt Hermannsburg und der Nationalsozialismus.
  Der Weg einer Lutherischen Milieuinstitution zwischen Weimarer Republik und
  Nachkriegszeit*. Münster: LIT Verlag.

Schendel, G. (2015). Exploring the territory between universalism, *Volkstum* and
  race policies. Discourses on South Africa in the Berlin and the Hermannsburg
  Mission Societies. In: H. Lessing, T. Dedering, J. Kampmann, and D. Smit, eds,
  *Contested relations: Protestantism between Southern Africa and Germany from the
  1930s to the apartheid era*, pp. 155–177. Wiesbaden: Harrassowitz Verlag.

Schluyter, H. (1951). *The history of the co-operating Lutheran missions in Natal
  1912–1951*. Durban: Moorleigh Press.

Schmidt, R. (1934). *Die Wertung des Volkstums bei Louis Harms (Vortrag gehalten
  anlässlich einer Freundesratstagung der Hermannsburger Mission) (The evaluation of
  Volkstum by Louis Harms, presentation at the occasion of friends of the Hermannsburg
  Mission Conference)*. Hanover: Verlag der Missionshandlung Hermannsburg,
  pp. 1–20.

Schultze, A. (2005). *'In Gottes Namen Hütten bauen': Kirchlicher Landbesitz in
  Südafrika: Die Berliner Mission und die Evangelisch-Lutherische Kirche Südafrikas
  zwischen 1834 und 2005*. Munich: Fritz Steiner Verlag.

Scriba, G. and Lislerud, G. (1997). Lutheran missions and churches in South Africa.
  In: R. Elphick and R. Davenport, eds, *Christianity in South Africa: A political,
  social and cultural history*, pp. 173–194. Berkeley: University of California Press.

Setati, M., Adler, J., Reed, Y. and Bapoo, A. (2002). Incomplete journeys: Code-switching and other language practices in mathematics, science and English language classrooms in South Africa. *Language and Education*, 16(2), pp. 128–149.

Sharpe, E. (2001). The legacy of Bengt Sundkler. *International Bulletin of Missionary Research*, 25, pp. 58–63.

Steiner-Khamsi, G. and Waldow, F. eds, (2012). *Policy borrowing and lending: World yearbook of education 2012*. London: Routledge.

Sundkler, B. (1960). *The Christian ministry in Africa*. Uppsala: Swedish Institute of Missionary Research.

Tabulawa, R. (1997). Pedagogical classroom practice and social context: The case of Botswana. *International Journal of Educational Development*, 17(2), pp. 189–204.

Tabulawa, R. (2009). Education reform in Botswana: Reflections on policy contradictions and paradoxes. *Comparative Education*, 45(1), pp. 87–107.

Thale, T. (1994). Of tribal boys and communists: Naboth Mokgatle's 'The autobiography of an unknown South African'. *Current Writing*, 6(1), pp. 43–56.

Thale, T. (1995). Paradigms lost? Paradigms regained: Working class autobiography in South Africa. *Journal of Southern African Studies*, 21(4), pp. 613–622.

Tikly, L. (1999). Postcolonialism and comparative education. *International Review of Education* 45(5–6), pp. 603–621.

Tjelle, K. (2013). *Missionary Masculinities, 1870–1930: The Norwegian Missionaries in South-East Africa*. Basingstoke: Palgrave MacMillan.

Vail, L. ed., (1989). *The creation of tribalism in Southern Africa*. Berkeley: University of California Press.

Van der Vlies, A. ed., (2012). *Print, text and book cultures in South Africa*. Johannesburg: Wits University Press.

Voges, H. (2000). Die Arbeit im Südlichen Afrika. In: E.-A. Lüdemann, ed., *Vision: Gemeinde Weltweit: 150 Jahre Hermannsburger Mission und Ev-luth. Missionswerk in Niedersachsen*, pp. 233–357. Hermannsburg: Verlag der Missionshandlung.

Volz, S. (2011). *African teachers on the colonial frontier: Tswana evangelists and their communities during the nineteenth century*. New York: Peter Lang.

Volz, S. and Mgadla, P.T. (2010). Conflict and negotiation along the lower Vaal River: Correspondence from the Tswana-language newspaper, Mokaeri oa Becuana. In: P. Limb, N. Etherington, and P. Midgley, eds, *Grappling with the beast: Indigenous Southern African responses to colonialism, 1840–1930*, pp. 157–212. Leiden: Brill.

Ward, K. (2012). German Lutherans and English Anglicans in Southern Africa to 1918: A shared and divergent history. In: H. Lessing, J. Besten, T. Dedering,

C. Hohman, and L. Kriel, eds, *The German Protestant Church in colonial South Africa: The impact of overseas work from the beginnings until the 1920s*, pp. 417–435, Wiesbaden: Harrassowitz Verlag.

Ward, K. (2015). Afrika! Mayibuye! Equality, freedom and humanity: The struggle for South African Christianity in the twentieth century. In: H. Lessing, T. Dedering, J. Kampmann, and D. Smit, eds, *Contested relations: Protestantism between Southern Africa and Germany from the 1930s to the apartheid era*, pp. 231–243. Wiesbaden: Harrassowitz Verlag.

Winfried, W. (1954). Der Fall Saron (The case of Saron). *Hermannsburger Missionsblatt*, 94, pp. 135–137.

Zimmerman, A. (2010). *Alabama in Africa: Booker T. Washington, the German Empire, and the globalization of the New South*. Princeton: Princeton University Press.

Unpublished Theses, Papers and Reports

Buckland, P. (1983). *Education policy and rural development in Southern Africa: A review of four regional commissioned reports on education policy*. Report submitted to the Committee on Rural Education, Human Sciences Research Council, Pretoria.

Bundy, C. (1992). *Schooled for life? The childhood and education of Govan Mbeki*. Yale University. Seminar Paper. 2 December 1992.

Chisholm, L. (1989). *Reformatories and industrial schools in South Africa: A study in class, colour and gender 1882–1939* (PhD dissertation). Johannesburg: University of the Witwatersrand.

Dhlomo, O. (1980). *An evaluation of some problems in teacher training with special reference to teacher training colleges in KwaZulu* (DEd dissertation). Pretoria: University of South Africa.

Fleisch, B. (1995). *The teachers' college club* (DPhil dissertation). New York: Columbia University.

Graaff, J. (1994a). Education as an instrument of war: The case of Kwazulu/Natal. In: H. Jacklin and J. Graaff, *Rural education in South Africa: A report on schooling systems in the Bantustans*.

Graaff, J. (1994b). Is Bop better? A case study in educational innovation in Bophuthatswana. In H. Jacklin and J. Graaff, *Rural education in South Africa. A report on schooling systems in the Bantustans*.

Herr, R. (1992). *Heinz Dehnke. Ein Missionar in der Auseinandersetzung um die Kirchwerdung und den Schwarzen Politischen Aufbruch in Südafrika* (MTheol thesis). Pretoria: University of South Africa.

Hofmeyr, J. (1983). *An examination of the influence of Christian National Education on the principles underlying white and black education in South Africa 1948–1982* (MEd thesis). Johannesburg: University of the Witwatersrand.

Holderness, B. (1986). *Upgrading primary education in the seventeen circuits, 1980–1985: A celebration of achievement.* Occasional publication 2. Potchefstroom: University of Bophuthatswana, Institute of Education.

Jacklin, H. and Graaff, J. (1994). *Rural education in South Africa. A report on schooling systems in the Bantustans.* Unpublished report for the National Education Policy Investigation (NEPI), Johannesburg.

Leeb, W. and Aitchison, J. (1990). *Report to the ELC Property Management Company: ELCSA (SED) farm schools – A development study.* Pietermaritzburg.

Lehobye, S. (1992). *An evaluation of the primary education upgrading programme in the two circuits of the Odi region.* Potchefstroom: University of Bophuthatswana, Institute of Education.

Luthuli, P. (1977). *The metabletic nature of the aim in education* (MEd thesis). KwaZulu-Natal: University of Zululand.

Luthuli, P. (1981). *The philosophical foundations of black education in South Africa* (PhD dissertation). Pretoria: University of South Africa.

Malao, J. (1983). *Planning an educational system for Bophuthatswana* (MEd thesis). Potchefstroom: Potchefstroom University for Christian Higher Education.

Malope, L. (1992). *Planning educational reforms in Bophuthatswana: An evaluation* (MEd thesis). Potchefstroom: Potchefstroom University for Christian Higher Education.

Mbenga, B. (2009). *Dutch Reformed Church mission education and the emergence of secular schooling among the Bakgatla-ba-Kgafela Community of Rustenburg District, South Africa, 1903–1930s.* Paper presented to the African Studies Association (ASA) of America Annual Meeting, Roosevelt Hotel, New Orleans, Louisiana. 18–22 November 2009.

Melck, M. (2012). *Die Afrikadeutschen of Kroondal, 1849–1949* (MA thesis). Pretoria: University of Pretoria.

Ndaba, E. (1975). *A psycho-paedagogical study of differentiated education and its significance for education in KwaZulu* (DEd dissertation). KwaZulu-Natal: University of Zululand.

Ngwenya, T. (1996). *Ideology and form in South African autobiographical writing: A study of the autobiographies of five South African authors* (PhD dissertation). Pretoria: University of South Africa.

Polakow-Suransky, S. (2002). *Historical amnesia? The politics of textbooks in post-apartheid South Africa.* Paper presented at the Annual Meeting of the American Educational Research Association, New Orleans, Louisiana 1–5 April 2002.

Prinsloo, J. (2002). *Possibilities of critical literacy: An exploration of schooled literacies in the province of KwaZulu-Natal* (PhD dissertation). Johannesburg: University of the Witwatersrand.

Schlemmer, L. (1982). A venture in educational development: An external evalua-
    tion report on the Bophuthatswana teacher upgrading project, mounted by the
    SACHED Trust. Durban: University of Natal, Durban Centre for Applied
    Social Science.

Scriba, F. (n.d.). *The Ehlanzeni Mission Station, 1856–1973*, ed. and trans. J.H. Scriba,
    April 2014.

Simpson, G. (1986). *Peasants and politics in the Western Transvaal, 1920–1940* (MA
    thesis). Johannesburg: University of the Witwatersrand.

Starfield, J. (1987). *Dr S. Modiri Molema (1891–1965): The making of an historian*
    (PhD dissertation). Johannesburg: University of the Witwatersrand.

Taylor, N. (1989). Falling at the first hurdle: Initial encounters with the formal
    system of African education in South Africa, Research Report No 1. Education
    Policy Unit, Johannesburg: University of the Witwatersrand.

Swartz, R. (2015). *'Ignorant and idle': Indigenous education in Natal and Western
    Australia, 1833–1875* (PhD dissertation). London: University of London.

Interviews

Bodenstein, Christel. (6 and 16 August 2009). Johannesburg.

Bodenstein, Hans. (6 and 16 August 2009). Johannesburg.

De Clercq, Francine. (2 July 2009). Kempton Park, Johannesburg.

Holderness, Bill. (5 August 2009). Telephonic interview.

Kistner, Ulrike. (14 January 2017). Johannesburg.

Kohn, Christian and Heidelore. (11 November 2016). Hanover, Germany.

Meyberg, Horst. (1 October 2015). Pretoria.

Motstatsi, Mittah. (2 July 2009). Kempton Park, Johannesburg.

PEUP teachers who wished to remain anonymous (2009). Mahikeng (Mafikeng).

Scriba, Georg. (December 2015). Howick.

Voges, Heinrich. (2 September 2015, 9 October 2015, 23 August 2016). Pretoria.

INDEX

Page numbers in italics indicate photographs, maps and tables. The letter 'n' indicates a note.

Printed and bound by CPI Group (UK) Ltd, Croydon, CR0 4YY

09/06/2025

14685834-0002